The Journal of a Sea Captain's Wife
1841–1845

The snow brig *Sarah Abigail,* 210 tons. It was built at Cohasset, Massachusetts, 1834, by Jonathan B. Bates. The ship in the foreground carried Mrs. Nye to Hawaii.
Courtesy The India House, New York, New York.

The Journal of a Sea Captain's Wife
1841–1845

During a Passage and Sojourn in Hawaii and of a Trading Voyage to Oregon and California

by
LYDIA RIDER NYE

Edited with a
Prologue and Epilogue
by
DOYCE B. NUNIS, JR.

THE ARTHUR H. CLARK COMPANY
Spokane, Washington
2004

Arthur H. Clark Company
P.O. Box 14707
Spokane, WA 99214

LIBRARY OF CONGRESS CATALOG CARD NUMBER
ISBN-0-87062-309-5

Library of Congress Cataloging–in–Publication Data

Nye, Lydia Rider, 1811-1891.

The journal of a sea captain's wife, 1841–1845: during a passage and sojourn in Hawaii and of a trading voyage to Oregon and California / by Lydia Rider Nye; edited with a prologue and epilogue by Doyce B. Nunis, Jr.

p. cm.

Includes bibliographical references (p.) and index.

ISBN 0-87062-309-5

1. Nye, Lydia Rider, 1811-1891—Diaries. 2. Ship captains' spouses—United States—Diaries. 3. Nye, Lydia Rider, 1811–1891—Journeys—Hawaii. 4. Nye, Lydia Rider, 1811–1891—Journeys—Oregon. 5. Nye, Lydia Rider, 1811–1891—Journeys—California. 6. Hawaii—Description and travel. 7. Oregon—Description and travel. 8. California—Description and travel. 9. Hawaii—History—To 1893—Biography. 10. Oregon—History—To 1859—Biography. 11. California—History—To 1846—Biography 1. Nunis, Doyce Blackman. II. Title.

DU627.17.N94 A3 2001

910'.9164'092—dc21

[B]

2001042092

For
GLORIA RICCI LOTHROP
Student, Colleague, Friend
and
In Memory of
MARIA ANGELI RICCI

Contents

Illustrations

Acknowledgments

The genesis of this publication dates back to the year 1967. I was forwarded a typed letter from Mrs. Grace F. Pearson, Jacksonville, Oregon, directed to the executive secretary of the Historical Society of Southern California. It was a letter of inquiry: would the Society be interested in publishing a manuscript she had prepared. The letter was passed on to me as editor of the Society's publication, the *Southern California Quarterly*. I responded, inviting Mrs. Pearson to send her manuscript for evaluation. In a subsequent mailing, she forwarded her edited version of the journal of Lydia Rider Nye, with annotations of the text, along with a bibliography of sources consulted.

In reviewing the material, I came to realize that the manuscript certainly was worthy of publication because of its uniqueness: a journal kept by an active Alta California mariner's wife. However, in reading Mrs. Pearson's manuscript, I found she had edited out a considerable portion of the original text which she felt was uninteresting or repetitive. It was also clear to me that her annotations were either discursive or inadequate to what was required to complement the journal properly.

Reaching these conclusions, I suggested to Mrs. Pearson that we might co-edit the manuscript along more historically accepted editorial lines with the expectation that it would meet the standards required for publication in the *Quarterly*. The length of the manuscript also suggested that it would have to be split into at least two parts and run in consecutive issues. Mrs. Pearson agreed. I set to work.

However, because of other professional demands and writing

commitments, coupled with a sabbatical leave abroad, I was unable to give the revision the priority attention Mrs. Pearson apparently had expected. She grew impatient; in her view, rightly so. Regrettably, in 1969 the arrangement was abruptly terminated. I returned her manuscript with a concluding communication; she reciprocated with a curt but poignant farewell letter. To this day, I regret that the collaboration ended on such a sad note.

Since I had already commenced working piecemeal on the Nye journal, especially in the spring of 1969 when I was on sabbatical leave, spent primarily in England, I decided to continue to give it attention as time and circumstance permitted. I must confess that the attention rendered to the project has been intermittent. Perhaps that was just as well since the editorial requirements were considerable. This protracted endeavor had some advantages. It afforded inclusion of important materials from British sources on several research trips to London. Second, it afforded more extended research in California depositories, including search of newspapers.

Last, but not least, a research trip to Honolulu was essential if the editorial quality I had as an objective was to be realized. I was fortunate enough to receive a Haynes Foundation Summer Faculty Research Fellowship from the University of Southern California that made possible a Hawaiian visit. It proved the capstone of almost twenty years of intermittent research.

The task now completed, I wish to pay my respects to Mrs. Pearson for calling this journal to my attention. I also express appreciation to her for several notes which I have made use of in the annotated text which follows, and duly acknowledge my indebtedness to her initial effort.

In respect to my own work, a word appears in order. First, I prepared a complete new transcription of Mrs. Nye's journal, written in the form of letters to her mother and family, as well as several variant fragments. These variant texts have been utilized in the editing of the journal and where included are so noted. In addition, all her surviving letters found in the Lydia Rider Nye Collection in the Hawaii State Archives, Honolulu, were transcripted anew and are included as part of the manuscript.

A second task was to structure the manuscript in a meaningful arrangement. To that end the text was broken into chapters, with the last based exclusively on Mrs. Nye's post-Hawaiian letters. The manuscript has been set in a historical mounting, framed by a Prologue and an Epilogue which round out biographical and historical details deemed necessary to set off and complete the documents which form the corpus of the work itself.

Lastly, editorial guidelines of a specific nature were rigidly applied. First, a verbatim transcription of the documents. However, to make the documents more readable, punctuation and bracketed spelling corrections have been supplied. In addition, occasionally paragraphing has also been necessary for narrative clarity.

Equally important, to make the narrative meaningful to a contemporary reader, the text has been annotated. These annotations are primarily informational elaborations deemed appropriate by the editor so as to provide missing historical dimensions which would otherwise be either unfamiliar or possibly misleading. The single purpose of the annotations is to illuminate the manuscript itself.

In bringing this work to fruition after so long a time, I wish to express my appreciation to the following depositories, institutions, and libraries for their many courtesies and invaluable assistance: in London, the British Library and the Public Record Office (Richmond, Surrey); National Archives, Washington, D.C.; New England Historic Genealogical Society, Boston; California State Library, Sacramento; Henry E. Huntington Library, San Marino; Bancroft Library, University of California, Berkeley; California Historical Society Library, San Francisco; California Room, San Diego Public Library; in Honolulu the staff in the Hawaii State Archives, the Hawaii State Library, and the Bishop Museum.

Individuals who have made contributions both large and small include the late James de T. Abajian, San Francisco; my longtime friend, the distinguished Hawaiian collector, Paul Markham Kahn, San Francisco (now deceased); at the California State Library, the former head of the California Section, now retired, Allan R. Ottley, and Gary F. Kurutz, present Head, Special Collections; Jean F. Munroe, Reference Librarian, Scripps Institution of Oceanography Library, University of California, San Diego; Mary Jane Knight, Librarian, and her assistant, Lela Goodell, Hawaiian Mission Children's Society, Honolulu; also in that city, Marguerite K. Ashford, Associate Librarian, Bishop Museum; Barbara Dunn, Hawaiian Historical Society; and Mrs. Arlene S. Ching, Hawaii State Library. (Most of the arforesaid individuals have long since retired or may have died since they extended to me their collaborative assistance. Nonetheless, I still stand in their debt.) A special thank you is due to the Reference Department, Doheny Memorial Library, University of Southern California, for their prompt attention in handling my requests for interlibrary loan materials. For a critical reading of the draft manuscript I am grateful to Will Bagley and Robert A. Clark.

Lastly, I am most grateful to the secretarial staff in the USC Department of History for their professional care and caution in rendering a final typescript. I tip my hat to Sharon Mather and Brenda R. Johnson who have moved on to other employment challenges.

For permission to publish the journal and letters of Mrs. Lydia Rider Nye gratitude is expressed to the Hawaii State Archives. Ruth S. Itamura, at the time State Archivist, also gave permission for reproduction of a number of illustrations in her care, including two original sketches by Mrs. Nye. India House, New York City, provided a photograph of a ship painting among their holdings and gave permission for its reproduction.

To one and all mentioned above, my appreciation for your professional expertise and gracious assistance in helping me perfect for publication a more polished manuscript. Any blemishes which may mar what follows are mine alone.

DOYCE B. NUNIS, JR.
Distinguished Professor
Emeritus of History
University of Southern California

Prologue

On September 21, 1842, the brig *Sarah Abigail* came to anchor in the harbor at Honolulu after an uneventful passage of 142 days. Captain Justus Doane had set sail from Boston harbor on May 2. His ship carried the tenth company of American missionaries dispatched to the Hawaiian Islands by the American Board of Commissioners for Foreign Missions. Also on board as a passenger was Mrs. Lydia Rider Nye, wife of Captain Gorham H. Nye, bound for a reunion with her long-absent mariner husband.

Gorham Hayden Nye, a native of Massachusetts, reportedly came to Valparaíso, Chile, in 1823 on a whaleship. The following year he returned to the Pacific as master of a whaler out of Nantucket. Reputedly, he made three round trips between California and Massachusetts by 1831. It was on one of these return voyages that he married Lydia Rider Drew on July 26, 1828, in Plymouth. A native of that town, the bride, one of the daughters of Atwood and Lydia Drew, was born on January 15, 1811. Shortly after their nuptials, her seafaring husband, discontented with land life, returned to his maritime pursuits. By 1833, he was definitely sailing along the California coast as master of the *Loriot*. Thereafter he became a regular visitor, sailing between California and Hawaii, and later Oregon. His wife's arrival would end a separation that had lasted at least nine years. No doubt Mrs. Nye was eager to be reunited with her spouse, for Captain Nye was a rather striking individual. Of him, a young maritime clerk recorded this glowing description in his diary: "He is what I call a handsome man. He has black hair and eyes, and a very pleasing look. I have hardly ever seen a man that pleased me more at first sight than he ."[1]

[1]Biographical facts on Nye have been drawn from the Sacramento *Union*, July 8, 1871; the San Francisco *Alta California*, July 10, 1871; and the San Jose *Pioneer*, November 16, 1878. The descriptive quote is from the "Diary of Francis Mellus," January 1, 1839, MS, Henry E. Huntington Library, San Marino.

A photograph of Captain Gorham H. Nye probably taken during his last residence in the Hawaiian Islands, 1865–1868. *Courtesy Hawaii State Archives.*

To amuse herself and inform her family, Mrs. Nye kept a journal of her Pacific odyssey, a portion of which was in the form of a letter to her mother, to record her voyage to Hawaii, her life in Honolulu, and later, her voyage on her husband's ship to Oregon and California. Prior to her husband's arrival in Honolulu, Mrs. Nye found herself quickly included in the social life of the community, especially by the missionary group which had been sent to the Islands by the American Board of Commissioners for Foreign Missions, the first party arriving in March 1820. The Board, based in Boston, was an interdenominational body which sponsored both clergy and lay missionaries. The majority of these were predominately Presbyterians and Congregationalists. Mrs. Nye felt readily at home with the community since all shared a common Puritan New England background. There is no question: Mrs. Nye was a devout Christian; religion was a fundamental element in her life. Her journal reflects a deep sense of genuine piety and firm belief.

Mrs. Nye did not like shipboard life on the voyage to Hawaii. She remarks in her journal that the vessel was "a floating prison." Her writing gave vent to her sea-bound confinement. In writing her mother she told her that she would record "the dark side as well as the bright side." However, there is no dark side in her narrative. And rightly so, for Mrs. Nye was a product of her age: she was a Victorian lady. Yet underneath her piety and primness her Victorianism did not suppress her humanity. When her husband finally was reunited with her in Honolulu, they went to church. She described her feelings on that occasion in these words: "Many years have elapsed since we walked to the house of God in company. Twelve years since the Hymeneal torch was lighted by the altar of love—yet it burns with unabated fervor. Old Oceans may not quenched it nor time smothered it in our bosoms."

During the four months of waiting on Oahu for Captain Nye's arrival, Mrs. Nye became widely acquainted with the residents of Honolulu. Her social acceptance is obvious from her journal. One notable aspect of her personal qualities stands out: she was an expert horsewoman; riding was one of her principal leisure-time activities. Later, her husband saw that she had a splendid California horse of her own.

Honolulu in 1842–1843 gave every appearance of a thriving community. It boasted two Protestant churches built of stone, each with a seating capacity for 3,000, and an unfinished Roman Catholic cathedral, also of stone, capable of holding 1,500–2,000. In addition the European-American residents of the community had the use of the Seaman's Bethel as a chapel.

For the education of half-caste children, the city residents, through generous contributions, built and maintained a school. The children of the chiefs had a separate school and residence as well. Not content with these educational institutions, the town had the Sandwich Islands' Institute, a small museum and library, and a reading room for seamen who called at the port.

As evidence of its growing importance in the commerce of the Pacific, consulates were maintained by the British, French, and American governments. The center of government was in the king's house and in the government office. And to cap Honolulu's splendor, it had a fort, mounting sixty guns. This fort afforded residence for the governor and also contained a prison, presenting a sense of security.

Mrs. Nye had not come to a barren island. Honolulu had some twenty retail shops, not to mention four wholesale stores. It could boast a hotel, two billiard rooms, seven bowling alleys, a bath house, and two taverns where "demon rum" was dispensed. Sailors could find twelve boarding houses and grog shops catering to them while on shore leave.

Nor was Honolulu lacking in professional talent. Three physicians and two apothecary shops were at hand. On a more mundane level, the community had a bakery, two barber shops, four blacksmith shops, two butchers, cigarmakers, masons, and sailmakers. Ships would find fourteen ships' carpenters available along with three caulkers; shore residents had the services of five house carpenters, four shoemakers, two cabinet makers, three tailors, and a watchmaker. Mrs. Nye even could find a saddle and harness maker to supply her riding needs. A timber yard, copper foundry, and paint-oil factory were the only "heavy" industries. And the arts were represented by a blockmaker, printer, and engraver.

For the first time in her life, Mrs. Nye came into contact with multi-ethnics. The native population numbered near 8,000. Some forty Chinese were residents, a few operating businesses. Yearly ships from various parts of the world rounded Diamond Head for the safe anchorage in the splendid harbor. In 1842, some forty-five ships called; three were from Chile and Peru; from China, one; Mexico, twenty-two; Guatemala, two; New Zealand and Tahiti, four; England, two; United States, five; Columbia River, six, for a total tonnage of 9,435 tons, with goods on board valued at £40,000 sterling.

Whaling vessels also made Honolulu a frequent port-of-call. Sixty-six vessels visited once or more in 1842: forty-four American, sixteen English, five French, and one Danish, a total of 25,462 tons, with crews numbering about 2,000 and their whale oil catch valued at $400,000. By such visitations, Hawaiian commerce flourished, especially in Honolulu. Chief among the entrepreneurs were the "keen New Englanders." However, the British were probably more prosperous. Their capital assets, including land and houses, was estimated at £80,000, while the Yankees could boast only about two-thirds of that amount, excluding missionary property.[2]

Thus while Mrs. Nye counted the days, weeks, and months waiting for her sea-captain husband, she found much to occupy herself, socially and religiously. Sewing and horseback riding also provided enjoyable respite.

Finally, the long awaited day arrived: Gorham Nye's ship the *Bolivar Liberator* came to anchor. On March 14, 1843, her long "expectations were soon to be realized." She spied the vessel from Punch Bowl Hill, "riding proudly over the blue waves, of the yet heaving ocean," and watched it come safely to anchor. Soon she heard "a well known step approaching . . . the next moment, I was in the arms of my husband." After the years of separation she found "in him the same kindness and affections which were so natural to him." Her only distress was that a dancing party was being given that evening for thirty or more couples and there was no alternative—"*we must go*." The next day she vented her feelings: "I don't enjoy parties." Soon the rhythm of married life was established. But not on shore!

April 1st, while she was writing to a friend, Gorham appeared and announced that he had taken command of the brig *Fama* and, within three weeks, was sailing to Oregon and California. He inquired if she would like to join him. "Oh yes!" was her quick reply. Thus began Mrs. Nye's new odyssey, which would take her to the Columbia River for a brief stay, followed by a longer visit to San Francisco, including an inland trip to the Napa Valley, then Monterey, and Santa Barbara. Her journal carefully chronicled those experiences.

The *Fama* returned to Honolulu November 30, 1843, from Monterey via Santa Barbara with a cargo including twenty-six horses, lumber, and hides. The passage took eighteen days.[3] Captain Nye quickly acquired a charming cottage, furnished it com-

---

[2]These details on Honolulu have been drawn from Alexander Simpson, *The Sandwich Islands*... (London, 1851), pp. 108–109.

[3]*The Friend*, 1 (Dec. 2, 1843), [76].

fortably, and ensconced his wife in her new home. Mrs. Nye reveled at the prospect of a well-ordered existence. She carefully chronicled the visitors who paid courtesy calls at the cottage high up in Nuuanu Valley. Life brightened on January 30, 1844, with the birth of "a beautiful daughter, with black hair—black eyes—fair complexion, and in every way a good and quiet child." The baby was baptized on May 4 in the Seamen's Chapel by the Reverend Samuel C. Damon and was named Lydia Atwood Nye.

Shortly thereafter, Captain Nye returned to California on the *Fama*, but this time without wife and child. However, Mrs. Nye and baby Lydia did accompany him on a second voyage in 1845, the *Fama* leaving Honolulu on May 6. It would prove a disastrous voyage; the vessel was wrecked near Santa Barbara on February 26, 1846. Fortunately, the captain and his family were not on board, and all of the crew were saved. It was not until September 30 that they could take another ship and return to the Islands. The *Fama's* loss, however, was a financial reverse of grave consequence to Captain Nye.

Whether or not life was resumed in the Nuuanu Valley cottage is unknown. In late January 1847, Captain Nye sailed for California on the *Joven Guipuzcoana* as its master, and he went alone. Upon his departure, Mrs. Nye and little Lydia took room and board with Reverend Samuel C. Damon. Preparations ensued for their return to New England, and on May 25, 1847, they took passage on the *Montreal*, bound for the United States via Hong Kong. Eventually, they reached their destination, but sight is soon lost of them after their return to Massachusetts.[4]

As for Captain Nye, he returned east in 1853. How long he remained there is unknown, but he returned alone to California, and resided a number of years at Santa Cruz. A three-year interlude in the Islands followed before he finally moved to St. Helena in 1871. There he died, age seventy-six, on October 31, 1878, alone and estranged from his wife and daughter. What produced the estrangement is not known.[5]

---

[4]Details of Mrs. Nye's return passage and later life are discussed in the Epilogue, *post*.

[5]Details of Captain Nye's later activities are also discussed in the Epilogue. One possible factor in the obvious estrangement between Gorham and Lydia may have been his drinking. His maritime clerk, Faxon Atherton, records a number of incidents when Nye went "on

(*continued on next page*)

Mrs. Nye lived to be eighty. She died at Plymouth, Massachusetts, on February 27, 1891. Her daughter, Lydia, married Allen Bradford of Dighton, Massachusetts, on January 3, 1872.[6] Their daughter, Lydia Bradford Parker, presented her grandmother's journal and papers to the Hawaii State Archives, a fitting repository. Thus Mrs. Nye returned in death to a place she loved and treasured during four years of her long life.

Lydia Rider Nye's journal is unique: it is presently the only known journal kept by a wife of a ship captain during a voyage along the Pacific Coast prior to 1848. Indeed, it may be the only known journal kept by an American hide and tallow sea captain's wife while voyaging along the Pacific Coast in the first half of the nineteenth century.[7]

However, Mrs. Nye cannot claim to have been the first American wife to accompany a seafaring husband on a Pacific coastal voyage. That distinction belongs to "Harriet," the wife of the carpenter's mate, who sailed on the *Lelia Byrd*, Captain William

---

(*continued from previous page*)

a spree" or was "drunk". He records a July 4, 1837, celebration on shipboard this way: at 2, "pretty happy"; at 3, "well corned"; at 5, "most gloriously so"; at 7, "most confoundedly *drunk*." Doyce B. Nunis, Jr., ed., *The California Diary of Faxon Dean Atherton, 1836–1839* (San Francisco, 1964), p. 55. Mrs. Nye's religious convictions definitely included adherence to strict temperance. Whether or not Nye took the pledge and abstained from his favorite gin during his wife's voyage and visits on shore is unknown. If he did drink around her, she remains stoically silent, mayhap ashamed for such unseaming conduct in her husband for she records not one word on the subject, let alone any criticism of her spouse.

[6]Mrs. Nye's birthdate and that of her sisters and brothers is found in Plymouth, Massachusetts, Vital Records, copied by Mrs. Ella F. Huntoon in 1897, p. 89, MS, New England Historic Genealogical Society, Boston. Her marriage is recorded correctly in her journal. Her death date and the marriage of her only child are recorded in *A Genealogy of the Nye Family* by Nye and Best, published in 1907, p. 310 (which dates the marriage 1829).

[7]I have not undertaken a close examination of non-American voyages to the far Pacific Northwest-Alaskan Coast or the Pacific Basin as a whole. Therefore, I must caution the reader that my focus is strictly on the Oregon/California segment of the Pacific Slope prior to 1848, with particular attention to California. I am aware, of course, of the voyage of the *Imperial Eagle* to the Northwest Coast in 1787, captained by Charles William Barkley, who had on board his newly wed sixteen-year-old bride, Frances Hornby Trevor, accompanied by a maid hired in the Hawaiian Islands, Winee. Apparently, Mrs. Barkley kept a diary of the voyage and later prepared a reminiscence. The diary itself was lost in a fire, but Captain John T. Walbran read it and copied out passages which survive in the holdings of the British Columbia Provincial Archives, Victoria. Derek Pethick, *First Approaches to the Northwest Coast* (Vancouver, 1976), pp. 107–109, 194; W. Kaye Lamb, "The Mystery of Mrs. Barkley's Diary," *British Columbia Historical Review*, 6 (Jan. 1942), 31–59.

Shaler, in 1804, visiting first off the Columbia River, then Trinidad Bay, San Francisco, and San Buenaventura in Alta California.[8]

Nine years later, the first sea captain's wife, Mrs. George Washington Eayrs, and her infant son were on the *Mercury* during its 1813 voyage. It was not until 1825 when the *Sachem* visited Mexican California that an American wife was aboard again; this time, Mrs. William Alden Gale, whose husband was serving as supercargo on the vessel during a voyage that lasted two years.

In 1830, Mrs. Henry Delano Fitch and her young son, San Diego residents, joined her husband, master of the *Leonor*, remaining on board until 1831. Thereafter, she refused any further invitations, although Captain Fitch continued to be an active sailing master on the California coast.

From the mid-1830s, mariners' spouses appeared more frequently as traveling companions to their sea-going husbands. Mrs. Joseph Oliver Carter sailed with her husband on the *Diana*, accompanied by her young son, in 1835–1836, and on the *Rasselas* later that year, returning for a longer voyage with her children on the latter vessel in 1837–1838. Mrs. Carter was joined in the 1836 voyage by Mrs. William Hinckley on the *Don Quixote*. But, like Mrs. Fitch, one voyage proved one too many. It was her last. Like Mrs. Fitch, whose husband's home port was San Diego, Mrs. Hinckley resided in Monterey, her husband's base of operations.

Mrs. John Wilson, sailing on the *Ayacucho,* 1837–1838, tired of life at sea as did Mrs. Joseph Francis Snook, aboard the *Catalina*, 1838–1839, but the latter was persuaded to undertake a second voyage on the *Joven Guipuzcoana*, 1841–842.

Prior to Mrs. Snook's second passage, Mrs. James Stevens came to California from Boston on the *Roger Williams*, captained by her husband. The vessel had been purchased for José Antonio Aguirre, Santa Barbara, where the ship arrived, February 8, 1840, having departed Boston, September 13, 1839. Whether or not Mrs. Stevens continued the journey to Monterey a few weeks later is unknown. At that port, Joseph Steele, who had purchased the ship for Aguirre, turned it over to the new owner who renamed it the *Joven Guipuzcoana*. Reaching San Francisco on March 22, 1840, Joseph F. Snook

---

[8]See Chapter IV, *note* 35, *post* for more details.

became master. Thus Mrs. Snook became the second ship captain's wife to sail on that ship which was now flying the Mexican flag.

As for Mrs. Stevens, she stayed in Santa Barbara while her husband sailed north to deliver the vessel he had brought out from Boston for the purchaser. This appears a reasonable deduction since Stevens took passage on Captain Nye's *Bolivar Liberator* at Santa Barbara on January 17, 1841, returning after a passage with calls at San Pedro and San Diego, February 3. Captain Stevens was apparently beached, for his only other command was a brief stint, August 31 to November 18, as master of the *Bolivar Liberator* on a sea-otter hunting voyage from Santa Barbara to the west coast of Baja California and return. It is doubtful if he took his wife along.

William Glen Rae, supercargo for the *Cowlitz*, a Hudson's Bay Company ship, one belonging to the Department of the Columbia, was accompanied by his wife, Eliosa, who was Chief Factor John McLaughlin's daughter, on his 1841–1842 travels. The latter year, Mrs. Alpheus Basil Thompson finally sailed with her seafaring husband, then serving as owner and supercargo on the *Fama*, for a one-time-only trip. Like Mrs. Fitch and Hinckley, one was enough; besides, like the other two, she resided in her husband's home port of Santa Barbara. That same sentiment applies to Mrs. Stephen Smith who voyaged with her husband in 1843–1844 on the *George and Henry*, accompanied by her mother. This was that vessel's first and only passage to California, sailing round-trip from Baltimore, Maryland.[9]

A counterpart to Mrs. Thompson was Mrs. William Davis Merry Howard, whose husband finally based his operations in what was to become San Francisco, then called Yerba Buena. She traveled with her husband when he was first a clerk and assistant supercargo on the *California* for a two-year voyage in 1842–1844, and then continued as his companion when he became supercargo on the *Vandalia*, 1844–1847. Another counterpart was Mrs. Henry Mellus,

[9]The details concerning the names, vessels, and dates of mariners' spouses sailing with them have been drawn, unless otherwise noted, from the monumental work by Adele Ogden, "Trading Vessels on the California Coast, 1786–1848," typed manuscript, Bancroft Library, University of California, Berkeley. This voluminous work is arranged by yearly chronology, with ships listed alphabetically. There is also a splendid ship and person nominal index. *Ibid.*, pp. 102 *et seq.*, for the ships and names that follow in the text.

who stayed with her husband for three years while he served as supercargo on the *Tasso*, 1845–1848.

In all this litany of sea voyages along the Pacific Coast, mainly the California coast detailed above, prior to 1849, including Mrs. Nye's two trips, none could be called newsworthy in the modern sense of that journalistic term. However, there is one notable exception which needs to be recounted. The newsworthy distinctive voyage belongs to the wife of Captain John Bancroft, a man well-known to Captain Nye. It was Bancroft who succeeded Nye as captain of the ninety-ton American brig *Loriot* in 1836. A year later he assumed command of the *Llama*.[10] It was on that vessel that Mrs. Bancroft made her first and only voyage in 1838–1839.

Little is known about Mrs. Bancroft. She is reported to have been half-Hawaiian and a sister of Nathan Spear's wife. Since Spear married Jane Holmes, then Bancroft married her sister, Mary, apparently in the Islands, as had Spear.[11] When Mrs. Bancroft took passage on her husband's ship, little did she realize the tragedy which lay ahead.

On January 13, 1839, a contemporary diarist recorded the fate which befell the *Llama*:

> About 10 A.M. a vessel was seen off Di[a]mond Head with colours half mast which proved to be the Brig Llama which sailed from here in June last for N[orthwest] coast and California, otter hunting. It appears from the mate's (Mr. Robinson) account that they had arrived at the Island of Santa Rosa but a few days before the Indians [from the Pacific Northwest] had some dispute with Capt. Bancroft about provision. After dinner of the day succeeding the

---

[10]Hubert H. Bancroft, *History of California* (7 vols.; San Francisco, 1884–1890), II:708; V:730.

[11]*Ibid.*, II:708. Mrs. Bancroft was a daughter of Oliver Holmes, one of the earliest American-born island settlers. He sailed from Plymouth on the ship *Margaret*, Captain James Magee, engaged in the sandalwood trade and was discharged on Hawaii, October 8, 1793. He relocated to Oahu, arriving on the *P.W. Henry*, January 3, 1796. When the island was conquered, the island's defenders were driven to their death on the rocks at the foot of the Pali. Among the victims was Kalanihooulumokuikekai, high chief of Koolau. He had a beautiful daughter, Mahi Kalanihooulumokeki. Under Hawaiian custom, the women of the vanquished were spared, and Mahi entered the court of the conqueror. There she met Holmes, and they were married. They had five daughters, one married Nathan Spear, another Captain William Heath Davis, Sr. See Chapter IV, *note* 66, *post*.

> dispute, as Capt. B[ancoft] was standing in the starboard gangway, the Indians who were standing forward, fired at him. One of the shots appeared to enter his breast, as he there placed his hand as he was falling to the deck and exclaimed, "I'm a dead man," which was the last words he uttered. Mrs. B[ancroft] who was below at the time, on hearing the report of the musket, rushed on deck and seeing what had happened, fell on her husband's body to protect him from the Hell hounds who fired 10 muskets at him in that state, the shots from some of which entered the thigh and heel of Mrs. B[ancroft]. Besides Capt. B[ancroft], they killed one of the men who had endeavored to get a musket from the armchest. They also spit on Capt. B[ancroft], kicked him, threw fish at him and abused him most shockingly. They offered no violence to any more of the crew who they permitted to sew up in canvass the remains of Capt. B[ancroft] and throw them overboard, after which they forced the mate to take them back to Kigarney, where before leaving, they robbed the vessel of every thing they could take away and released them.

Thus, Mrs. Bancroft returned to Honolulu a widow.[12]

A happier fate befell Mrs. Nye. Her first voyage along the Pacific Coast proved a safe and pleasant one. Her activities, places visited, and people met are fully recorded in her journal entries. And those entries contain important sidelights on the history of Hawaii, Oregon, and California. That her voyage took place on the *Fama* is equally coincidental. A Boston whaleship of the same name, commanded by Captain Hoyer, touched at Honolulu, September 13, 1840, after twenty-three months' voyage. The newspapers reported that his wife had accompanied him on his extensive cruise.[13]

Mrs. John Paty, whose residence and home was Honolulu, her husband's home port, frequently accompanied Captain Paty on his regular trips to California. Indeed, for a seafaring wife she undoubt-

---

[12]Nunis, ed., *The California Diary of Faxon Dean Atherton*, pp. 123–124. An eye-witness account by a crewman, J. Molteno to [Eliab] Grimes , was published in the *Hawaiian Spectator*, 2 (April 1839), 236–239. Also see the *Sandwich Island Gazette*, Jan. 19, Feb. 2, 1839, and a letter from Atherton to Thomas O. Larkin, Jan. 13, 1839, in George P. Hammond, ed., *The Larkin Papers* (10 vols.; Berkeley and Los Angeles, 1951–1964), I:3.

The island of Santa Rosa lies off the southern California coast while the "Kigarnery," referred to by Atherton in his account, is Kaigni, the Indian name given to a Haida Indian village at Cape Muzon, Dixon Entrance, Alexander Archipelago.

[13]*The Polynesian*, 1 (Sept. 19, 1840), 59.

edly holds the record. She made two voyage visits in 1834, one on the *Avon*, the latter on the *Don Quixote*, which her husband had just acquired. She made a second two-months passage in the *Don Quixote* in 1840, again in 1842–1843 with her son; in 1843–1845 with two children, with a second trip in 1845; and finally two short voyages, March–April and July–November in 1846, accompanied by her young daughter. But there is no evidence she ever kept a journal of such a voyages.[14]

In 1844, two vessels called at Honolulu with wives of the captains on board. The first was the 321-ton *Congaree*, Captain Weston, from Boston, bound to Kamschatka. Arriving April 8, it sailed on May 3, returning September 13. During its first visit, Mrs. Weston called on Mrs. Nye. Finally, on November 20, the *Congaree* weighed anchor for its home port.[15] The brig *Laura Ann*, bound for the Marquesa Islands, made a stopover, June 13 to July 27. The ship's master, Captain Thomas, was accompanied by his wife.[16]

The year following, 1845, another mariner's wife anchored at Honolulu on board ship. Mrs. Ricker, wife of the supercargo on the *Bull*, a Swedish brig commanded by Captain Wrengren, reached Honolulu after a passage from the Columbia River and Monterey on September 27, sailing on October 20 for Lahaina.[17]

Three other vessels called at Honolulu in 1847 that had on board wives of the captains. The New Bedford whaler *Saratoga*, sailing from New London, Captain Smith, made Honolulu on January 5, 1847. The ship, already fifteen months at sea, had accumulated 1,500 barrels of whale oil. It departed on May 3 to resume its voyage.[18] The *Xylon*, Captain Millington, from New York, arrived at Oahu on February 10 after a passage via Rio, Valparaíso, Callao, and Mazatlán. On February 24, it set sail for San Francisco where it tarried during

[14]There are a number of newspaper notices respecting Mrs. Paty's voyages with her husband to California.

[15]William Paty's Harbormaster Records, Hawaii State Archives, Honolulu; *The Friend*, 2 (May 1, 1844), 52; (June 1, 1844), 60; (Dec. 2, 1844), 120; *The Polynesian* (new series), 1 (Sept. 14, 1844), 71; Mrs. Nye's guest list, see Appendix I.

[16]*The Friend*, 2 (July 1, 1844), 68; *The Polynesian*, new series, 1 (Aug. 3, 1844), 43.

[17]*The Friend*, 3 (Oct. 1, 1845), 152; (Nov. 15, 1845), 175.

[18]*Ibid.*, 5 (Jan. 14, 1847), 31; (March 15, 1847), 47.

March and April before departing.[19] The brig *Eveline*, Captain Stephen T. Goodwin, from Newburyport, arrived at Honolulu, July 18, and it, too, sailed for San Francisco on August 2, reaching that port on August 31.[20]

These examples illustrate the fact that occasionally wives of sea captains accompanied their husbands into the Pacific on voyages prior to 1848, but it was an exception rather than the rule.[21] But none kept a journal of their experiences. Mrs. Nye did—and that makes her very special indeed.

---

[19]*Ibid.*, 5 (Feb. 15, 1847), 31; (March 1, 1847), 39. The *Xylon* returned to Honolulu on May 20, after a twenty-one-day passage from Monterey and sailed on May 26 for Manila. *Ibid.*, 5 (June 1, 1847), 87. Also see Bancroft, *California*, V:581*n*.

[20]*The Friend*, 5 (July 29, 1847), 110; (Aug. 12, 1847), 175; Bancroft, *California*, V:578*n*. The *Eveline* apparently continued to traffic along the coast of Alta and Baja California, sailing sometime after October 11, 1847, from Monterey to Mazatlán. It returned in February 1848 to San Diego; by early March, the ship was at San Diego and Monterey, before sailing to San Francisco. On June 8, 1848, it weighed anchor for Oregon. After the initial California arrival in 1847, Mrs. Goodwin apparently took up residence on shore, for she is not recorded as traveling with her husband after his departure to Mazatlán, the subsequent return to California and the voyage to Oregon. *Ibid.*, VI:112*n*; Ogden, "Trading Vessels on the California Coast," pp. 1326, 1370.

[21]Prior to 1848, wives of whaling ship captains began to venture to sea with their mariner husbands. No doubt the length of the typical whaling voyage, three years, may have influenced the decision of husband and wife to sail together. The earliest known American whaling couple was Captain William and Caroline Mayhew who sailed on the *Warren*, *Luminary*, and *Powhatan*, 1834–1849. After 1850, increasing numbers of mariners' wives joined their husband on one or more passages. Emma M. Whiting and Henry B. Hough, *Whaling Wives* (Boston, 1953), pp. 10 *et seq*. (The authors relate over three dozen husband/wife voyages up to 1913.)

Chapter I

The Voyage to Hawaii

Brig *Sarah Abigail* at Sea
Lat. 29°51', Long. 37½°

Monday 2 o'clock, May 16th, 1842. To you, my dear *Mother*, brothers and sisters are these pages written. If the perusal of them can afford you any comfort, I shall be doubly rewarded. I wish to write with the same familiarity with which I should sit and talk with you, were I at home. *Surely*, you will not let this be read by any who would be disposed to criticize. I feel assured *you* will excuse all mistakes, and everything that is incorrect. Hoping you will regard my feelings in this respect, I now commence my story.

Two weeks today, since I left the shores of Boston, and this is the first time I have been able to write. But what shall I say? Shall I describe to you my feelings on leaving the home of my childhood—my only earthly parent—brothers—sisters—and friends; in short, the stone that points to the resting place of my dear Father? NO! It is not easy to clothe in language the heart's deep sorrow. You will not be surprised when I tell you it was a heavy trial, leaving home so suddenly. I had anticipated spending one more Sabbath with you and with my Christian friends (it being the first Sabbath in the month). I suppose brother told you I was not able to go to Church with him, kept chamber during the day, sorrowing most of all that I might never behold you again. Yes! A few more hours more and I leave my quiet home to go to heathen lands, not knowing the things that may befal[1] me there. But trust is in the Lord, "As the day is, so shall thy strength be."

Monday morn rose with the sun, much refreshed; went on board at nine o'clock and sailed as was expected on the 2d day of May.[1] The weather was fine. There was a great collection of people on the wharf to witness our departure. A prayer was offered by Rev. N. Adams, accompanied with remarks—closed by singing the 97th psalm.[2] All were solemn; even the missionaries, though their object was so desirable, could not bid adieu to their friends without a struggle. There was, however, much calmness on every countenance. About twelve o'clock, the vessel moved from the wharf, and we bade a silent but affectionate farewell to one—to another—in short, to all. The pilot left us early that night, and on the following morning we were out of sight of the American shores.

Thursday, May 19th. The first week after my embarkation, I was confined with sea-sickness; that was a gloomy week to be obliged to keep in one place, and, I might add in one position; for there were five of us sick and our rooms being very small, would not admit the fresh air. Often, would my mind wander to my dear home—to the room I have always enjoyed when sickness prostrated me—the kind friends that stood around me. What a contrast! No kind mother to smooth my pillow or administer to my wants (though the attendant was very kind). I would then, try to think of sufferings of the Saviour, who had no where to lay his head. But I could not keep my mind on anything. The constant rolling of the vessel, the disgusting smell of bilge water, and the continual vomiting, made our situation more uncomfortable than you can well

[1]The brig *Sarah Abigail*, 210 tons, Captain Justus Doane, was carrying as passengers the tenth company of American missionaries to be dispatched to the Hawaiian Islands by the American Board of Commissioners for Foreign Missions (hereafter cited A.B.C.F.M.). As mentioned in the Prologue, the A.B.C.F.M. was interdenominational, with Presbyterians and Congregationalists being the majority of the missionaries sent to the Islands. *The Missionary Herald,* XXXVIII (June 1842), 253.

[2]Reverend Nehemiah Adams, residing at 4 Boylston Place, Boston, by 1843 was serving as pastor of the Union Church on Sussex Place. *Simpson's Boston Directory 1840* (Boston, 1840), p. 57; *Simpson's Boston Directory 1843* (Boston, 1843), p. 27.

imagine. Oh! what a place for sickness is the cabin of a vessel—your head stowed away in the berth of a narrow stateroom—a little door in front, to be sure, but that opening, *not* into a nice airy apartment, but into a little cabin strongly perfumed with bilge—that peculiar odor, which all who have been to sea will understand. On Friday morn, the storm being over, the sun shone clear. We were advised by the Captain to go on deck; but oh! what a universal weakness; it seemed as though my whole system had undergone a thorough change, and indeed, the thought that when I was last on deck *land* was still in view. *Friends* were waving their handkerchiefs until sight was lost in the distance. But now, I seemed to be in a new world! The beauty and grandeur of the mighty ocean for the first time presented itself to my view. Beautiful! Indeed it was: nothing but sky and water as far as the eye could reach. The large, deep blue, rolling waves, crested with white foam, were seen in every direction. Their appearance was truly magnificent. Sunday it rained a little; cleared in the afternoon. Monday was very stormy and rough. Sea-sickness, that dreadful ordeal, confined me to my bunk until Wednesday. I had vainly hoped to have escaped passing through this ordeal a second time, but find one week's experience of a sea-life, will not prove a sufficient antidote, must herefore submit a second time to the tribute exacted by old neptune of those who are to become his loyal subjects. But it is dreadful, and as there is no cure for the malady but time, and am accustoming to the ship's motion, etc. I have nought to do, but keep quiet as possible—eat as much as I can, and exercise all the patience I can command.

Saturday, May 21st. But I will no longer dwell on the dark side of the picture. Here I am on board a vessel, in a neat little cabin, occupied by passengers only, and in whose company I delight to dwell for they are seemingly true followers of Christ, which renders my situation very pleasant. Though I have for a reason bade adieu to the land of my forefathers and entered the vessel which will be the place of my abode until I reach the place of my destination, think not my dear friends that I am now sitting in silent sorrow. Oh no! The thought that I have left my sweet home is indeed painful. Yet I think I can say I have found the grace of my Redeemer sufficient for me. God has not left me in this trying hour, though I cannot but grieve at causing you so much anxiety. But why should you feel anxious, my dear Mother? Let me entreat you to dry your tears you have shed on my account. Put your trust in the Lord—he will sustain you and you will be made happy. Though I never can repay you for all the kindness and love you have shown me during my life, you have my sincere thanks for every favor, and O! forgive every instance of ingratitude, and bury in oblivion every thought or word wherein I may have caused you pain, and may the Lord reward you a hundred fold in the life which now is and that which is to come. But I must leave you for the present. I already feel dizziness coming over me which will oblige me to lie down. It is not a very pleasant sensation, I assure you, though I am in hopes in time to get rid of it entirely; neither am I used to the motion of the vessel to write with any ease.

Monday, May 23rd. The first two weeks made rapid progress; the last five days gained but little, though the weather is fine, attended occasionally with showers of rain. I cannot as yet give you a description of a storm at sea for I have not realized one—though the second night out it was very rough, with a strong wind—have been at the rate of nine and ten miles an hour. Today a little more than three, which makes it rather dull. How is it possible that I wish for those winds that will convey me farther from my dear friends and all that I have in my much loved Country. Alas! it is a joy and sorrow connected. I am beginning to get a little used to the vessel, though I frequently have a turn of sea-sickness—have not yet regained my strength. We have almost every thing for our comfort which I suppose can be had at sea.

Wednesday, May 25th. The Capt. and officers are very kind and agreeable—try to make everything pleasant for us; our accommodations better than I expected, and our spiritual privileges very great. Last Sabbath we had a meeting on deck in which all on board united. The occasion was interesting, aside from the charm of novelty. It was an imposing sight to witness such an audience on the great deep. One of the sailors made a public profession of religion, the Sabbath previous to embarking. He took a letter from the pastor of the Church, recommending him to the care of the Capt., who is hopefully pious, but has not united with any church. But I have not given you the names of the Missionaries—Rev. G. B. Rowell and lady, Doct. J. W. Smith and lady.[3] I find them very pleasant and agreeable. We enjoy each other's society very much. I feel I have great cause for gratitude to our Heavenly Father for his kindness in thus providing for me. The Steward is very kind, and always appears to be ready to do anything for our comfort. This morning I was awakened by the cry of a sail! a

[3]The Reverend George Berkeley Rowell, born in Cornish, New Hampshire, January 22, 1815, graduated from Amherst College in 1837 and Andover Seminary four years later. He was ordained October 22, 1841. The previous April he married Malvina J. Chapin (born Newport, New Hampshire, April 30, 1816). On arrival at the Islands, he was stationed at Waioli until 1846, then at Waimea, Kauai, until 1865. There he died, June 15, 1884. His widow removed to southern California in January 1893, and died at Craftonville, October 20, 1901.

The Reverend James William Smith, M.D., was born in Stanford, Connecticut, July 8, 1810. A graduate of the New York College of Physicians and Surgeons, he took as his bride Milicent Knapp (born Greenwich, Connecticut, October 15, 1816) in 1841. After his Hawaiian arrival, he was stationed for the rest of his life at Koloa. Ordained to the ministry in 1857, he died at his station on November 30, 1887. His wife survived until September 24, 1891. Summary chart at end of Hiram Bingham, *A Residence of Twenty-One Years in the Sandwich Islands* (Hartford and New York, 1848), n.p. (hereafter cited *Bingham Missionary Chart*; a second edition was printed in Canandaigua, NY, 1855); Hawaiian Mission Children's Society, *Portraits of American Protestant Missionaries to Hawaii* (Honolulu, 1901), pp. 76–78 (hereafter cited *Protestant Missionary Portraits*); *Missionary Album: Portraits and Biographical Sketches of American Protestant Missionaries to the Hawaiian Islands* (Honolulu, 1969), pp. 166–167, 176–177 (hereafter cited *Missionary Album*).

sail! I assure you I was on deck in a moment. I thought of the charge you gave me, keep a letter written. Though I had not forgotten your request, I never had any heart to write. However, it proved not to be a "homeward bound" as we supposed. We are now in a region where I should expect to find a climate much warmer than we find ours today. It is pleasantly warm and no more. But we shall not enjoy so cool an atmosphere many days, for we are fast approaching the torrid zone where we shall find heat enough.

Saturday, May 28th. We are still blessed with fine weather, and fine winds, and as we are making good progress, hope in a few days to reach the line [the equator]; which appears to me like the first stage in my long journey.[4] It is now the hour of twilight. I have been gazing at the moon; saw her slowly appear from behind a cloud near the horizon, and thought how often I had watched her first appearance from the window in our east room with one and another, some whose faces I shall never more behold. Had I not been interrupted I know not how long I should have remained. It is not a satisfaction to each of us to fix our eyes on the same glorious orb and gaze at the same heavens filled with the wisdom and power of Jehovah! If we can but say, from the heart, this God is ours, it is enough.

The sun sets nearly three hours earlier with us, than with you, so the days seem quite short. I hardly know how I spend my time. I have not felt able to knit or sew, or rather do not feel inclined to do either. My eyes will not admit of my reading much. The constant roar of water has affected my head that I am obliged to be very careful. Have several pieces of music on board and some fine voices, so we pass much of our time in singing—can play several tunes on the accordion. By the way, my music box is a great comfort to me. There are so

---

[4]The reference to the "line" is, no doubt, to the equator. Mrs. Nye's ship would not reach Honolulu until September 21, 1842.

many sweet associations connected with it, in days that are past, that I sometimes think there is pain mingled with the delight it affords. I know, Ma, you wished me to leave it at home, but then you will not regret it if it affords me any pleasure. The sounds are so familiar. I, for a moment, imagine myself at home, "sweet home," nearer to me than ever.

O happy, thrice happy, are they,
Who dwell there in friendship and peace,
Contented with friends and kindred to stay,
Till the flow of life's current shall escape.
They are the happiest 'neath the blue sky,
Dwellers at home—but ah! they know it not
As do they that have wandered to try
Far away, amid strangers, their lot.

Wednesday, June 1st. It is very warm today, and were it not that we are blessed with a fine constant breeze, the heat would be insupportable. Passed a brig this morning bound to America as we suppose, but did not come near enough to speak her; this is the fifth vessel we have seen this week, but I have not been favored with the privilege of sending letters. Could you my dear Mother know how nicely I get along, it would not only add to my comfort, but would lessen the anxiety, I know, you feel on my account. But that privilege is denied me: and O! how I would like to hear from *you* and all my friends at this time, "but the winds and waves tell all the same in varying tale." We have a nice finished room on deck, use it for a sitting room, dining room—in fine weather we are glad to leave the cabin early in the morning for the fresh air that draws through the Saloon (as we call it) keeps us very comfortable. I sometimes think I am one of the privileged few to meet with such good company & accommodations. I feel no disposition to murmur. Caught two fish today. They resemble a mackrel in size and taste. It is really amusing to watch the Portuguese men of war; they are transparent, look something like a balloon, floating on the water, with small fish following them. Have not seen many of the monsters of the deep.[5]

Friday, June 3rd. Here I am more than three thousand miles from home. When I think of it, the distance seems annihilated, and I feel as though it was but a step between us. Although I think much of you by day and often dream of you, yet do not think my time passes unpleasantly. No! I can truly say goodness and mercy have followed me thus far. I am blessed with a tolerable degree of health. Could I take more exercise, it would be better. I have heard it remarked that sailors lived rather an idle life, but I find it the reverse—they are constantly employed. I sometimes think can I be on board a vessel! It seems so still and quiet—no loud talking—no profane language; in short, they differ from the common sailors. The Sabbath is reverenced by all all together at sea; it wears an aspect different from all other days. After washing the decks in the morning, there is nothing done of the ship's work, each one is free to do what he wills. Last Sabbath, I handed them some magazines—hymn books, etc. It is really pleasant to hear them singing and reading until time for the services to commence. They likewise have a Bible class twice a week in the forecastle. When eight bells strike, all on board assemble for prayers. How much like home! O brother! I feel encouraged to know, that when gathered around the family altar, that I am daily remembered by you. Think not my friends you also ever forgotten by us. O no! I trust our prayers for you and your prayers for us, ascend together to the throne of grace.

Saturday, June 4th. Another Saturday! and we are yet north of the line. How trying to be thus delayed in so scorching a latitude. It is about as warm as our extreme hot weather at

[5]Most likely the reference is to whales.

home. We have an awning, and I assure you, we do not try to do anything more than to keep comfortable. I do not wonder people in warm climates are indolent, if they feel such languor as we do, not only one, but all. However, to complete the adventures of the day. After prayers in the evening, we were all sitting in our parlor on deck, when we were aroused by the cry of porpoises. We all sallied forth, when to our amazement we saw the ocean teaming with living creatures. Porpoises! Porpoises! In every direction, large beautiful fish, in a great frolic. They seemed to have taken the evening that they might be undisturbed. They throw themselves out of the water, then dive under several feet. They came fearlessly around the ship, & appeared as if they were tempted to pay us a visit. However, we concluded not to disturb them, and they, after showing their activity & beauty, passed off & left us to amuse ourselves.

Monday, June 6th. Spoke ship *Sultan*, thirty days from Glas[g]ow, for Cape Good Hope.[6] We have had no opportunity to send to our friends at home. How earnestly I wish they might know of our pleasant and thus far prosperous voyage. I now begin to realize some of the pleasures of a sea life, and to feel that it has its charms; have become accustomed to snug apartments, ships motion, etc., and begin to think a sailor's life must, on the whole, be a pleasant one. I think I never shall regret going to sea and having an opportunity to view the wonders of the deep—marking the traces of an almighty hand upon the mighty waters.

Wednesday, June 8th. The weather is rainy, sea runs high. I do not know why it is, I do not suffer more from fear than I

[6]The *Sultan*, a 327-ton bark, under command of Captain J. Poole, had been built in 1837. *Lloyd's Register of British and Foreign Shipping from July 1, 1843 to June 30, 1844* (London, 1844), Entry No. 754. This British vessel should not be confused with an 1840 American-built bark of the same name. William A. Fairburn, *Merchant Sail* (6 vols.; Center Lowell, ME, 1945–1955), V: 2912–2913.

do. Were I on shore and saw a vessel tossing and rolling, seas breaking over her—as they have for a few hours—should I not feel alarmed for the safety of those on board? Now, I remain unmoved; knowing there is one whom the waters and the seas obey; one who protects us on the sea, as well as on the land.

Spoke ship *Mary Kendric*, thirty days from London, bound to Van Dieman's land.[7] This morning went on deck to look at some blackfish.[8] They were very plump and fat, and I should suppose would yield a considerable oil. It was quite amazing to watch them as they swam about us in pairs—appeared quite inclined to be sociable—coming around our stern, passing under the vessel, and returning again to amaze us. Wished, brother George, you were here to throw the harpoon. I am often reminded of you, and Mr. Nye, knowing that for many years he made it his business to capture those mighty monsters of the deep. But, I hope, dear brother, you are *now* at home enjoying your friends, but most of all the light of God's countenance. Or are you still enjoying the daily round of amusements? If so, listen, I entreat you, to a sister who ardently wishes for your everlasting happiness. Make the friend of sinners your friend. Be persuaded to repent, believe and live; *now*, while an opportunity is presented. Do all you can to comfort the heart of our dear Mother; and make her declining days as happy as possible.

Saturday, June 11th. Crossed the line [equator] about twelve o'clock last night. I think Neptune pays a particular regard to the Sabbath by not making his appearance. The weather is hot in the extreme. I retire about nine in the evening and rise early, to enjoy the morning air. I see the sunrise much oftener than when at home. A sunrise at sea is

---

[7]Although there is no entry for it in *Lloyd's Register*, this vessel, probably of English registry, was enroute to Tasmania.

[8]Blackfish is one of the various delphinoid cetaceans, notably the black pilot whale.

beautiful but what a contrast: at home we hear the singing of birds—the sound of the hammer—footsteps approaching—carriages rolling—but at sea naught is heard save the roaring of the water, the heaving of the ocean. There is one exception, the crowing of the fowl—the squealing of the pigs. When I first awake, for a moment, I imagine myself on shore, but soon learn to the contrary by the sound of Yo heave ho; clew up the royals and top gallant sails.[9] Haul down flying jib; haul up the mainsail, and clew down the mizzen topsail, etc.

Wednesday, June 15th. The last few days have been rather squally, attended with rain, a heavy sea going. I wish I could in truth say I did not feel the return of sea-sickness, but not to that extent I did at first; enough to make me feel depressed, and loathe my food. Otherwise, I enjoy a tolerable degree of health. We are now sailing at the rate of nine miles an hour. For one moment, I almost wish I were not going from you with such rapidity. Then again, the thought presents itself, ought I not have my friends for a while and be more solicitous to obtain the *one* I have in view? Do you wish to know whether I regret so arduous an undertaking? O no! I have not yet had sufficient trials to shaken my faith. Providence has smiled upon me, and O that God would grant me the accomplishment of my wishes in again meeting my husband after so many, many years of separation. I am glad, my dear friends, at length were so willing to part with me, and that no obstacle prevailed with me to relinquish the undertaking.

Saturday, June 18th. Yesterday, we had the pleasure of seeing a ship at a distance. We hope to have spoken her and I was on the point of getting letters ready, when we found she was inclined to say naught to us, and as the wind would not allow us to go to her, we must remain strangers. But it is much to *see* a distant sail, and feel that we have a neighbor within *seeing* distance.

---

[9]Clew up is a nautical term which means to run a sail up a yard.

Today a steady breeze; the light trade wind, clouds over our heads, a clear sun—clear moon and stars each night—new constellations rising in the south, and familiar ones sinking in the north. We have already sunk the north star—are now watching in the south for the Magellan clouds.[10] When, dear Sister, we are gazing at the heavens, how much it reminds of those happy hours we spent at Wilbraham Academy[11] when a large number of us would go a star-gazing. Then, I did not feel that interest I now do. I have become quite familiar with many of the constellations. I regret I had not taken the geography of the Heavens and your Spanish books with me. I have much time to study, but my head will not admit of it. There are a great variety of books on board—many music books—how much I enjoy singing; it wiles away a dull hour. Often from a remote corner will issue forth some plaintive note; we no sooner catch the sound than one and *all* join in full chorus, making the very heavens to resound with the echo. Nothing to disturb us, save the scorching rays of the sun which obliges us to retreat.

Monday, June 20th. Yesterday was a very pleasant day. We assembled as usual in the house on deck and joined in the worship of God. The presence of Jesus is not confined to a temple made with hands. Many go to his house every Sabbath. They go and return without a blessing; while the believing two or three, who are gathered together in his name, are blessed with his presence. This thought revives me when lamenting my *long absence* from the house of the Lord.

There is a delightful breeze today. I love, when the weather is fine, to watch the silvery flying fish, in small shoals, winging their short and sparkling flights by the ship. Last night

[10]A collection of star-clusters and nebulae near the South Pole in the sky, looking like a piece of the Milky Way.

[11]The reference is a Wilbraham Academy which was in Wilbraham, Massachusetts, some six miles east of Springfield.

several flew on board; during the day many more struck the sides of the vessel, but happily for them, though unfortunately for us, did not succeed in getting over. By the way, they made a fine breakfast for all, that is we cabin folks. The men in the forecastle do not expect to taste all the dainty bits, however, when a large quantity of fish are caught, they have some, but when not enough for all, of course, we are the favored ones.

Thursday, June 23rd. Wednesday, we had a fair wind, but not too much to be able to write, vessel pitched exceedingly. Today a calm. Should you not suppose that in a calm we had the satisfaction of lying still? Alas! it is far otherwise, the sea has a great swell after the wind is silent, so that the ship lies entirely at the mercy of the waves and is knocked about from side to side with a force you can form no idea of without experience. I fear the trade wind is breathing its farewell and with sadness shall I catch its expiring tones.

Saturday, June 25th. Lat. 30° 20', Long. 41° 40' W. A light breeze from the south, have made but small progress for the last twenty-four hours—lowered the boat, part of the ships company went to sail. O dear variety! How pleasing to the human mind is change. Caught two fish—passed the day quite pleasantly. Yet there will be hours of sadness, particularly Saturday nights at the hour of twilight, we delight to think and talk of our dear friends and home. One such occasions, we usually sing a favorite piece. I will just give the words.

Yes, my native land, I love thee,
All thy scenes I love them well,
Friends, connections, happy country!
Can I bid you all farewell?
Can I leave you—
Far in heathen lands to dwell?

Home! Thy joys are passing lively;
Joys no stranger heart can tell!

Happy home! 'tis sure I love thee!
Can I—can I say—farewell?
Can I leave you—
Far in heathen lands to dwell?

Scenes of sacred peace and pleasure;
Holy days and Sabbath bell,
Richest, brightest, sweetest treasure!
Can I say a last—farewell?
Can I leave you—
Far in heathen lands to dwell?

No! I hasten from you sadly,
From the scenes I loved so well!
Far away, ye billows, bear me,
Lovely native land—farewell!
Sad I leave thee—
Far in distant lands to dwell.

Bear me on thou restless ocean,
Let the winds my canvass swell—
Heaves my heart with strange emotion,
While I go far hence to dwell.
Sad I bid thee,
Native land!—Farewell—Farewell![12]

I have transposed *some* of the sentences that they correspond exactly with my own feelings. I *never* can forget the first time I joined in singing them. I could not refrain from weeping; in short, when I think of the object of my undertaking and the motives which induced me, there is a satisfaction which no trial can destroy. The sacrifices I have made are very great; but with the light of God's countenance, the path of duty is made pleasant. A consciousness that this is the path God has chosen for me; I can only say— "Give me a calm and contrite heart, from every murmur free."

[12]The hymn "Yes My Native Land" was composed by Samuel F. Smith (1808–1895) who also wrote "My Country 'Tis of Thee," adapted from the original English version. (I am grateful to Lance Bowling, Director, Cambria Records and Archives, for this *note.*)

Tuesday, June 28th. We have passed most of the time since we left Boston in very pleasant weather, but are now approaching the high latitudes of the S[outh] Atlantic where there is nothing but gales and squalls, of which we have today the first, or rather the heaviest. It commenced in the morning with heavy clouds in the S. West, with thunder and lightning—took in the light sail and reefed the top sail, which had not been done since leaving the same latitude in the N[orth] Atlantic. There is one enjoyment I must be deprived of for a season: the pleasure of going up on deck in the evening and viewing the bright constellations as they glisten between the tropics, and behold the moon as she glides majestically through the heavens, unobscured by clouds; and in various ways do I behold the works of God, of which I am ready to exclaim! with the Psalmist: "Lord what is man, that thou art mindful of him, or the Son of man that thou regardest him."

Thursday, June 30th. A heavy sea today. Last night we had a gale, which Capt. D[oane] called severe. When I last wrote, the weather was boisterous, but today it has been trying. Repeated squalls, and high winds have raised the sea so much as to keep the vessel tossing with violence. There is no such thing as rest, and when sitting up, are obliged to sit braced. Even the chairs & other loose furniture often take legs and travel to and fro; however, I do not suffer from sea-sickness—appetite is good. Doct. Smith makes but a poor hand at sea. Scarcely a day but what he is sick some part of it—has no hope of recovery until we pass the Cape. We do not suffer from the heat as we have done—shall be obliged to have the stove put up. I often think what a pleasant month it is with you, and how delightful our front yard looks at this time with the flowers all in bloom, while I have seen nothing but sky and water for *sixty days.*

Monday, July 4th. Lat. 40° 16', Long. 47° 05'. Nine weeks this morning since I took passage on board the *Sarah Abigail.*

If I could look back without measuring time, it would seem *four* months instead of *two* since I left my "sweet home" and friends. Some of them I left without seeing, but they are all in my thoughts, and often pass before me in imagination. This you will observe is the day of our National Independence. Though far from my beloved land, in the South Atlantic Ocean! I think not, I can forget you. Many were the suggestions in regard to celebrating the day, but it finally passed by in the same monotonous way, except the National banner was displayed. Occasionally, the report of a gun was heard in honor of the day or rather in pursuit of birds. However, in the evening instead of fireworks; had a fine view of the Magellan clouds; seen only this side of the Equator, they are very distinct tonight as the sky is very clear. For several days, it has been dark and dreary, but this morning the sun rose bright and clear, and never did it appear more beautiful. Capt. Doane got an observation, which he had not done for several days. The air is very piercing while you are sitting with your windows and doors open. I am obliged to sit wrapped in a cloak or shawl. During the services yesterday, it being the first Sabbath in the month, my mind would often revert to those seasons I have so often enjoyed with my dear Christian friends. It was encouraging to hope the pastor would not forget to intercede with God for an absent sister, while at the communion table, where I have so often had a seat, especially while on the tempestuous ocean, and destined to heathen lands. This eve we shall observe the monthly concert, though it will be some hours before our friends at home—shall think of them at the time they are making their petitions for us and for the world.

Thursday, July 7th. A heavy squall this morning, attended with a violent tempest. I know not how it is, but I hear the thunder roll—see the lightning flash and the waves threatening to swallow us up, still I am calm, or rather unmoved. I feel better to be in the room on the deck than to be shut up in the cabin, for you little know what a confusion a squall makes! In short, I would rather suffer a little more if I can but witness the wonderful power of Jehovah! The Capt. says this is but a touch of Cape Horn weather. We are now within ten days sail of the dreaded Cape. Would we had already doubled this tremendous bug-bear. I shall not be a little glad when we have achieved this, for I do a little dread the passage round with its short dark days and long gloomy nights. Took our meals in the cabin today for the first time beside a cheerful *fire* in the lovely month of *July*. Find woolen clothing comfortable.

Saturday, July 9th. This is a comfortable morn. There is a pleasant breeze and we are sailing seven miles an hour. Saw a ship yesterday. She passed astern of us, bound probably to the United States. There seems to be no chance of our speaking a "homeward bound" vessel. Indeed, I fear we shall not be able to send letters to the U.S. until we arrive at Valparaiso. Saw several cape pigeons flying around us and as they are found principally about the Cape we cannot but look upon it as a harbinger of our approach to this point.

Tuesday, July 12th. I have been so weary from the excessive rocking of the vessel that I have done but little more than to lounge about for several days. Snow, hail, and sleet were driving upon us most of the night, and the seas were "mountain high." Today the sun rose clear—about three P.M., the joyful exclamation of land! land! was heard. My feelings can be more readily imagined than expressed after seeing nothing but sky and water for ten weeks! It proved to be the Falkland Isl[ands]—had not much time to behold them before night came upon us.[13] I am now writing by candle light and it is but four o'clock. However, we passed them in safety though I

[13]These islands, about three hundred miles northeast of the Straits of Magellan, were firmly placed under British sovereignty in 1832.

could not but feel some fear, for I observed the Capt. was more than usually anxious as it had the appearance of being a dark stormy night. At length the bustle of the steward reminded me morning had again dawned. Soon the bell rang for breakfast and I had the pleasure of ascertaining we were out of danger. Truly I have reason to be thankful to God, that no danger has befallen us, and that I have another opportunity of recording his tender love and mercy.

Sunday, July 17th. Lat. 56° 14', Long. 67° 20'. This has been a pleasant Sabbath—services as usual. Prayer meeting in the morning, preaching in the afternoon. Mr. Rowell addressed us from these words. "Behold the lamb of God which taketh away the sin of the world." Find that God is not confined to the Sanctuary; can say, it is good to be here. Passed Staten Island, yesterday[14]—at sunrise, the cry of land ho! land ho! was again announced. Surely I thought, it must be Cape Horn is upon us. Yes! true enough, after a passage of seventy six days, I now behold what you and even myself thought an impossibility. Heretofore, the very mention of Cape Horn sounded heavily upon my ears. Now I find my anxiety is not to become a reality; in short, we passed it in less than twenty-four hours. It was a most delightful day; the sun shone upon the mountain tops which were covered with snow. Occasionally the clouds would be seen hanging about them which made the scene truly picturesque. For tea the steward favored us with a loaf of nice cake; the frosting was uncommon white. Of course, his design was to represent the snow on the mountains of Cape Horn.

Wednesday, July 20th. Give me joy, my dear friends, I was not weeks, nor months, off the Cape, but one day only. Yes! I am now in the South Pacific Ocean; the weather is clear and cold, occasionally a little snow, no ice as yet. At four o'clock

[14]A rocky island eighteen miles southeast of the tip of the main island of Tierra del Fuego. It rises to a height of 3,000 feet.

A.M. we were called to notice an eclipse of the moon, two thirds of its disk being obscured. (It was not visible with you.)[15] Then my muff and boa would [have] been very comfortable. However, I staid awhile—went to my berth, lay until the bell rang for dinner. Do not think I spend every day so, no! I am becoming quite industrious. Have not been really seasick since the first month, but feel a universal languor. Find a vessel is no place for me to embroider or do fine sewing, work muslin, I cannot! My head will not admit of it. Last eve someone remarked, it is fine weather for candy. No sooner did the steward catch the sound than he set about making some. In a few hours he brought forward a plate of as nice candy as was ever eaten on board ship—which afforded not a little amusement.

Monday, July 25th. I cannot give you something more of a sea life than when I last wrote. On Friday night of last week, I was awakened by the noise on the deck. Presently I heard the wind roaring heavily through the rigging, and our light vessel was reeling from side to side, as if unable to bear the mighty burden. The Capt., with a stern, clear voice, giving orders, while the sound of quick footsteps over our heads, showed they were speedily executed. For a moment nothing would be heard but the heavy noise of the wind, soon a formidable wave would break over the side of the vessel. *Sarah Abigail* would seem to pause for a moment, as if astonished. She keenly felt the injury. Soon, however, she would recover from the shock and again be abused in the same manner. She seemed to put forth all her strength to endure it. At length the fury of the storm increased; the wind howled fearfully. I felt afraid that her strength would fail. But He, who rules the winds and waves, regarded us in mercy. Gradually the wind subsided although it still continued rough. I felt calm for

---

[15]The eclipse was visible only in the southern hemisphere.

sometime, but when I thought where we were, thousands of miles from *home* on the mighty ocean! tossed by waves which were threatening every moment to plunge us into its unfathomable depths. When thoughts like these passed through my mind, I felt a little fearful. But I raised my supplications to him who heareth the ravens when they cry, and he heard my prayer and delivered me from my distress. Doct. S[mith] observed, if our Mothers knew our situation, how they would feel. I replied, if they controlled the storms, we should have nothing to fear. I then thought, our Heavenly Father did control them, and if we were his children, all things would work together for our good. Thus He granted support & consolation in the hour of need.

Saturday, July 30th. We have had a most delightful breeze for the last few days. Saw a whale last evening—judged to be eighty feet in length; however, it soon passed by, and glad were we to retreat to our rooms; the weather was cold and boisterous. Looking over my trunk today, I discovered several mementos given me the morning I left. How shall I sufficiently thank you, Sister Jane, for your kind token of remembrance, another from my little niece. I shall ever remember with gratitude the favors you and brother bestowed upon me. Do talk to your little ones about me that I may not be forgotten by them. May you long enjoy them, and every temporal blessing, heart can wish. But above all, may you enjoy them, the richer blessings of the Gospel. May you have the peace of mind which is known only by the followers of Jesus. Last Tuesday was the fourteenth anniversary of my marriage which ever brings with it recollections most interesting.[16] Is it not still vivid in your remembrance? Ah! we were a merry company then; shall we ever meet again?

Wednesday, August 3rd. Are within a few days sail of Val-

[16]This reference provides the marriage date of the Nyes—July 28, 1828.

paraiso; shall spend the week in writing in hopes to meet with American ships in port that will convey letters to my dear friends. I wish you could just look in upon us this evening and see how pleasantly we are sitting around the table, each one engaged in writing. The weather has been remarkably fine for a few days. Very fortunate for us, cannot write with any ease when the vessel is tossing about. Some days we do not take our meals with any degree of comfort, for everything will be sliding about—cannot have but one dish on at once, when that has passed round, the steward takes it and brings on another. If anyone should see us, they would think we were doing any thing but eating. But I would not have you suppose this is often the case. No! Most of the time the table is set handsomely—food very nice—have an excellent appetite—not sea-sick at all.

Last week, I amused myself in the millinery line—found my gingham bonnets not comfortable at all times—made a hood; when finished, it was really handsome, made of the most fashionable silk (Mazarene blue). In short, we carry on various kinds of work. Mrs. R[owell] is making her husband a cloth cap—Mrs. S[mith] is dress-making, while I am busy making patchwork—have 125 stars finished.[17] Doct. S[mith] is trying to entertain us with reading the history of the Sandwich Islands.[18] Do not find much time for work—Bible class twice a week, singing school, reading society, besides we must play and exercise for our health. Well, I must bid you good night, could I know you were all well, how much sweeter would be my sleep. Shall not write again until my arrival in Valparaiso.

---

[17]Mrs. Nye was making a patchwork quilt of stars—today a fast-fading American folk art.

[18]Most likely the book was the work of Ephraim Eveleth, *History of the Sandwich Islands, with an account of the American mission established there in 1820,* published in Philadelphia in 1831 by the American Sunday-School Union. A second edition, somewhat enlarged by the inclusion of an appendix, was issued about 1839. James J. Jarves, *History of the Hawaiian or Sandwich Islands* (Boston, 1843) would eclipse Eveleth's volume.

Saturday, August 6th. This morning Capt. D[oane] called the company together to consult their feelings in regard to going in to Valparaiso. The wind being fair for the Islands, it was his wish to keep on, as it would detain us three or four days, and we were not in any particular want of anything; by the way would like to replenish our water, for we have drained the casks on deck, and it will save us the trouble of breaking up the cargo; for a vessel is not allowed to go to sea without having so many gallons of water below decks; as for vegetables, the sight of them would be a luxury. In short we have plenty of beans, dried apples, rice, which is served up with cod-fish, a fine substitute for potatoes. However, Capt. D[oane] soon learned we would be greatly disappointed (though we were neutral, left it entirely to him). O! he said, I can't endure such long faces—and immediately decided in the affirmative. It was not merely to gratify my curiosity that I wished to stop, nor once more to set my foot on terra firma, though I had been an inhabitant of a floating prison for months. No! It was solely that you might hear from me sooner. Here was my package of letters to read, and knowing how gladly they would be received (feeling your anxiety must be great) no doubt my looks expressed more than I would like to utter. But hark! The cry of land! land! again bursts forth—in a moment, I was on deck, and to my surprise, saw the Andes in full view. You are already aware those are the highest range of mountains in America; the tops of which are covered with many feet of snow.[19] But I will not take time to describe them, suffice it to say they were beautiful and sublime—they not only filled the mind with pleasing emotions, but awakened feelings of awe and astonishment. We entered the harbor just ninety-six days from the hour we left Boston;

[19]The Andes, a mountain system over 4,000 miles long, contain the highest peak in the Americas, Aconcagua.

are so near land as to see the green bushes and trees. Can hear the birds singing—the smell of the land is reviving—the idea of again walking on the earth is truly pleasing.

Saturday, August 13th. When I last wrote, we had just entered the harbor of V[alparaíso]. Anchored about a mile and a half from shore, [we] were soon visited by the Custom House officer, who demanded our passports. In a moment it occurred to me that I had not taken any. Each one handed theirs, while I remained impassive, began to think I should not be admitted to go on shore—should only have a view of the city from the harbor. Could count forty-eight vessels lying at anchor. Two English, one French, one Chilian, ships of war, lay near us, each with a band of music.[20] Had not anchored but a short time when they struck up "God Save the King" or *America*. What could have been more applicable? But I am digressing from my subject. The officers ascertaining we did not wish to board ashore gave back the passports; so my fears did not become a reality.

The Capt., Mr. R[owell] and the Doct. went on shore. We were left to ourselves—not long, however. Soon they returned, bringing with them a basket of fine fruit, but better than all else besides, the joyful news an American ship would sail for N[ew] York the following morning. On looking my letters over, found none addressed to Father Nye. I immediately went to writing; wrote until eight bells struck (which was twelve). I could but imagine, my dear Mother, I heard your voice in accents mild and clear, saying, as you were wont to, *Lydia! go to bed!* you are tired. Indeed, I was tired—perhaps a little excited.

Wednesday, August 17th. Among the ships lying in the har-

[20]The naval vessels were H.M.S. *Carysfort*, Lord George Paulet, commanding; H.M.S. *Dublin*, Commander Fucher; the French *Adonis*, Commander Bayeur; the Chileans were the frigate *Chile*, Commander Martínez. Valparaíso *Mercurio*, August 11, 1842, p. 1, cl. 1.

bor, was the *Victoria*, Capt. Spring, from N[ew] York, with eighteen passengers;[21] among whom was Mrs. Thurston, who had been a missionary at the S[andwich] Isles for twenty years, and was now returning from a visit to America.[22] Likewise Rev. S. C. Damon (and lady) going as Seaman's Chaplain for the port Honolulu.[23] Do you recollect this is the ship I talked of sailing in? I think it is all for the best I did not—she had a tedious passage—sailed the 10th of March, fifty days before we did, and is now going to Callao, thence to Columbia River—does not expect to get the Isl[and]s until Dec[ember], which if nothing prevents, we shall arrive in Sept[ember]. In the evening, Capt. Spring and several of the passengers visited us, among whom was Mr. Damon, who invited us to go to church with him. He was staying at Capt. Waltches [Walsh's?], who had kindly invited him to make it

[21]The *Victoria* left New York on March 10, 1842. It was detained nearly two months at Valparaíso and Callao in selling its outbound cargo assigned to those two port cities. It anchored at Honolulu, October 19, 1842. *Protestant Missionary Portraits,* p. 76.

[22]Mrs. Thurston, whose maiden name was Lucy Goodale, was the wife of the Reverend Asa Thurston. They were married October 12, 1819. Born in Marlborough, Massachusetts, October 29, 1795, she embarked with her husband on board the brig *Thaddeus* from Boston, October 23, 1819. The vessel carried the pioneer band of American missionaries to the Islands. Reaching their destination, Kailua, Hawaii, April 4, 1820, they were assigned to that community on April 12. She lived until October 13, 1876, when she died in Honolulu. Her husband had died on March 11, 1868.

Mrs. Thurston had sailed from Honolulu with her five children for New York on the bark *Flora*, Captain Shaw, August 3, 1840, in company with Hiram Bingham, his wife and three children, who were leaving the Islands permanently. They arrived at their destination on February 4, 1841. *Ibid.*, p. 2; *The Polynesian*, 1 (Aug. 8, 1840), 3.

[23]Samuel C. Damon, born in Holden, Massachusetts, February 15, 1815, graduated from Amherst College in 1836. After a year as principal of the Academy in Salisbury, he entered Princeton Theological Seminary in 1837, but finished his religious training at Andover Theological Seminary. Ordained on September 15, 1841, he married Julia S. Mills (born August 20, 1817, in Torringford, Connecticut) on October 6, at Natick, Massachusetts. The following year, March 10, 1842, the couple sailed from New York on the *Victoria*, Captain Spring, for Honolulu. Delayed some months at Valparaíso and Callao, they reached their destination on October 19. Assigned as chaplain for the American Seamen's Friend Society, in 1850 Reverend Damon became the pastor of the Bethel Union Church, Seamen's Chapel. He died in Honolulu, February 7, 1885. His wife survived until June 10, 1890. She died in Cheyenne, Wyoming. *Missionary Album*, pp. 76–77.

his home while in port.[24] Accordingly, on Sunday morning we dressed ourselves in our best and set out in a little row boat, or more properly speaking, the Capt.'s yawl boat. Soon we arrived at the mole—found them waiting, it not being time for services to commence. Mr. Damon proposed walking. Visited the Roman Catholic church—a most magnificent building—the bells all chiming as we entered—the females kneeling to the Virgin Mary.[25] We met them on their way, with splendid mats in their hands to kneel upon—dressed very rich—a shawl thrown loosely over their shoulders—heads very much drest; they wear no bonnet. We then called at Capt. Waltches, had to ascend a high hill with a steep meandering road. It was, to me, very tiresome, but cheering to be again on land—everything was green, although it was winter, or rather the rainy season.

On reaching it, the scenery was delightful. A full view of the harbor, and the highest hills on the top of which was a row of fine buildings occupied by Foreign residents. In front was a delightful yard, filled with orange trees, rose bushes in full bloom, geraniums, and a great variety of flowers, which seemed refreshing—seeing nothing of the kind for months. Mrs. W. appeared to be a fine woman—a native of Boston. Their house is furnished elegantly. We next proceeded to the English chapel; it is situated high up the side of a hill, perhaps 250 feet above the level of the sea. It is a plain wooden structure, looking more like a school house than a church. The Chilians are bigoted Papists, and allow no other worship. The English residents were forbidden to build a church; they had, however, permission to build a place for *instruction*

---

[24]I have been unable to identify Captain Walsh (?), a resident of Valparaíso.

[25]Valparaíso, at this time, was a 1,659-square-mile civil province within the Archdiocese of Santiago de Chile. Its cathedral, Our Lady of the Assumption, a beautiful three-nave stone edifice, was built in the eighteenth century and restored in the latter part of the nineteenth.

in [this] place [so long as] they did not *call it* a *Church*. No natives are permitted to enter it. If an Englishman or an American marries a native, not even she is allowed to attend this place of worship. The congregation consisted of about 120 persons, the services were such as are usual in Episcopal churches.

Saturday, August 20th. This morning saw a large turtle floating on the water, apparently asleep. Might have captured it easily, but *Sarah Abigail* was riding proudly over the foaming billows at the rate of nine miles an hour. Soon lost sight of it. In fine, have had pleasant weather ever since we left port. Took the Southeast trades three days out. If the wind and weather continue as favorable as they have hitherto been, we expect to make the Isl[and]s in thirty days. This is a vast tract of Ocean which we have to traverse. I have contemplated it with its various appearances and think it one of the sublimest objects in nature. Well! my dear friends, if you are not tired with following me, I will carry you back to Valparaiso where I attended divine service. Really glad was I that I could, after so long an absence, again tread the courts of the Most High and I hope I felt not unthankful for the mercies I had received. Sermon from Rev. C. Armstrong from Acts 13th, 18th.[26] Ser-

[26]Since April 23, 1841, the Reverend William Armstrong had served the English Anglican community in Valparaíso. Admitted as a pensioner at St. John's, December 16, 1833, he matriculated at Cambridge in 1834 and took his B.A. four years later. After ordination as deacon in 1839, he was appointed curate at Leigh, Essex, 1839–1841. Ordained by the Bishop of London, June 19, 1840, Armstrong had a brief turn as assistant chaplain at Buenos Aires before accepting the Valparaíso post. The resident English had petitioned London for support and the locals were generous in their contributions to the Church of England "parish abroad."

Reverend Armstrong remained at Valparaíso until his acceptance of the rectorship at St. James in New Brunswick, 1857. Later he held the same position at St. John's. He retired in the Canadian diocese of Fredrickson in 1887 and probably died there several years later (c. 1890?). Letter from Valparaiso English Residents to Lord Aberdeen, December 9, 1840. F.O.16/46 fos. 141–141b (additional data is found in fos. 135–140, and in annual reports thereafter), Public Record Office, Kew, Richmond, Surrey, England; J. A. Venn, comp., *Alumni Cantabrigienses, Part II From 1752 to 1900* (6 vols.; Cambridge, 1940–1954), I:74.

vices being ended, we immediately repaired to the boat, which being in readiness were soon placed on board the *Sarah Abigail*, all as one exclaiming, "There is no place like home."

Dinner being announced, we seated ourselves around the table, which was set with great taste. At each end was a vase of fine flowers, fruit of various kinds—in short, it was furnished with an abundance of good things for the palate. So you may well judge in what manner they were disposed of after being ninety six days upon the wide ocean, rolling and tossing—not able to sit at the table with any degree of comfort, but now we are free from all intrusion, therefore you may be sure we did the dinner justice. At 8 P.M. all hands went on board the *Victoria* which lay about a mile from us, expecting to hear Rev. S. C. Damon preach. But on our arrival, it was agreed between the clergy that our minister, Mr. Rowell, should officiate. The number on board the ship consisted of forty; our company, fifteen. I assure you, it was rather an interesting sight to witness such an audience on the deep. Most all were present, and appeared to hear the word gladly—text Gal. 8th 6th. All the exercises were solemn and impressive. Services being ended, we were introduced to the passengers, among whom was E. T. Webster, an acquaintance of Mr. Nye's, who was very social.[27] Capt. S[pring] kindly invited us to stop and take tea, but most of us declined. Accordingly, we set off for home, leaving Mr. & Mrs. Rowell. At twilight they returned, bringing several to pass the evening with us. Capt. S[pring] regretted the singing was no better—said there was but few of his company could sing—wished we would favor them with a few tunes, to which we very readily complied. They then bade us good night. I immediately withdrew, feeling exceedingly exhausted.

[27]Possibly this was Edward C. Webster enroute to Honolulu. *The Friend,* 3 (April 1, 1845), 54.

Thursday, August 25th. It is now nearly eight o'clock, the usual time for prayers, but I will write a few lines as I have not written any so long. Have been indisposed to write or do any thing. In my last I told you I was much fatigued. The exercise I took was too much for me—have been sick. Though I have called myself well, yet I find I cannot bear but little fatigue, compared with what I used to at home. Find my strength here is weakness. In short, I thought I would ask Doct. S[mith's] advice. Said he had observed my debility. He finally persuaded me to put myself under his care a few days, promising me rosy cheeks before I got to the Isl[and]s, which I consented to. Had every possible attention. Now, dear Mother, I do not worry about me for I am much better. You know I promised to write things just as they were, the dark side as well as the bright side. But to return to my history of Valparaiso, I must go back to Aug[ust] 8th, which was Monday. Rose much earlier than usual. Weather not so favorable as I could wish—cloudy with every appearance of rain. At 8 A.M. a salute was fired from each ship, then the music followed which was delightful. Capt. D[oane] thought of sailing at 3 P.M. Breakfast being over, all went ashore, or rather, the two ladies went a visiting on board the *Victoria*, while I chose to remain at home and write letters to leave with some one who would put them on the ship *Coquimbo*, which was expected soon, and was going direct to America.[28] I had already sent letters by the *Eunomus;* then it was possible you might not receive them.[29] I had hardly finished when I heard footsteps approaching, the sound of well known voices greeted my ear. I went to the door and gladly did I again welcome our dear little band who had been gone but a

[28]The American ship *Coquimbo*, 671 tons, Captain Knowles, reached Valparaíso on August 25, twenty-one days from Africa, and sailed on the 29th for Boston for A. Hemenway & Co. Valparaíso *Mercurio*, Aug. 26 and 30, 1842, p. 3, cl. 3; p. 3, cl. 3.

[29]The American brig *Eunomus*, 240 tons, Captain Cookery, eighty days from Realejo and Panama, arrived August 1 and sailed for New York on August 8. *Ibid.*, Aug. 2 and 10, 1842, p. 3, cl. 2; p. 3, cl. 3.

few hours only, but it seemed an age almost, in short, have become very much attached to each other. We have spent near four months together, and we are as happy as the sea will permit us to be. Soon a boat came alongside loaded with fresh supplies or by the cackling and squealing I should say livestock—several little Chilian pigs, three or four dozen fowls, beef, vegetables, fruit—water we had already been supplied with. Took dinner. Wind ahead. The Capt. went ashore but soon sent off word he should not sail until morning. We then queried, what way we should amuse ourselves, finally concluded to go ashore once more. Then the question arose, would it answer? The Commander was gone. However, we obtained leave of the first officer and was soon set ashore. First visited the market, which was quite a curiosity, tended mostly by females; we could not understand a word they uttered. While passing through one of the principal streets, I accidently met a gentleman whose countenance seemed familiar. Upon further acquaintance found it to be Mr. Atherton, who went out in the *Don Quixote*—had sailed with Mr. Nye; is now keeping store in Valparaiso.[30] Having walked a while, stopped at Mrs. Walches [and] stayed until sundown—had a pleasant sail home—no rain—set on deck through the evening, and enjoyed ourselves finely—music all around—and the view of the city when lighted was delightful. It stands at the base of a

[30]Faxon Dean Atherton was born in Dedham, Massachusetts, January 29, 1815. After an apprenticeship to several leading Boston merchants, he sailed for Valparaíso on Captain A. L. Simpson's ship, the *Mercury*, in early August 1833. He remained in that Chilean port as an embryonic mercantilist from November 9, 1833, to December 16, 1835. On the latter date he shipped to Oahu on Captain B. F. Snow's schooner *Victoria.* Arriving February 6, 1836, his sojourn was brief. By March 26 he was enroute to California on the brig *Bolivar Liberator,* Captain John Dominis. During that interval he became intimately acquainted with Captain Gorham Nye, meeting him first on May 28, 1836. A year's trip to New England to visit family and friends, a passage taken on Captain John Paty's *Don Quixote,* found him back in Valparaíso on December 28, 1839. Married to Dominga Goñi, a daughter of one of Chile's leading families, July 7, 1843, he would raise a sizeable family. In 1860, he moved to California with his family and settled south of San Francisco at what is today called Atherton. There he lived the life of a country squire. He died on July 18, 1877. Nunis, ed., *The California Diary of Faxon Dean Atherton,* pp. xiv–xxxi.

steep hill. On first seeing it, I was not much pleased with its appearance. The houses were low, and appeared to be built without any regard to taste, or regularity. On going ashore, I was more favorably impressed. The streets were laid out in order, occasionally paved but so unpleasant were they to our feet we rejoiced to find them but rarely. The houses principally are made of one story of wood, built in Spanish style with an open court in the center, and rooms around it. They all have a balcony in front—are covered with tiles in place of shingles. Spanish and native ladies all appear in the streets without bonnets; the head is generally adorned with flowers; they dress very rich, with not a little taste. Thus far, I have given you (but not a very brief) description of V[alparaíso]. Hope when I write again to be on the foaming ocean with outspread sails, making rapid progress to the place of my destination.

Tuesday, August 30th. Are within twenty-four hours sail of the equator enjoying a most delightful breeze. There is indeed real pleasure in being at sea, such fine weather as we have enjoyed these three weeks past. Not seen any storm since we left Valparaiso. I was aroused this morning by the pleasing intelligence of a sail. Though we have been but a few weeks at sea, it is delightful to know that we are in sight of a friend. As he approached, we saw by her flag she was not an American, for she displayed a most singular banner which we found to be Dutch. She came so near as we could easily discern her crew, which were of a swarthy complexion. We were not a little disappointed in finding it was not a vessel bound to the United States. Those only who have been to sea many days and seen naught but their own moving habitation and its inhabitants can imagine the delightful exultiment produced by speaking a vessel. Whatever be the country, colour, or rank of the strangers, when we thus meet, they assume the character of friends and we part from them not without reluctance.

Saturday, September 11th. There has been but very little wind during the day, but it is now freshening and that gentle dashing about the prow of the ship tells me her canvas is full. Yesterday the waves came dashing over the bow sprit, washing *Sarah Abigail's* face finely. I, for the first time, received a little splashing. We were sitting on the side of the vessel watching the foaming billows, not aware of any danger, for she was riding proudly over the sparkling waves and seemed to rejoice, when she came in contact with the noble billow, then, with a significant toss of the head, would show she triumphed over it. Towards evening, the clouds began to collect in the South—looked very dark, a shower was approaching. All hands were busily employed taking in studding sails and top gallant sails. The men would run up the top mast like squirrels. The Capt. would give the orders to the mate and he would repeat them to the men; each one appeared to perform his part well. Had a shower of rain without much wind. Orders were then given to replace a part, at least, of the sails. The Capt. appears to be very cautious, careful of every body on board, watchful that they run no risk, kind and humane to his men who are as still and quiet as any private family; nothing cross or dictorial in his manners. We have had a cool day though sufficiently warm to admit of our remaining on deck this evening. The sky presents a most beautiful appearance in this region, being of the clearest blue with a few fleecy clouds in the horizon, a beauteous form and transparency. The evenings are really delightful; and never did moonlight appear so enchanting to my eyes as upon the sea. Would that I could do justice to some of them in words.

Wednesday, September 14th. Last night we were visited by a squall of rain, accompanied by severe thunder, and lightening which was very vivid. A ball of phosphoric fire, in appearance, rested on each mast for a few seconds. I should like to have been an eye witness, but Capt. D[oane] did not like to give us a call thinking we might be alarmed. The thunder was extremely heavy, and one can hardly imagine aught more deafening than its tremendous peals. I had, before experiencing a thunder storm at sea, thought I should feel more alarm in witnessing the lightning glare and listening to the thunders peal. It is surprising how soon one becomes sufficiently accustomed to the sea, as to feel the same security as they would on the more stable earth. I lie down at night feeling as secure as I would were I on terra firma, though the roaring wind—the dashing waves—continually sound in my ears. I sleep as soundly as any landsman. The belief that in all places we are alike under the watchful eye of an omnipresent Providence is sufficient to quell all fears and confidence in Him who notes even the falling of a sparrow, calms my agitated feelings that threatening danger may arouse.

Today it is very pleasant with a clear sun and a smooth sea. I always write whenever I can catch a quiet time. Reading tires me; work I do sometimes. I shall keep my journal open until I arrive at the Isl[and]s and put it on board the first ship bound to America. It is impossible for me to find any variety at sea to entertain my friends with, so that this Journal, with all its inaccuracies, must be submitted to them. I am now sitting with my writing desk before me at a large table, at one corner of which is Doctor S[mith] playing on the accordion; at the other, Mr. R[owell] reading, and at the fourth, the Capt. writing with his hat on. The steward bustling about, making some lemonade, and preparing some ham for lunch, and last of all, at the least importantly employed, Mrs. R[owell] and Mrs. L[owell] in their rooms asleep, and this at eleven o'clock in the day. O shame!

Saturday, September 17th. This day is one that we can enjoy highly. The fine trade wind, which is blowing from the Southeast, is invigorating. My health has been remarkably good since we crossed the equator the last time. Are making rapid progress. A few days more will bring me to the place of my destination. I feel a mixture of pleasing and melancholy sensations the nearer I approach the Isl[and]s. The thought that I am not to meet with that *dear friend* (for some months after my arrival) for whom I have relinquished a life of ease and tranquility for the fatigues of a voyage across the Atlantic and a habitation among a people of strange language. Often does my imagination wander to the morning of my departure from home. A widowed mother's heart with anguish run; tears flowing from the eyes of brothers and sisters dear, while the last farewell was uttered. But as abler pens than mine have attempted to do justice to such parting scenes, I shall say nothing of my own sensations when I found myself fast receding from my own country to find another home, many, many miles from the land of which was my birthplace, the home of my dearest friends, and the sport which will ever be the greenest in memory's treasures. But why do I indulge these painful feelings? Is it because my Heavenly Father is unkind? His ear is ever open to the prayer of the fatherless. He can support his children in the darkest hour and cause their sinking hearts to rejoice. Last evening I went up on deck to view that phenomenon of nature, the ocean on fire! In appearance, a light flame spreads over the ocean with thousands of sparkling gems, resembling fire flies in a dark night. It had a most splendid appearance.[31]

Monday, September 19th. We have all been preserved another week, and yesterday was permitted to open our eyes on another Sabbath, the last we shall probably spend on board ship. Mr. Rowell preached a farewell sermon, which was very affecting. Yes, in a few hours! (and it may be days) will land us at the Sandwich Islands. Have been packing some of my things today, feel very tired. It reminded me of

[31]Mrs. Nye was witnessing oceanic bioluminescence: "The emission of visible light by living organisms. The flash of the firefly, the brilliant 'phosphorescence' or 'burning' of the ocean, or the eerie glow of mushrooms deep in the forest at night are but a few examples of bioluminescence." *McGraw-Hill Encyclopedia of Science and Technology* (3rd ed., 4 vols.; New York, 1971), II: 232. "Oceanic bioluminescence is produced by dinoflagellates, a single-celled organism having some of the properties of both plant and animal. They are unique in using the sun's energy for photosynthesis and expending energy in the same form, as light. The light is created by oxygen combining with a substance called luciferin; the complicated chemical reactions produce light without heat." Robert W. Taber and Harold W. Dubach, *1001 Questions Answered About the Oceans and Oceanography* (New York, 1972), p. 138.

your kindness, dear Sarah, in packing my trunks so nicely. 'Tis true I have assistance, but then how different is the hand of a brother or sister. By the way, the flagroot you gave me brother, was the best preventative I ever found for sea sickness, and I would not like to go sea without it. How are your little ones? Does Sarah ever talk about Aunt Nye? Do not let them forget me, in short, may they prove a lasting blessing to you. Impress their infant minds with a knowledge of the Saviour. And may the peace of God which passeth all understandings find a place in your heart.

But I should say to my brothers and sisters who are on land to be very thankful, contented and happy. I hope you will not infer from this that I am not contented. I am, and as happy as my wicked heart will allow. Would that I could be more thankful for the blessings I am favored with. But you know not how to prize the privileges you are enjoying at home. I know you are not exempt from trials, nor ought you to expect to be. In short, any one on land with good health and a little cottage, "be it ever so humble," should feel highly privileged.

It is now near the close of day, as I may not witness another sunset at sea, I have brought my portfolio on deck that I may enjoy it to the full. The sunsets here are beautiful owing to the many light clouds that are round the edge of the horizon, tinged with the most beautiful shades that one can imagine. Above these golden tints may be seen one of purple, the most delicate, while overhead the eye finds the heavens decked with the deepest blue. Could all which renders these sunsets so delightful at sea be found on shore among the beautiful scenery in many parts of our own country, the scene would be enchanting. And magnificent as it is on the ocean, it would be doubly so when the eye could turn from so lovely a sky to majestic mountains, shady greens, cultivated fields, and the dwellings of man. I see in the ocean much which strikes me with awe, fills me with reverence for that Being who holds the mighty waste of waters in the hollow of his hand. Some visitors from land today—several birds and a butterfly. It is supposed we are about seventy miles from land.

Wednesday, September 21st. Who can describe the thrill of delight that rushes to the heart, the glow that animates once more the cheek, the hope that again sparkles in the eye, when after 142 days at sea, the welcome sound of land ho! is heard from the main-mast. Yes, that joyful sound was announced this morning, at three o'clock. In a moment, we were on deck, and saw to our surprise that our expectations were soon to be realized. Oahu! the long desired haven, was in full view, the place of my destination. Welcome, indeed, were the varied beauties which now met my eye—the mountains, clothed with the most beautiful green—occasionally a glimpse of some cottage. I could almost fancy I heard the distant sound of heathen voices. But our gallant bark rode proudly over the blue waves of the yet heaving ocean. Then a favoring wind bore her rapidly onward, and ere the morning dawned, were safely anchored in Honolulu, Oahu. Can I realize, my dear Mother, I am so far from you that you cannot be a partaker of my joys and sorrows? And must be deprived of the pleasure of alleviating your cares in the decline of life when you will most need my assistance? Ah! no; you can still feel that tender solicitude of a parent and I the love and gratitude of a child.

I hope the contents of this little book will be interesting to each of you. Remember they were written while the events were passing, and that they were the feelings of the moment. You will therefore feel disposed to pass over all errors and think it like the private conversation of your

Afft. daughter and sister
Lydia R. Nye

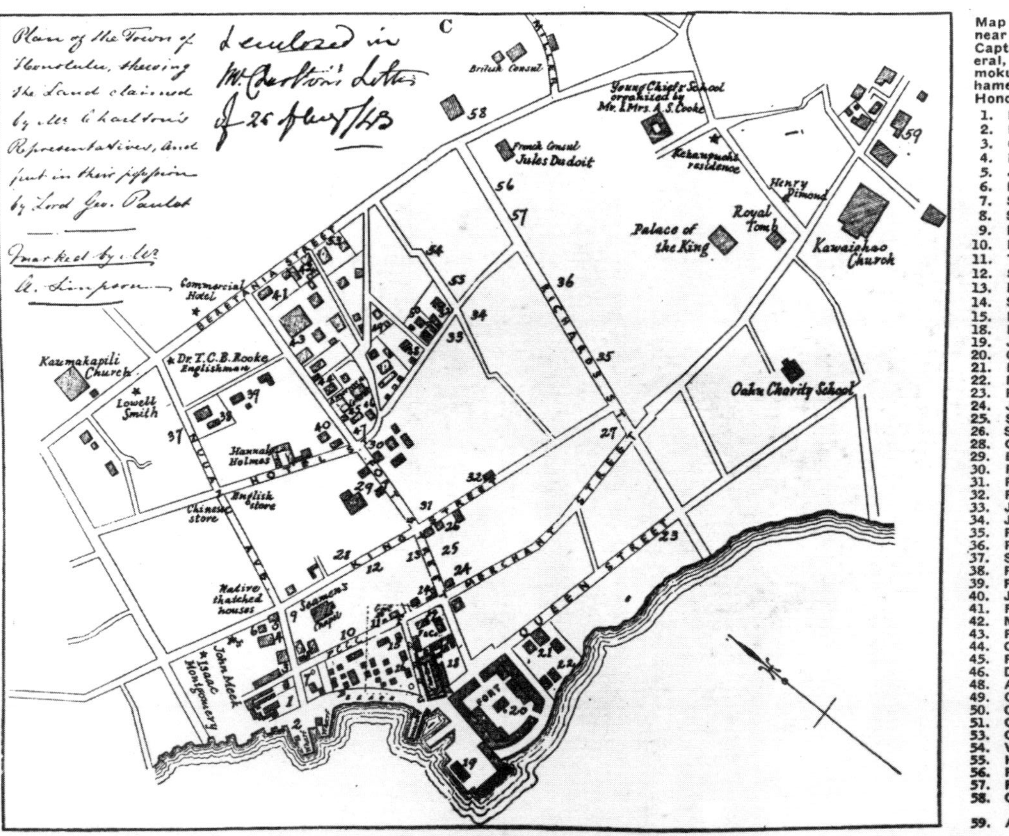

Map showing tract of land (rectangular piece near wharf, marked off with dotted lines), which Captain Richard Charlton, British consul general, claimed had been given to him by Kalaimoku, high chief and right hand man of Kamehameha I. Original in the British Consulate, Honolulu.

1. Brinsmade, Ladd & Co.
2. Brinsmade, Ladd & Co. wharf
3. Grimes Store, American
4. Hudson Bay Co.
5. Joe Booth's saloon
6. Native houses
7. Straw houses used as fish market
8. Stephen Reynolds' Store, American
9. Native thatched houses
10. Mr. and Mrs. John Paty
11. Two-story building with lookout
12. Seamen's chapel
13. Pierce & Brewer
14. Small wooden buildings
15. Empty lot 16. Sheds 17. French & Co.
18. Henry Skinner & Co.
19. James Robinson & Co.
20. Old fort and residence Governor Kekuanoa
21. Hale Kauwila, Government House
22. Mauna Kilika, Government House
23. Residence, Kekauouli
24. John Cummins Store
25. Sung & Co. bakery
26. Store 27. Anton Silva
28. C. H. Nicholson, tailor
29. E. C. Webster Store
30. Robert Davis, American
31. Residence, High Chiefs Paki and Kónia
32. Residence, High Chiefs Paki and Konia
33. Judge Robertson's residence
34. James Jackson Jarvis
35. Residence, Princess Victoria
36. Residence, William Sumner
37. Scattered native houses
38. Residence, Mr. Skinner, Englishman
39. Father Damon
40. John Colcord, blacksmith
41. Residence, Charles Brewer
42. Mr. Jones
43. Roman Catholic Church
44. Captain John O. Dominis
45. French Hotel
46. Dr. R. W. Wood ..47. Stove
48. Alexander Adams, Englishman
49. Captain Dowsett, Englishman
50. Odd Fellows Hall
51. George Pelly 52. William Wond
53. Captain and Mrs. J. O. Carter
54. William French residence
55. Hawaii Theater
56. Residence, Chief Kaeo and Lahilahi
57. Residence, Chief Haalelea
58. Captain Dominis residence; now Washington Place (residence, governors of Hawaii)
59. American missionary houses

Map of Honolulu 1843. *Courtesy Hawaii State Archives.*

Chapter II

Hawaiian Interlude

September 21, 1842. Arrived at Honolulu, Oahu, after a passage of 142 days in the *Sarah Abigail* (Capt. Doane). Anchored about one mile from the shore; was soon visited by several Americans, among whom was Mr. Brewer, who bade me welcome to his house. On arriving at the wharf, a carriage was in readiness, which soon conveyed me to my new house; was introduced to Mrs. B[rewer] who appeared a very polite and sensible woman, easy and social.[1]

[1]Charles Brewer, born in Boston, March 27, 1804, after a rather decent education, took to sea when seventeen, shipping out as a green hand on the brig *Palmer*, bound to Calcutta. Captain Hall's command had been built at Medford in 1820, "and proved to be a fine vessel in every respect." The young man's first voyage, sixteen months in duration, was followed by a second, five-month round trip from Boston to Liverpool.

On February 23, 1823, he sailed from Boston on the *Paragon*, Captain William Cole, for Hawaii and China. On board as second mate was John Dominis, a man destined to sail the Pacific coast for years to come, as well as Thomas Crocker, U.S. Consul to the Sandwich Islands, and his clerk, Robert Elwell. The ship reached Honolulu on August 1, 1823, and departed in February 1824 for China. After circumnavigating the globe, the *Paragon* again made a trans-Atlantic crossing from Charleston, South Carolina, to Liverpool. Brewer signed on the 130-ton *Chinchilla*, Captain Thomas Meek, bound for the Hawaiian Islands in 1826. Leaving New York on December 25, 1826, the Islands were reached the following April, after a 150-day passage. A voyage to Sitka proved lucrative before the vessel headed across the Pacific on the rest of its journey. The *Chinchilla* repeated the same pattern in 1827 and 1828.

Two lengthy tours of duty on the *Ivanhoe*, 1829–1831, in Pacific commerce ended when Brewer accepted command of the *Victoria*, based out of Honolulu, engaged in trading along the Alta California coast. A long career in Pacific trade was now assured.

In 1840, while on a visit to New England, he married Martha Turner. He also purchased the ship *William Gray*. On March 14, 1841, Brewer sailed the ship for Valparaíso, with his wife on board, then Tahiti, and finally, Honolulu.

Entering a partnership with Henry A. Peirce, Brewer prospered. In 1843, Peirce retired, and C. Brewer & Co. continued, with a nephew as an associate until 1845. In that year, Brewer liquidated his holdings and sailed for Boston, via the Pacific, on the *Montreal*, with his family. Three years later he returned on the *Samoset* for an eight-month business

(*continued on next page*)

[*September*] *22*. Some disappointed in not finding Mr. Nye at the Isl[ands] though in reality I did not anticipate it. Not well today—feel the change very sensibly.

23. Most of the Foreign residents called on me today.

24. Unpacked my things—feel quite fatigued.

25. Went to the native Church in the morn;[2] to the Bethel in the evening.[3]

26. Finished unpacking; found everything in good order.

27. Received calls from Foreign and Missionary ladies and gentlemen.

(*continued from previous page*)

sojourn. He continued to maintain his financial interest in shipping. In 1884, he was living on a ten-acre estate at Jamaica Plains, New York. Charles A. Brewer, *Reminiscences* (Jamaica Plains, NY [c. 1884]), *passim*. His death date is unknown [c. 1884–1891?].

[2]The Reverend Lowell Smith was pastor at the native church. He had sailed on board the *Mentor*, Captain Rice, from New London, Connecticut, with his wife, the former Abigail Willis Tenney (born December 4, 1809) of Barre, Massachusetts, on November 21, 1832. Born in Heath, Massachusetts, November 27, 1802, he graduated from Williams College in 1829, completed his theological studies at Auburn Seminary in 1832, and was ordained on September 26.

Arriving at the Islands, May 1, 1833, as part of the sixth party of missionaries sent by the American Board, he served at Kaluaaha, Ewa, from 1834 to 1836, when he was transferred to Honolulu and was pastor of the Second Church (Kaumakapili) for thirty years. He lived out his life in church service, dying at Honolulu, May 8, 1891, while his wife lived only until January 31, 1885. *Bingham Missionary Chart*; Judd, *Voyages to Hawaii before 1860*, p. 28; *Protestant Missionary Portraits*, pp. 44, 48; *Missionary Album*, pp. 178–179.

[3]The Bethel, a chapel for seamen, had been built under the auspices of the American Seamen's Friend Society. Land was donated by the king and the construction was handled by Charles Burnham, a carpenter newly arrived. On November 28, 1833, the Reverend John Diell, who initiated the project, dedicated the structure. It was a two-story building, a library and reading room below, a meeting room above. Bradford Smith, *Yankee in Paradise* (Philadelphia and New York, 1956), p. 184.

Reverend Diell, born August 1, 1808, in Cherry Valley, New York, completed his education at Hamilton College in 1827 and his religious studies at Andover Seminary, 1832. With his wife, Caroline Platt (born Plattsburg, New York, in 1807), he reached Honolulu on the *Mentor*, Captain Rice, with the sixth missionary party, May 1, 1832. He departed in 1839 for a voyage around the world for his health, and returned to the Islands on the bark *Flora*, June 20, 1840, having sailed from New York on January 7. On December 2, 1840, he sailed for the United States, with his wife and three children on the ship *Lausanne*, Captain Spaulding, but died at sea, January 18, 1841. His widow died at Adriance, Virginia, on January 16, 1901. *Bingham Missionary Chart*; Judd, *Voyages to Hawaii before 1860*, p. 27; *The Polynesian*, 1 (June 27, 1840), 2; (Dec. 5, 1840), 3; *Protestant Missionary Portraits*, p. 45; *Missionary Album*, pp. 80–81.

28. Made a few calls; took tea to Mrs. Knapp's, Missionaries.[4]

29. Rode up Nuanna [Nuuanu] Valley with Mrs. M[oore][5] to call on Mrs. Paty.[6]

---

[4]Mrs. Knapp, whose maiden name was Charlotte Close, like her husband Horton O. Knapp (born March 21, 1813; died March 28, 1845), was a native of Greenwich, Connecticut (born May 26, 1813). The couple embarked on the *Mary Frazier*, Captain Charles Sumner, from Boston, December 14, 1836, as members of the American Board's eighth missionary company. Arriving at the Islands, April 9, 1837, they were assigned to Waimea, Hawaii, and later to Honolulu. After her husband's death, Mrs. Knapp married the Reverend Daniel Dole, June 22, 1846. She died July 5, 1874. *Bingham Missionary Chart*; Bernice Judd, *Voyages to Hawaii before 1860* (Honolulu, 1974), p. 30; *Protestant Missionary Portraits*, p. 63; letter from Miss Agnes C. Conrad, State Archivist for Hawaii, March 19, 1969; *Missionary Album*, p. 133.

[5]Mrs. Moore was Charles Brewer's aunt. She and her husband came to Honolulu with Brewer on the *William Gray* in 1841, leaving New York on April 1 and reaching Oahu October 9. Her husband, George M. Moore of Providence, Rhode Island, died at Honolulu, November 2, 1849. Brewer, *Reminiscences*, pp. 50, 52; *The Polynesian*, 1 (Oct. 9, 1841), 3; *The Friend*, 7 (Nov. 15, 1849), 77.

[6]There were three Paty brothers, Henry, John, and William, all Massachusetts-born, sons of a seafaring father. On December 27, 1833, the three departed Boston for Honolulu aboard the brig *Avon*. By May 1834, they reached their destination and commenced careers as Pacific traders.

Henry, born in 1809, jointed with his brothers in mercantile careers involving commerce between the Islands, California, and New England. He committed suicide on his brother John's vessel, the *Don Quixote*, while enroute from Valparaíso to Honolulu in 1841. Mrs. Edward C. Green, ed., "Journal of Captain John Paty, 1807–1868," *California Historical Society Quarterly*, XIV (Dec. 1935), 292, 314–315, 322.

John, the eldest, born in Plymouth, February 22, 1807, early took to the sea. At the age of twenty-one he was a captain. In 1837, he took his first ship to Alta California from the Islands, sailing his brother Henry's schooner, the *Clarion*. He was to be a frequent visitor thereafter on his own vessel, the bark *Don Quixote*, 1838–1848, and on subsequent ships up to 1866. He claimed to have made the Hawaiian-California passage over eighty times—and without losses of any kind. He died in Hawaii at the age of sixty-one, November 11, 1868. He married Mary Ann Jefferson, August 18, 1831. She often traveled with him and made the voyage to Hawaii in 1833. She would survive her spouse until 1891. *Ibid.*, pp. 292 *et seq.*; Mrs. F. H. Day, "Sketches of the Early Settlers of California: Captain John Paty," *The Hesperian*, III (Sept. 1859), 289–300; Sacramento *Union*, Sept. 10, 1859; Sacramento *Bee*, Sept. 17, 1961.

William, born in 1814, the youngest, joined with John in forming the firm of Paty & Company in Honolulu in 1841, with John as the sea captain making voyages to and from the West Coast, while William was the storekeeper. Eli Southworth, another New Englander, was the third partner. He first visited California in 1838 on the *Don Quixote*, possibly earlier (1833–1835) on the *Loriot*. As a business partner, he was in San Francisco, 1843–1845. Later he entered the lumbering business and from 1853 lived with William Heath Davis at San Lean-

(*continued on the next page*)

30. Rode in the valley with Capt. D[oane] to Mrs. Brewer's cottage about 3 miles.

October 1. Cannot but feel sad today, as I took my leave of the frail bark, which had, through the mercy of God, borne me safely more than 18,000 miles across the mighty deep. The *Sarah Abigail* sailed for St. Blas, thence to the U.S.; sent letters on the Coast, likewise to America.[7]

2. Today heard an excellent sermon from Mr. Dole.[8]

3. Rode horseback for the first time up to Nuanna Valley, more than two miles, and spent the day to Mrs. Paty's.

4. A vessel unexpectedly stopped here from the coast.[9] Saw Mr. Nye at Montera [Monterey] 25 days since, all well. While I was lamenting at not having a letter, Mr. B[rewer] said he

---

(*continued from previous page*)

dro until his death in 1857. William maintained his residence in Hawaii. Bancroft, *California*, V: 729; *Sandwich Island Gazette*, May 26, p. [3]; Nov. 17, 1838, p. [3].

John was commissioned Naval Supervisor by King Kamehameha III and requested to "see to the welfare of the Hawaiian natives in California and Mexico"; while William, on January 1, 1843, was appointed Harbormaster and Collector General of Customs in Honolulu. William married his cousin, the former Martha A. Paty, of Plymouth, in May 1839. They lived in a pleasant grass-thatched house in Nuuanu Valley, a favorite place of residence, then as now, because it is much cooler than the sun-drenched plain Honolulu occupies. John's wife also lived on Oahu. Their home was situated in Honolulu not far from that of Captain Brewer. Paty Journal in Harbormaster: Arrivals and Departures, Honolulu Harbor, Oct. 21, 1842–Dec. 31, 1849, including the journal kept by William Paty, Jan. 1, 1842–Jan. 28, 1845, Hawaii State Archives, Honolulu (hereafter cited Paty's Harbormaster Records and/or Paty Journal and HSA); Green, ed. "Captain John Paty's Journal," pp. 292 *et seq.*

[7]The *Sarah Abigail* returned to Honolulu on January 5, 1843, sailing on the 9th. *The Friend*, 1 (Feb. 1843), 8.

[8]The Reverend Daniel Dole, a native of Bloomfield (now Skowhegan), Maine, was born September 9, 1808. A graduate of Bowdoin College, 1836, and Bangor Seminary, 1839, he was ordained in 1840. With his wife, Emily Hathaway Ballard (born Hallowell, Maine, June 11, 1808), whom he married on October 2, 1840, he came to the Islands in the ninth missionary party on the *Gloucester*, Captain Estabrook. Departing Boston on November 14, 1840, the vessel arrived in Honolulu, May 21, 1841. On the death of his wife in Honolulu, April 27, 1844, he married the widow, Charlotte Close Knapp, June 22, 1846. Dole was stationed first at Punahou, Oahu, later at Koloa. He died at Kapaa, Kauai, August 26, 1878. *Protestant Missionary Portraits*, p. 73; Judd, *Voyages to Hawaii before 1860*, p. 33; *The Polynesian*, 1 (May 22, 1841), 3; *The Friend*, 2 (May 1, 1844), 52.

[9]The vessel was probably the whaler *General Scott*, 333 tons, out of Fairhaven, Massachusetts, commanded by Captain Fosdick. Already at sea over two years, it called at Monterey in early September 1842, then departed. It reached Fairhaven on June 18, 1843. Ogden, "Trading Vessels on the California Coast," p. 1019.

had one for me; on reading it, found it dated at Montera and sent to this Isl[and] to meet me on my arrival.

5. Went a shopping this morn; rode horseback on the plain this afternoon.

6. No dressmaker here. Everyone makes their own dresses. O dear! can I? Well, I must try; today fitted the lining to a white dress.

7. Accepted an invitation from Mr. and Mrs. Hooper to tea this eve., the American Consul.[10]

8. Have been dressmaking all day. Singing school this evening.

9. Heard Rev. Lesley preach (Methodist) from Columbia River, Oregon.[11]

10. Been a shopping; found a nice piece of merino for riding dress.

11. This morning Mrs. Paty sent her carriage for me to come to Nuanna Valley and spend the week. Shall take my

[10]William Hooper, from Boston, voyaged to the Hawaiian Islands with his two business partners, Peter A. Brinsmade and William Ladd. In December 1832, they entered into partnership, forming Ladd & Company. By late July 1833, they were Honolulu residents. All in their twenties, Hooper was the youngest, twenty-four. Two years later the firm shifted its interests from trade to agriculture and obtained a plantation at Koloa in the southeastern corner of the island of Kauai, with young Hooper placed in charge. A new dimension in the economic life of Hawaii was thus established: the Islands' first permanent sugar cane plantation. Unfortunately, Ladd & Company would be forced into bankruptcy by November 1, 1844, and a sheriff's sale on April 18, 1845, would foreclose on Koloa. Hooper served as U.S. consul, 1842–1844. Harold W. Bradley, *The American Frontier in Hawaii: The Pioneers, 1789–1843* (Stanford, Calif., 1942), pp. 236*n*, 244–246; Bernice Judd, "Koloa: A Sketch of Its Development," *Forty-Fourth Annual Report of the Hawaiian Historical Society* (Honolulu, 1935), pp. 51–80; Bradford, *Yankees in Paradise*, pp. 274–275.

[11]The Reverend David Leslie was born in New Hampshire in 1797. He sailed for the Oregon Methodist Mission on the ship *Sumatra* from Boston, January 20, 1837, accompanied by his wife and three young daughters. They reached Fort Vancouver on September 7. In 1838, he was elected justice of the peace by the American settlers. Later he served as chaplain for the first Territorial Legislature, which met in July 1849, and for twenty-five years was on the board of trustees of Willamette University from its founding in 1845 as the Oregon Institute. He died at Salem, May 1, 1869. Caroline C. Dobbs, *Men of Champoeg* (Portland, 1932), pp. 60–63; Hubert H. Bancroft, *History of Oregon* (2 vols.; San Francisco, 1886–1888), I: 161.

He was in Honolulu at this time as escort to two young daughters whom he brought to place in school, having lost his wife several months before. Gustavus Hines, *Oregon: Its History, Conditions and Prospects*... (Buffalo, 1851), p. 137.

riding dress and make it while there. Mr. P[aty] takes breakfast and does not return until evening; has his dinner sent to the store.[12]

14. Have [had] a nice still time. Did not think I should succeed so well in dress-making, shall trim with velvet and buttons. Fortunate for me I took the [button] moulds with me.

15. Well, my habit is all pow [*pau*], a native word; means finished, done—sets finely too. No riding caps to be bought here, shall try my skill in making one.

16. Rode home early this morn (Sunday) heard Rev. G. Rowell preach at the Bethel, Rev. L. Smith at the native church.[13]

17. Rode on horseback up to Mrs. P[aty] with several to pass the evening only was prevailed upon to spend another week.

18. I enjoy the country very much, it is so quiet and cool. The scenery, too, is beautiful, and we make quite a little band of Plymouth folks, four with Mr. Gleason.[14] Every day I think of something new to relate to Mrs. P[aty] about friends and home which is very gratifying.

---

[12]The eating habits of foreign residents of Oahu were those of New England at that time—namely, a very substantial breakfast that included meat or fish, and potatoes as well as numerous other items; dinner, which was even more substantial, and which was served sometime between 12 noon and 3 P.M.; and tea, which consisted of tea with bread and butter unless guests were present, in which case, the menu was more varied. This was served around 7 P.M.—sometimes earlier—and was a favorite time for entertaining, if one may judge from the number of invitations Mrs. Nye received.

[13]Not to be confused with the stone church, Kawaiahao, dedicated July 21, 1842, and generally known as the King's Chapel. It was attended by Hawaiian royalty and nobility (the *ali'i*) as well as many missionary families. Ethel M. Damon, *Early Hawaiian Churches* (Honolulu, 1924), pp. 3–5, 16–19, 24–26, and in her in-depth study, *The Stone Church at Kawaiahao* (Honolulu, 1945), pp. 54–58.

[14]James Henry Gleason, born in Plymouth, Massachusetts, October 22, 1823, a nephew of William and John Paty, reached Honolulu on board the ship *California*, December 3, 1841. Entering the employ of Paty & Co., he served until 1845 in Hawaii, when he became the firm's resident agent at Monterey. With the advent of the gold rush, he struck out on his own as a merchant, first in San Francisco, then later in Monterey. He died in 1860, leaving a widow with four sons and four daughters. Duncan Gleason, ed., "James Henry Gleason: Pioneer Journal and Letters, 1841–1856," *Quarterly of the Historical Society of Southern California*, XXXI (March–June 1949), 11–52; Duncan and Dorothy Gleason, eds., *Beloved Sister: The Letters of James Henry Gleason, 1841 to 1859* (Glendale, Calif., 1978), pp. 79–88.

19. Ship *Victoria* arrived this morning. Sailed 50 days before I did from N.Y. with 18 passengers, among whom is the seamen's Chaplain, Rev. S. C. Damon.[15]

20. This morning a very rare occurrence, an engagement was announced between Miss Piper and Mr. Rickar; it will be quite a treat to have a *Yankee wedding.*[16]

21. Very rainy. Made a white cambric muslin dress this week.

22. Had an old fashioned ironing today of muslins only, dare not trust the natives to do them up.

23. Heard Mr. Damon's introductory sermon this morning. Mr. Richmond in the eve (a Methodist from Oregon).[17]

24. Took tea to Mr. Grimes, he is a nephew of Capt. Grimes.[18]

---

[15]See Chapter I, *note* 23, *ante*, for Damon biographical sketch.

[16]Sarah Piper and O. P. Ricker were married on December 19, 1842. See *note* 63, *post.* (Ricker is sometimes spelled Rickar.)

[17]John P. Richmond, physician and Methodist Episcopal Church missionary, a native of Illinois, sailed from New York with his wife and four children on board the *Lausanne*, October 10, 1839. The vessel, bound for the Oregon country, carried fifty-two passengers, including sixteen children. One June 1, 1840, Fort Vancouver was reached. Dr. Richmond and his family were stationed at the Nisqually mission for the ensuing months. On September 1, 1842, they sailed for Hawaii in the *Chenamus.* "Methodist Annual Reports Relating to the Willamette Mission, 1834–1848," *Oregon Historical Quarterly*, XXIII (Dec. 1922), 315*n*; Nellie B. Piper, ed. and trans., "Extracts from Explorations of the Oregon Country. . . ." *Ibid.*, XXVI (June 1925), 186*n*; John M. Cause, ed., "The Diary of Henry Bridgeman Brewer: Being a Log of the Lausanne and the Time-Book of the Dalles Mission," *ibid.*, XXIX (June 1928), 191, 194; (Dec. 1928), 358; Hines, *Oregon*, pp. 38–41.

[18]Eliab Grimes and his nephew Hiram, both Massachusetts-born, were two of Honolulu's leading merchants for over twenty years. Their partnership was a typical one: Eliab was the sea-going merchantman, Hiram the landlocked storekeeper. They early engaged in exploiting Alta California commerce, first as sea-otter hunters, then in the hide and tallow trade. Eliab, after a number of visits to the Pacific coast, applied to the Mexican government for a land grant which was conferred on him in 1844, the Rancho Paso, ten leagues situated northeast of Sacramento.

Hiram formed a partnership with William Heath Davis, San Francisco merchant, in 1845. After a brief California visit in February 1847, he returned on the *Euphemia* in July with his wife and child to take up permanent residence. Born March 20, 1780, in Fitchburg, Massachusetts, he died in San Francisco on November 7, 1848, at the age of sixty-eight. *California Star*, Nov. 18, 1848; Bancroft, *California*, III: 767–768; Robert G. Cowan, *Ranchos of California* (Fresno, 1956), p. 58; William Heath Davis, *Seventy-Five Years in California*, edited by Harold D. Small (San Francisco, 1967), pp. 76, 119–121, 141–142, 186.

James D. Dana, naturalist on the U.S. Navy Exploring Expedition, Captain Charles Wilkes commanding, sketched these three views of Honolulu which provides a panoramic sweep as seen by him in November 1840. Above: On the far left is the Honolulu fort and ship anchorage. Below: On the far right is the native church built by the Protestant missionaries. Above, right: Showing Diamond Head on the far right.

Courtesy Hawaii State Archives.

A lithograph of the fort guarding the Honolulu Harbor. Reproduced from Sir Edward Belcher, *Narrative of a Voyage Round the World* (2 vols.; London, 1843).

Two drawings by Mrs. Lydia Rider Nye: one of Captain Charles Brewer's house and the newly dedicated Cathedral of Our Lady of Peace in 1843 (above), and one of the Native Stone Church.
Courtesy Nye Collection, Hawaii State Archives.

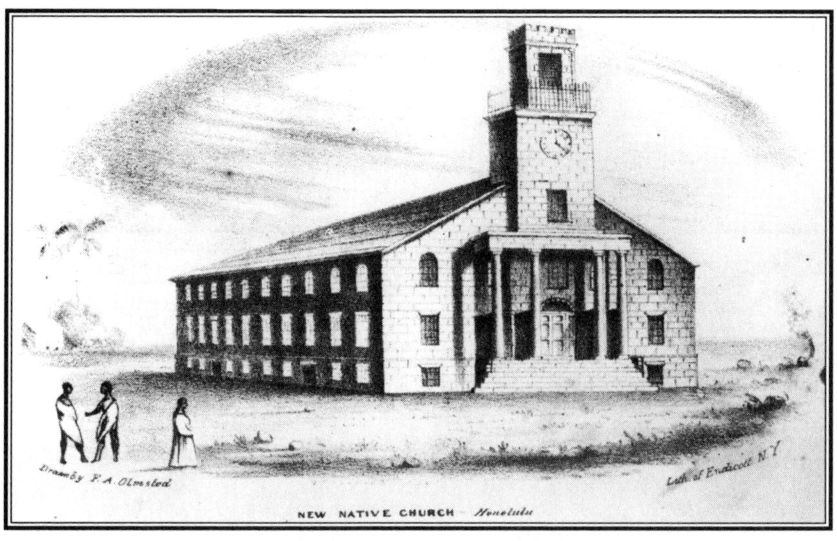

Lithograph of Kawaiahoa, the native stone church. It was formally dedicated on July 21, 1842. From Francis A. Olmstead, *Incidents of a Whaling Voyage* (New York, 1841). *Courtesy Hawaii State Archives.*

Lithograph of King Kamehameha III and Queen Kalama. They were married on February 14, 1837. The King ruled Hawaii from 1825 to December 15, 1854, when he died. From Steen Bille, *Beretning om Corvette Galathea's Riese Omkring Jorden 1845, 46 or 47* (Kjobenhav, 1851). *Courtesy Hawaii State Archives.*

25. Rode with Mr. and Mrs. B[rewer] horseback which I find I must often do for exercise, generally start at 4 or half past, P.M.

26. Company to dine, indeed, we have most every day.

27. This day will be long remembered by the natives in Honolulu, as an era in the great cause of temperance. At nine in the morning the cold water army (consisting of natives only) assembled at their place of meeting and having formed a procession, began their march through the principal streets, to the number of about 1400—dressed in their best, which was very comical, most of their heads trimmed with wreaths of green and yellow flowers, with a Temperance badge on their shoulders and their banners floating in the air—while they kept pace with the sound of martial music.[19] These were followed by a dense crowd of natives who thronged the side-walks. The multitude proceeded to the native church. His Excellency, Governor Kekuanaoa, addressed them in a brief and pertinent speech, which was received with great cheering.[20] He was followed by the (big mouth) Queen, who was received in like manner.[21] Rev. Leslie addressed them in

[19]Actually, the Temperance Society was established April 26, 1842. On that date, the king and others "pledged themselves to total abstinence from all that can intoxicate." The occasion noted by Mrs. Nye was a culmination of the movement. One enthusiast wrote: "Temperance laws are now triumphant, and the nation is a temperance nation, from the king on the throne down to the little children. All are collected into a 'cold-water army.' We have had a grand festival. *Fourteen hundred* children marched in procession with music and banners, dined together, made speeches, and hurrahed in the most approved style." Laura Judd, *Honolulu: Sketches of the Life in the Hawaiian Islands from 1828 to 1861*, edited by Dale L. Morgan (Chicago, 1966), pp. 157, 167–168. For further discussion of the temperance movement, see Ralph S. Kuykendall, *The Hawaiian Kingdom, 1778–1854* (Honolulu, 1938), pp. 161–163.

[20]Mateo Kekuanaoa (born c. 1791?), the last survivor of the early ali'i, served as Oahu's permanent governor for many years. His long and eventful life ended November 26, 1868. Two of his sons would be king, Kamehameha IV and Kamehameha V. Rufus Anderson, *History of the Sandwich Islands Missions* (London, 1872), p. 310.

[21]Miriam Kehauluohi (Auhea), 1794–1845, succeeded by sister, Jochabid Kinau, as *Kuhina-nui* on the latter's death in April 1839. Her sister was the second wife of Governor Kekuanaoa. That marriage begot two sons (Lot and Alexander) destined to be kings, and one daughter, Victoria. Kehauluohi acted for that infant girl as premier since the office of the title of queen by heredity descended to her. She held office until her death in June 1845, at the age of fifty-one. *Ibid.*, p. 138.

English—Rev. L. Smith interpreter. He was followed by several natives—closed with the young Chiefs and Chiefesses singing a hymn which they composed for the occasion. They next proceeded to the old grass church, formerly Mr. Bingham's, where we partook of a sumptuous feast.[22] The Governor had a table spread, instead of fine linen, green leaves were used as a substitute. Then it was loaded with various kinds of meat and fish—poe [poi] not excepted, which is their favorite dish. The Governor invited the spectators to take a seat to the table, while he seemed highly gratified in seeing us partake and drink so bountifully of *Cold Water*. Meantime the natives were seated on the ground (as is their usual way of eating) with their calabashes of fish and poe which is made of [baked] taro, first pounded, occasionally moistened with water, then molded into a mass like dough. It is then put in a calabash and water added till it is of the thinness of paste, then it is set by for fermentation. The poe may be used in a day or two, but a preference is given to that which has stood four or five days. It is eaten by thrusting the fore-finger into the mass, and securing as much as will adhere to it, then passing it into the mouth, all the while jabbering in a language best known to themselves. The repast being over, Rev. L. Smith took me home in his carriage, being highly gratified with the proceedings of the day.

28. Dined to Mrs. Hooper's. Attended preparatory lecture in the evening.

---

[22]Hiram Bingham, born in Bennington, Vermont, October 30, 1789, graduated from Middlebury College in 1816 and took his theological training at Andover Seminary; he was ordained September 28, 1819. He married Sybil Moseley (born Westfield, Massachusetts, September 14, 1792) at Hartford, Connecticut, October 11, 1819. The newlyweds came in the first American missionary party which reached the Islands on the brig *Thaddeus*, Captain Andrew Blanchard. Leaving Boston, October 23, 1819, the company landed at Honolulu, April 19, 1820. The Binghams served twenty-one years, returning to New England in 1841. His wife died at Easthampton, Massachusetts, February 17, 1848. In 1852, he remarried and lived on until November 11, 1869, in New Haven, Connecticut. *Protestant Missionary Portraits*, p. 2; Judd, *Voyages to Hawaii before 1860*, p. 22; *Bingham Missionary Chart; Missionary Album*, p. 41.

29. Very busy sewing. Rode horseback in the afternoon.

30. Attended church—once more have I been favored with the blessed privilege of coming around the table of the Lord; and partaking of its sacred elements. Yes, in this distant land! I enjoy the society of those who are followers of the meek and lowly Jesus.

31. Wrote to brother A. by the Brig *Constantia* across the land.[23]

November 1. Attended an auction for the first time. A box of fancy articles was sold which was given by a lady in the U.S. for the benefit of the Oahu Charity School, which I have not yet visited.

2. Called on several of the Missionaries—took tea to Mrs. Doct. Judd's who sailed from Boston in 1827.[24] This eve conference meeting to Mr. Chamberlain's who sailed in 1819 among the first band of Missionary laborers for the S[andwich] Islands.[25]

---

[23]This term refers to letters sent in ships destined for Mazatlán or San Blas, where they were disembarked and sent over land across Mexico to Vera Cruz, there to continue their journey in other ships. The brig was most likely the Chilean vessel, *Constante*, Francisco Unamano, master, which visited California in 1842. Bancroft, *California*, IV: 546n.

[24]Wife of Dr. Garrit Parmelee Judd, missionary doctor, who was serving as interpreter and adviser to Kamehameha III in the absence of William Richards, then on an embassy to the U.S., Great Britain, and France. Formerly Laura Fish, she was born in Plainfield, New York, April 2, 1804. She reached Hawaii with her husband, whom she married September 20, 1827. She lived until October 2, 1872, when she died at Sweet Home, the family residence in Nuuanu Valley. Her husband followed on July 12, 1873. *Bingham Missionary Chart*; Judd, *Voyages to Hawaii before 1860*, p. 26; *Protestant Missionary Portraits*, p. 25; *Missionary Album*, pp. 128–129.

[25]This was Levi Chamberlain, member of the second missionary contingent on board the ship *Thames*, Captain Reuben Clasby. Born in Dover, Vermont, August 28, 1792, he embarked from New Haven, November 20, 1822, and landed on April 27, 1823. Stationed in Honolulu, 1823–1847, he married Maria Patten (born Salisbury, Pennsylvania, March 19, 1803) in Honolulu, September 1, 1828. She came to the Islands in the third mission party on the *Parthian*, Captain Blinn, from Boston, November 3, 1827, and landed in Oahu, March 31, 1828. Levi Chamberlain died in Honolulu, July 29, 1849, and his wife, January 19, 1880. *Bingham Missionary Chart*; Judd, *Voyages to Hawaii before 1860*, p. 23; *Protestant Missionary Portraits*, p. 14; *Missionary Album*, pp. 64–65.

Mrs. Nye is confusing Levi Chamberlain with Daniel Chamberlain, who arrived with the first missionary party in 1820, but returned to the United States with his wife, Jerusha, March 21, 1823. *Ibid.*, pp. 62–63.

3. Wrote to Mr. Nye by Capt. Dominis, bound to Montera.[26] I find much more enjoyment in corresponding with him than formerly for letters will reach him in 18 or 20 days. Took tea to Mrs. Doct. Wood.[27]

4. Took tea to Mrs. Hooper's, party made on Mr. and Mrs. Damon's account. Tea was handed round, but very different style from us in America. It will require some time to become accustomed to Foreign etiquette.

5. Last night the bell rang for fire. However, it proved to be quite a distance from us. Today the streets are thronged with natives riding. They seem to take Saturday for a holiday. I find they are more civilized and farther advanced than I expected to find them.

6. Been to church twice. Have but two services, morning and evening, it is so warm in the middle of the day. I often attend one of the native churches.

---

[26]John Dominis came to the Hawaiian Islands as second mate and sail-maker on the *Paragon*, under the command of Captain William Cole in 1823, bound for China. Brewer, *Reminiscences*, pp. 17–18, 26–27. His subsequent and extensive career in the Hawaiian-Pacific coast trade is detailed in "Beginnings and Development of Trade on the Pacific Coast of North America," [Mercantile Trust Company of California] *Monthly Review*, XII, Pts. 8–9 (March–April 1923), 60, 78–79. He was lost on the *Noble* in 1845. Bancroft, *California*, II: 782. At this time he was in command of the *Joseph Peabody* and had returned from China on August 5. Davis, *Seventy-Five Years*, p. 278; Richard Carlton to Lord Palmerston, October 27, 1841, F.O. 58/12, fo. 1086, PRO.

Dominis' son would grow up to be consort to Liliuokalani, Hawaii's last queen. For the early family history, see Ante Kovăcević, "On the Descent of John Owen Dominis, Prince Consort of Queen Liliuokalani," *The Hawaiian Journal of History*, X, (1976), 3–24.

[27]Robert W. Wood, M.D., graduated from Waterville College (later Colby University) in 1829, and from the Medical School of Bowdoin College in 1832. He departed Boston for the Hawaiian Islands in October 1838, arriving at Honolulu in April 1839. For the ensuing ten years he was a physician of the Hospital for Seamen, serving as an appointee of the U.S. consul. By 1847, he acquired through foreclosure a plantation at Kaloa on Kauai. He can rightly be "called the father of successful sugar industry in Hawaii." He disposed of the plantation in 1872 and returned to New England, making Jamaica Plain, a suburb of Boston, his home. There he died, January 4, 1892, being survived by his second wife and a son. *The Friend*, 50 (Feb. 1892), 17; Judd, "Koloa: A Sketch of Its Development," pp. 77–79. Interestingly, at the time of Mrs. Nye's first Honolulu sojourn, Dr. Wood was serving as president of the Hawaiian Bible Society. *The Friend*, 2 (Jan. 1, 1844), 3, 48. The doctor's first wife, Delia M. Wood, a native of Machias, Maine, died in Honolulu, age fifty-four, on July 25, 1862. *Ibid.*, new series, 11 (Aug. 1, 1862), 64.

7. Made me a riding cap today. It is not the handsomest you every saw, but then it has two tassels and yellow strings; it is *not* a little becoming.

8. Sail ho! it is announced a whale ship from Plymouth. Alas, how many sweet associations did it bring to mind, when I found it to be the old ship *Fortune*.[28] Took a short ride on horseback, about five miles to the Kings cottage.[29]

9. Wrote most of the day. Shall endeavor to give you a sketch of the habits and dress of the natives. As to size, there is a great difference between the lower class of people and the chiefs or nobles. This difference in size is owing to difference in food and mode of living. Their houses are built by driving posts into the ground a short distance apart. The spaces between the posts are filled by small round sticks [like a large-scale wicker bird-cage] and the whole is then covered or thatched with dried grass. These houses have no windows for the admittance of light or air, and but one door, and that so small they are obliged to stoop whenever they enter or reenter. Their furniture consists of one or two mats that which serve as seats, as well as beds, with their calabashes, which contain their food and drink. The number of mats used for a couch, depend on the rank of those who are to lie upon it. The beds of the Chiefs consisting of from thirty to forty, while the lower class content themselves with a single mat. The calabashes, which are formed from the shells of gourds, are of various shapes, in consequence of the care taken by the natives to fasten bandages around them while growing. Some have the form of dishes, others are in the shape of long necked bottles, which they use for water, while

---

[28]This may have been the *Fortune*, built in Newcastle, Maine in 1826. Fairburn, *Merchant Sail*, V: 3358, 3459.

[29]Summer residence of Kamehameha III far up in Nuuanu Valley. Called *Kamakapupu*, its name, translated "Singing Shell," probably was derived from the land shells, a species of tree-dwelling snail, said to create a high, sweet singing sound under certain circumstances.

others still have close covers made of the gourd. Their dress I will describe at some future time.

10. Took tea to Mrs. DuToits [Dudoit], the French Consul.[30] Reports are in circulation that the French have taken Okhetic [Tahiti].[31]

11. The long looked for ship has just turned Diamond Head. What an excitement an arrival produces! Every eye is turned toward the frail bark, which is now rapidly bearing intelligence from our dear native land—every heart seems big with emotion—some are to hear tidings of joy! while others perhaps are to be made sorrowful. I was not expecting much by the *Wil[lia]m Gray*, as she sailed but one month after I left, but still, never was a letter so dear to my heart as the one I received from brother William.[32] Mr. and Mrs. B[rewer] received a great number, likewise two beautiful sofas which they had been looking for. Half past four, our usual time to ride, and how pleasant it is after so fine a shower as we have just had.

---

[30]Jules Dudoit was born in Port Louis, Ile de France (or Mauritius), February 28, 1803. After a maritime career in the southeast Asian area, he arrived on Oahu, March 25, 1835. In July 1837, he was appointed to the post of French consul by De Petit-Thouars, a position which he held until 1847. He became a Hawaiian citizen and perished in his sleep, July 20, 1866, the victim of his Chinese cook. He married a daughter of Peter Corney, Anna, a young Irish lass who was his second wife. (His first wife died of childbirth complications.) She long survived her husband; she died in June 1903. Leonce A. Jore, "Captain Jules Dudoit, the First French Consul in the Hawaiian Islands, 1837–1867, and His Brig Schooner, the *Clementine*," translated by Dorothy B. Aspinwall, *Sixty-Fourth Annual Report of the Hawaiian Hist. Soc.* (Honolulu, 1955), pp. 21 *et seq.*; Abel A. DePetit-Thouars, *Voyage du monde sur la frigate la Venus, pendant les annees, 1836–1839* (4 vols.; Paris, 1840–1845), I:347–348.

[31]Admiral Abel De Petit-Thouars imposed a French protectorate on Tahiti and the Society Islands in early fall of 1842. In April 1843, King Louis Philipps accepted the Protectorate and officially sanctioned French control. Donald D. Johnson, "Powers in the Pacific: Tahiti and Hawaii, 1825–1850," *Sixty-Sixth Annual Report of the Hawaiian Hist. Soc.* (Honolulu, 1957), pp. 15–16; J. R. Baldwin, "England and the French Seizure of the Society Islands," *Journal of Modern History*, X (June 1938), 212–231.

[32]The 157-ton schooner *William Gray*, built at Bangor, Maine, in 1816, was acquired by Peirce & Brewer in Boston 1841. Charles Brewer, who transacted the purchase, sailed it to Hawaii. Leaving Boston March 14, 1841, the vessel called at Valparaíso and Tahiti before reaching Honolulu. Fairburn, *Merchant Sail*, V:3539; Brewer, *Reminiscences*, pp. 49–51.

12. Saw two beautiful birds to sell for a *harpoona*, six cents a piece.[33] I was going to buy them, but Mrs. B[rewer] said they would not bear confinement for she had made several attempts. She has several Canary birds, which serenade us night and morning.

13. What delightful weather! Went to church in the morning—this afternoon, been reading Memoirs of Mrs. Huntington.[34] Oh, that I possess her views and feelings—sermon this eve by Rev. Mr. Leslie.

14. Have spent the day at home—this evening invited to Mrs. Dowsett's to sing.[35]

15. There is a report in circulation that the Americans have taken Monterey.[36] If true, the *Bolivar* will not be here as soon

---

[33]The correct Hawaiian word is *hapaumi*, meaning five pence. It is an erroneous Hawaiian usage.

[34]Mrs. Nye was reading the *Memoirs of the Late Mrs. Susan Huntington, of Boston, Mass. Consisting Principally of Extracts from Her Journals and Letters* . . . , by Benjamin B. Wisner (Edinburgh, 1826). This work went through three editions and also was published in an abbreviated form by Wisner under the title of *The Life of Susan Huntington* (1832).

[35]Mrs. Mary (Bishop) Dowsett was the widow of a sea captain. Sailing from Honolulu on the *Victoria*, June 1, 1834, Captain Samuel J. Dowsett laid his vessel in at the Pescadores Islands where he and four of his men were captured by the natives. Two escaped, but not the captain. Mrs. Dowsett died, age fifty-two, July 4, 1860. She was survived by her two sons, James I. and Samuel H. Dowsett, Honolulu merchants. *The Friend*, 9, new series (Jan. 1, 1860), 1; (July 7, 1860), 49, 56.

[36]This was the period when Great Britain, France, and the United States coveted California. Each nation had sent naval expeditions into the area on one pretext or another to reconnoiter. Since war between the United States and Mexico over the Texas question was considered imminent, Commodore Thomas ap Catesby Jones, commander of the Pacific Squadron, lying in the roadstead of Callao, Peru, understood that in the event of actual hostilities he was to seize Monterey, capital of Mexican California, and thus forestall any British attempt. Recently advised by John Parrot, American consul at Mazatlán, that war had begun, the abrupt departure of the British naval squadron under Admiral Richard Thomas, which was also at Callao, under sealed orders for an undisclosed destination, convinced Jones that Parrot's intelligence was correct. Cocksure that Admiral Thomas' destination was California (actually it was Nicaragua), Jones sailed immediately for Monterey.

Arriving October 19, 1842, Jones notified the Mexican officials that a state of war existed between their two countries and that he had come to occupy Monterey. This he proceeded to do, no resistance being offered, and on the following day the American flag was hoisted with proper ceremony. Later in the day, Thomas O. Larkin, U.S. consul to Mexican California, returned to Monterey and convinced Jones that he had made an error. Jones quickly

(*continued on next page*)

as was expected. O how I wish to know the truth of this assertion.

16. As it is very rainy and dull today, I will spend a few hours in writing. In my Journal shall I say—Well! I did not intend it to be thus, however, if it prove so to be, I shall regret having undertaken to note down every day's occurrences—You could not repress a smile were you to sit at the window and watch the kenackers[37] as they pass. Some with an umbrella open, while at the same time they will have no clothing on except a string of native cloth worn between the limbs, which is called a *malo* or *tappah*, and occasionally a *kihei* or mantle, about two yards square, which passing under one arm, is fastened in a knot on the opposite shoulder. Some in addition to this, will add an old cast-off vest, coat, pantaloons, or shirt, and with either one of these articles consider themselves in full dress, so that the street scenes in this place are as various as they are grotesque. The wahines (women) are always drest in a long loose gown with a pau or piece of cloth, several yards in length, wrapped about the body from the waist to the knees, over this loose dress. Very few of them will encumber their feet with shoes or stockings, but at the same time display well tattooed ankles. Both sexes are fond of ornaments. They decorate their heads and necks with wreaths, some of them very beautiful, formed of brilliant flowers, of a bright orange color.[38] When in full dress, they usually wear a very large shell comb and carry their bonnets in their hands or under their arm. The natives are exceedingly courteous in their manners. They seldom fail to greet you in the street with

---

(*continued from previous page*)
lowered the American flag and with full ceremony raised the Mexican flag, withdrew his land forces, and amidst profuse apology to the astonished Mexican authorities, weighed anchor and sailed. Theodore H. Hittell, *History of California* (4 vols.; San Francisco, 1885–1897), II: 317–319; George M. Brooke, Jr., "The Vest Pocket War of Commodore Jones," *Pacific Historical Review*, XXXI (Aug. 1962), 217–234.

[37]Kanaka, colloquial name for Hawaiians.

[38]This is the *slima* (*sida fallax Walpers*), Libiraic family.

a smile or a compliment—how do you do? Good morning. But I am happy to find that these people are acquiring the habits of civilized life, just in proportion as they enjoy the instructions and examples of the missionaries, and I might add the Foreign residents, but a long time must elapse before the people of these distant Isles can be reclaimed from sin and ignorance. Around each of the Missionary stations great changes have taken place, and I trust will continue. Ought we not be thankful that light has already begun to dawn on these benighted fellow creatures.

17. Last night I was awakened with the sound of three cheers! three cheers! and then a loud hurrah! hurrah! Without being in the least alarmed, I arose and saw from my window a procession of nearly two hundred sailors—headed by Rogers (an American) Capt. of a whale ship.[39] But I am not able to state particulars. The law requires every sailor to go on board ship at eight o'clock when a cannon is fired from the fort.[40] If seen in the streets after that hour, the constable takes them up. It seems that Capt. Rogers bid defiance to this law

---

[39]The New Bedford whaleship, the 321-ton *William and Eliza*, commanded by Captain Rogers, arrived at Oahu on October 21, 1842. Only six months out, the vessel had accumulated 2,300 bbls. of oil (which was sent back by the *Victoria*). It departed the harbor on January 2, 1843. Paty's Harbormaster Records.

[40]Effective January 1, 1841, the Hawaiian Islands governors were authorized to appoint constables and peace officers to enforce Island laws and ordinances. Lorrin A. Thurston, ed., *The Fundamental Law of Hawaii* (Honolulu, 1904), p. 35.

A Hawaiian resident, writing to a California friend, caustically remarked:

> Our Pious Consul owns—if not boasts, He got a law that a gun should be fired at half past seven—evening—when all Residents of Ships and all boats are to go off. At Eight a second gun fires—when the whole Police go in to every persons premises—Houses, outhouses & they think fit—to hunt for 'Residents' of Ships. If any are found, they are taken to the Consul of their Country who must pay two dollars for them, or they are put into the Fort. No Music after 9 o'clock. No dancing in private houses. In fact the Blue Laws of Connecticut could not touch the wise Laws of [the] Sandwich Islands. The faster they go, the sooner they will be at the end of the Race.

Stephen Reymonds to Thomas O. Larkin, Oahu, Aug. 16, 1841. Hammond, ed., *The Larkin Letters*, I: 107–108.

and got up this row, of which he afterwards was very much ashamed—even the natives were astonished! The Governor immediately appraised the American Consul of the circumstances, who, accompanied by others, proceeded at once to the scene of action and found the men were armed. Their presence checked them at once. Parties of soldiers patrolled the streets during the night and succeeding days but no other symptom of riot was manifested.

18. Today I had a call from cousin S. Worth, which was very unexpected—though we never saw each other before, the meeting was reciprocal on both sides.[41] O how much he looks like my husband. I can hardly be denied his seeing him, but he sails this afternoon on another cruise. Has been on this voyage three years, not been very successful.[42] It would have been pleasant for me if he could at least have spent a few days with us, but we met only to part.

19. Ship *Valleyfield*, Capt. Bolton, arrived today from the coast, saying the Americans have given up Monterey.[43] He saw Capt. Nye eighteen days since, was well, and spoke of me as being on my passage. He is collecting hides; will not be here until late this fall. Well, I feel thankful to hear this and of so recent a date too! Took tea to Mrs. Paty's.

20. Another week has glided away and again have enjoyed Sabbath and Sanctuary privileges. Though afflicted with a severe pain in my head, I have attended church, heard two admirable sermons from Rev. S. C. Damon.

21. Company to dine—Capt. Ingles and lady, with several passengers, who arrived on Saturday in the ship *Hopewell*,

[41]Unable to identify S. Worth.

[42]No doubt an American whaler.

[43]The English bark *Valleyfield*, 343 tons, owned by the Hudson's Bay Company, enroute from the Columbia River, touched at San Francisco in late October. Ogden, "Trading Vessels on the California Coast," p. 1049; Bancroft, *California*, IV:569*n*. *The Friend* does not record the arrival of the *Valleyfield*. (The reference to Americans giving up Monterey refers to Jones' abortive seizure mentioned in *note* 36, *ante*.)

Philadelphia, bound to China.[44] Mrs. I[ngles] appears very amiable, is admired and caressed by everyone; sings and plays sweetly on the piano. In the eve I attended the seaman's concert at the Bethel.[45]

22. Doct. Mead has just called (an Episcopal Clergyman).[46] Though in my dishabille, I cannot refuse seeing him, for he has come to bid us farewell. Is going to take passage in the *Hopewell* for China. A note from Mrs. Hooper to pass the evening.

23. Company from Mowee [Maui], Mr. and Mrs. Peck and family to spend a few weeks with us.[47] This afternoon went with Mr. and Mrs. Damon to call on the Governor. Were much disappointed in not seeing his Excellency. Had gone out to ride. However, his attendants waited on us. Showed us over the house, which was furnished with sofas, chairs, tables. The sleeping rooms, in place of bedsteads, a great number of mats were spread on the floor, Hawaiian style. I had before been introduced to his Excellency, the Governor, who is noble looking and speaks English well. Is a widower; has a pretty little daughter named Victoria about four years of age.

---

[44]The American ship *Hopewell,* 413 tons, Captain Engle, ninety days out of Philadelphia, reached Valparaíso July 10 and sailed August 6 for Callao. From there it would appear it sailed on to Honolulu. Valparaíso *Mercurio,* July 12, p. 3, cl. 3; Aug. 7, 1842, p. 3, cl. 3.

[45]A seamen's concert actually was a prayer meeting.

[46]Efforts to identify this clergyman have proved futile.

[47]Sherman Peck was born in Berlin, Connecticut, in December 1800. When of age, he began his mercantile career in Charleston, South Carolina. From there he ventured to Mexico City where he spent two years. He reached the Hawaiian Islands via California in 1829. The ensuing years found him engaged in a variety of mercantile enterprises which entailed voyages to Valparaíso, Manila, and the South Sea Islands. In partnership with Charles Titcomb, an ambitious attempt at silk culture was made at Koloa commencing in 1836, which ended in failure five years later. A new partnership with a ship chandler at Lahaina, Maui, followed. That successful business at the major whaleship harbor in the Pacific ended in the fall of 1847 when Peck sold his interest to Punchard & Co., before departing for the United States. Back in the States he lost his entire fortune and returned to the Islands in 1859 where he became the senior partner in the house of Brewer & Co. He died at Honolulu on June 17, 1871, survived by his widow. *The Friend,* new series, 20 (July 3, 1871), 51; Judd, "Koloa: A Sketch of Its Development," pp. 61–62.

She was dressed in a rich purple satin.[48] Spent the eve to Mrs. Carter's,[49] and to be sure! Capt. I[ngles] and lady were present.

24. Company to dine. Sewed all day. For a change took tea to Mrs. Duduoits. O how sweetly did Mrs. Ingles sing and play too! on the piano. Tomorrow a picnic is to be given at the King's cottage, about five miles in the valley of Nuanna.

25. A delightful day for the picnic. About nine o'clock the party left town together, between forty and fifty forming a strong cavalcade, and as they rode along the plain, presented a gay and cheerful appearance. Those who had not visited the Pari [Pali] (a very high precipice) concluded to ride a few miles further, for no person thinks of leaving the Island without a view from the Pari, which I found was sublime and beautiful beyond description. The lofty mountains, towering far above the clouds, the rocks, rivulets and cultivated fields; while the smoke ascended from the rude cabins of the natives. All awakened in my mind feelings of awe and reverence for that Being who formed the universe. But really it was the roughest road I ever traversed, filled with ravines and then the path so narrow one would entangle in the trees on each side, and gentlemen concluded they had worked their passage. Mrs. Damon remarked she had ascended mountains and rode in valleys, but none equaled this. However, we returned safely, just in time too. The house was tastefully decorated. The rafters and posts were prettily festooned with shrubbery, the vines of which drooped gracefully, forming rustic arches over the viands. The dinner was cooked in

---

[48]Mateo Kekuanaoa was the father of Kamehameha IV and Kamehameha V. Victoria was their sister and was called Princess Victoria Kamamalu. Ralph S. Kuykendall, *The Hawaiian Kingdom, 1854–1874* (Honolulu, 1953), pp. 33, 36, 96, 118, 239. See *note* 20, *ante*.

[49]The wife of Captain Joseph O. Carter often accompanied him with their son on his voyages. Their son, Henry A. Carter, would serve as Hawaiian minister to the United States in 1884. Captain Carter died in Honolulu, July 31, 1850. *The Polynesian*, 1 (Aug. 8, 1840), 35; Bancroft, *California*, II: 748; *The Friend*, 8 (Aug. 1, 1850), 64.

native style, and the manner of partaking of it nearly so. The dishes were placed upon mats on the floor. Residents, guests, and all, arranged themselves around this primitive table in such attitudes as best suited their ease and convenience. A blessing being asked by the Rev. S. C. Damon, all as one laid hold, some on roast pig—luaued dog—thought delicious by some—Governor suspicious of its being pig in disguise.[50] After dinner, promenaded around shadowy trees—purling streams—quite rural. But after all, I felt inclined to seriousness. I felt that I was *alone*, notwithstanding Mr. and Mrs. B[rewer]'s polite attention, besides others, who with pleasure are every ready to wait on me. Still I could not but feel sad. About seven o'clock we rode into town—orders from the chief marshall to escort Capt. Ingles and lady to the shore, where, forming a line, they rode through, were soon placed in the boat, wending their way toward the ship. Nothing occurred to interrupt the harmony of the day, although not confined exclusively to Americans, every one appeared to be united.

---

[50]Mrs. Nye does not state whether she was one of the partakers of the "luaued dog" (a term indicating it had been wrapped in ti leaves and roasted in an *imu* or underground oven)—nor does she express the extreme distaste held by most foreigners, especially the missionaries, for this choice Hawaiian delicacy.

Ruschenberger, who spent some time in the Islands in the mid-1830s, stands virtually alone among foreign visitors in expressing a fondness for it. In describing a typical Hawaiian feast, he writes: "Near my place at table was a fine young dog luaued, the flesh of which was declared to be excellent by all who partook of it. To my palate, its taste was what I can imagine would result from mingling the flavor of pig and lamb, and I did not hesitate to make my dinner of it, in spite of some qualms at the first mouthful... the edible dog... is a dainty animal fed exclusively on vegetables, chiefly taro in the form of poi, and at the age of two years, is considered a dish wherewithal to regale royalty." W[illiam] S. D. Ruschenberger, *A Voyage Around the World* (Philadelphia, 1838), p. 463.

Mrs. Lucy Thurston, who arrived in 1820 with the first missionary band, states, "Hawaiians never offer luaued dog to foreigners, who hold it in great abhorrence. Once they mischievously attached a pig's head to a dog's body and thus inveigled a foreigner to partake of it to his great acceptance." *Life and Times of Lucy C. Thurston* (Ann Arbor, Michigan, 1882), p. 40. Perhaps Governor Kekuanaoa was recalling this incident when he suspected he was being served "pig in disguise" rather than authentic dog.

26. Dined to Mrs. Paty's. Singing school in the eve.

27. Have just returned from meeting. Sermon this morning from Mr. D[amon]; this evening Mr. Leslie addressed us. What unspeakable privileges do I enjoy. Even here in these distant Isles, Jesus is proclaimed as "ready and willing to save all those who come unto God by him." Though darkness and error still prevail, I with faith look over these mountains and behold with joy the dawning of the Sun of Righteousness.

28. This morning an invitation is given to all the residents (from Capt. Ingles and lady) to a party on board ship this evening. I declined going, but found it did not meet the approbation of some. Accordingly, we set off about sun down, in company with doctors, lawyers, and ministers. Never was I on board so splendid a ship. An awning overspread the deck, arranged so as to present a lofty and spacious hall, which formed a delightful promenade, for those not engaged in the more active exercises below. Everything was tastefully arranged. The chandelier which was formed around the capstan presented the appearance of a pyramid of lights, in regular rows, gradually diminishing in number, as they rose in height, attracted much admiration for its ingenuity and taste. At nine o'clock, we sat down to an elegant supper, a profusion of everything the island afforded. Between ten and eleven, the party began to disperse highly gratified with the evening's entertainment.

29. Passed the evening to Mrs. Hooper's, expecting to hear Mrs. I[ngles] sing once more, but her little one could not be left, was quite sick. Sails tomorrow.

30. Spent the forenoon in writing to Brother George by the way of China; what a fine chance to go home—what a thought! I do not allow myself the pleasure of thinking of it at present. By the way I would like to have Gorham decide. Rode on horseback as far as Punerho [Punahou], three miles.

December 1. Last night was awakened by the cry of fire! fire!

proved to be nothing more than a straw house which was soon demolished. Just returned from the Thursday evening meeting which is held in the vestry of the Bethel, particularly for seamen.

2. Rev. G. Rowell, fellow passenger [in the *Sarah Abigail*], from Wailua, dined with us today. At three P.M. by appointment, Rev. L. Smith called to take me down to the mission to a feast which was appointed by the missionaries at this time, there being several from the other stations. Had a very social and interesting meeting.

3. Mrs. More [Moore] and I took the gig and drove to Pururho [Panahou] and spent the day with Mr. and Mrs. Dole, who keep a boarding school for the missionaries' children.[51] Saw two of Rev. Leslie's daughters, which he told me he should have under their parental care and instructions, while he will return to his labor in Oregon.

4. This morning Mr. Gulick preached to us from Kauai.[52] This afternoon attended the native church, Rev. L. Smith—shall ever remember with peculiar emotions, my enjoyment

[51]Prior to the founding of this school in May 1841, children of the missionaries in the Sandwich Islands had been sent on the long voyage around the Horn to New England, often as early as six or seven years of age, there to reside with relatives or friends while they secured an education. This involved hardship and long years of separation that left their mark on both parents and children. Punahou School, situated at the mouth of Manoa Valley on land originally given by Chief Boki (a gift of his wife Liliha from her father Hoapile), through the intervention of Queen Kaahumanu, for use of the mission, offered a solution to this problem. It still exists as one of the foremost private schools in Hawaii. Correspondence respecting missionary schools is in the Sandwich Island Mission Collection, Hawaiian Mission Children's Society Library, Honolulu. An excellent history of the school can be found in Mary C. Alexander and Charlotte P. Dodge, *Punahau, 1841–1941* (Berkeley and Los Angeles, 1941).

[52]Reverend Peter Johnson Gulick was destined to spend his life in the service of his faith. Born in Freehold, New Jersey, March 12, 1976, he graduated from Princeton College in 1825 and two years later from the seminary. He was ordained October 3, 1827. Married to Fanny Hickley Thomas (born Lebanon, Connecticut, April 16, 1798), September 5, 1827, he took his bride with him to the Islands in the third A.B.C.F.M. party which sailed on Captain Blinn's *Parthian*. From 1828–1835, he was stationed at Waimea, Kauai; at this time he was serving at Kobe, Japan. There he died December 8, 1877; his wife followed on May 24, 1883. *Protestant Missionary Portraits*, pp. 20, 24.

of this day in communing with sixteen hundred natives who have confessed Christ before the world, and entered into the most solemn engagement to be the Lord's. Even here in this once heathen land, Jesus has a people redeemed by his precious blood. Yes, these converted heathen appeared to enjoy the precious season greatly. To hear them sing, to see them kneel and listen with such eagerness to the word of life, was enough to draw tears from the eyes of all who were witnesses of this solemn transaction. I said to myself such a sight as this would silence the scruples and the opposition attending missions.

5. Ship of war! U.S. Frigate, Capt. Armstrong, arrived last night, twelve days from Monterey.[53] Several of the officers dined with us today, saying Mr. Nye was on board the evening they sailed, heard him speak of his wife, said he was much disappointed in not finding my name among the list of passengers which sailed the 10th of March in the *Victoria*, as I wrote him to that effect, had not heard of my arrival in the *S[arah] Abigail*. I met the Chaplain, Mr. Bartow, at the monthly concert this eve., who was very interesting in his remarks; was introduced.[54] What, Capt. Nye's wife!! very well acquainted with him, why he is expecting you, when lo! you are already here.

6. Spent the day to Mrs. Chamberlain's, who came out in

---

[53]The U.S. frigate *United States*, Captain James Armstrong, was the flagship for the Pacific Squadron and had on board Commodore Thomas ap Catesby Jones. It had departed California after an abortive attempt at seizing the country for the United States, under the misunderstanding that war with Mexico was underway. When apprised of the error, Jones retained the vessel on the coast for several weeks to placate the situation. The vessel and its sister ship, the U.S. sloop-of-war *Cyane*, paid a second call at Honolulu, August 3–19, 1843. The former's destination was Tahiti. *The Friend*, 1 (Aug. 11, 1843), 42; (Sept. 16, 1843), 50.

[54]The chaplain on board the *United States* was the Reverend Theodore B. Bartow, U.S.N. He was appointed on September 8, 1841, so this was probably his first extensive sea duty. He became a life member of Temperance Advocate and Seamen's Friend on the second visit of his ship to Hawaii in August 1843. Bartow's death is recorded as May 18, 1869. Thomas H. S. Hamersley, *General Register of the United States Navy and Marine Corps* . . . (Washington, D.C., 1882), p. 56; *The Friend*, 1 (Aug. 11, 1843), 42.

1819 among the first band of Missionary labors for the S[andwich] Islands.[55] This evening have been writing to Gorham by the U.S. frigate which sails tomorrow.

7. Ship *George*, Capt. Cash, sails tomorrow.[56] Have been writing to Ma, sister, and cousin I.[57] It is now two o'clock. Going to dine to Mrs. Carter's.

8. Finished my letters. Love to think they are on their way back to America. This afternoon rode horseback. Was caught in a shower, had no poncho. Got a fine sprinkling. I was literally wet through and through. This evening have been to Mrs. Doct. Judd's to a sing.

9. True! I did get a wetting yesterday, but then I took no cold; feel very well today. This afternoon Mr. and Mrs. Johnstone (teachers of the Charity School) took me out in their carriage.[58] Shall take tea to Mrs. Armstrong's who is to have quite

---

[55]Mrs. Nye is in error. Levi Chamberlain reached the Hawaiian Islands in the second missionary company which sailed from New Haven, Connecticut, November 20, 1822. See *note* 25, *ante*.

[56]No information found on this vessel.

[57]In a second copy of her journal, actually a long letter, which begins on December 7, 1842, and ends on January 14, 1843, Mrs. Nye has a few additional statements or phases penned which do not appear in her journal copy. At this point in the second copy, Mrs. Nye wrote: "This morning an invitation is extended to *all* the residents (from Capt. Ingles & lady) to spend the eve on board their ship. I declined going, but found it did not meet the approbation of *some*. Accordingly about twelve of us ladies set off about sundown in company with doctors, lawyers, and ministers. An awning overspread the deck, arranged so as to present a lofty and spacious hall, which formed a delightful promenade—everything was tastefully arranged. The chandelier or rather the capstan presented the appearance of a pyramid of lights in regular rows, gradually diminishing in number as they rose in height, attached much admiration for its ingenuity and taste. At nine o'clock we sat down to an elegant supper, profusion of every thing the Isl[and] afforded. Between ten and eleven the party began to disperse, highly gratified with the evening's entertainment."

[58]Born in Dundee, Scotland, in 1794, Andrew Johnstone immigrated to the United States in 1813. Thereafter, he lived six years in the West Indies and spent a year in Mexico before reaching Honolulu on June 7, 1831, in the fourth American Board missionary party on the ship *New England*, Captain Parker. The vessel sailed from New Bedford, December 28, 1830. Johnstone became assistant superintendent for secular affairs, 1831–1836. When released from his missionary status in 1836, he became principal of the Oahu Free School, at Honolulu, where he taught for twelve years. His wife, Rebecca Worth, who had been born in Nantucket, Massachusetts, in 1792, labored beside her husband as a teacher. On his death, July 10, 1859, she continued her profession. She died at Honolulu, October 5, 1879. *Protestant Missionary Portraits*, pp. 28, 31.

a company of American ladies. Mr. A[rmstrong] preaches for Mr. Bingham during his visit to the United States.[59]

10. Have wrote the live long day—Mrs. More [Moore] has given me the appellation of *quill* driver—says what do you find to write—I do not want for *matter*, but *language*, O that I had the pen of a ready writer.

11. After services today a Sabbath school was organized. Mr. Damon, Superintendent, classes being formed and numbered. My name was called for the first class, which I with pleasure accepted. Found it made up of half cast! Amalgamation! Sure enough! However, I found them quite advanced.

12. Been sitting all day. For exercise took a walk at sunset, the air being mild and the clouds brilliant. The abundant and beautiful foliage of this Isl[and] is a constant source of admiration to me. Flowers nursed in the house with us, grow wild here. The cactus is now in blossom while geraniums and other plants spring up spontaneously in the fields! There are few reptiles to be seen, the lizard, centipedes, frightful looking scorpions I have not yet seen, spiders of an immense size, but very harmless, they destroy the cockroaches.[60]

13. Just received a note from Capt. Grimes (who has but just returned from the Coast) saying if agreeable, he would call for me to ride at four P.M.[61] The weather was fine, and as we rode along the plains toward Witeta [Waikiki] groves of lofty coconut trees interspersed with the dark green hou [hau], and the graceful kuikui [kukui] (candlenut), was delightful.

---

[59]Richard Armstrong, ordained October 27, 1831, on completion of his studies at Princeton Seminary, was born in Turbotville, Pennsylvania, April 13, 1805. Prior to his religious call, he graduated from Dickinson College in 1827. On September 25, 1831, he married Clarissa Chapman, born in Russell, Massachusetts, May 15, 1805. As members of the fifth mission company, they arrived at Honolulu on Captain Swain's whaleship *Averick*, May 17, 1832, after a 172-day voyage. In 1833–1834, he paid a visit to the Marquesas Islands. He was assigned to Honolulu as pastor of Kawaiahao Church in 1840. He died at his post, September 23, 1860. Twenty years later, his wife took up residence in California. She died in San Francisco on July 20, 1891. *Ibid.*, p. 35.

[60]From the second copy of her journal, this phrase is added here: "which are very numerous."

[61]It is not recorded on what vessel Captain Eliab Grimes took passage.

Groups of thatched houses were everywhere observable surrounded by tarrow [taro] patches, in which the natives were at their toil. We could but remark as the sun was fast sinking below the horizon—the brilliant verdure of the plain, bounded by low and luxuriant hills, transferred us in imagination to dear N[ew] E[ngland].

14. Oh the fashions! Been all day puzzling over a white dress to make it set pretty; got tired, left it for a ride on horseback with a dozen or more in the valley of Nuana; came home quite refreshed.

15. Spent this forenoon very pleasantly in writing to Gorham by the *Fly* bound to Monterey.[62] This afternoon took tea to Mrs. Judd's.

16. Wind is very high with frequent showers of rain—feel a little lonely as one would suppose. Perhaps a little homesick! Mr. Brewer says you want to see your man! True, you are not aware how constantly I bear you in mind, wherever I am, and whatever I behold, particularly when I find anything that would be gratifying to my dear mother. I cannot but help wishing she were with me, or at least, that I could sit down with her in the evening and relate to her listening ear my adventures.

17. Wind has not abated in the least. One would be surprised to see the clouds of dust. I call them dry snowstorms. Notwithstanding, I have made the best of my way to singing school, it being necessary, there are but few that sing, or I should have said, will sing.

18. Last night I was awakened by the cry of fire! fire! and the ringing of bells. I ran out on the verandah and saw to my

---

[62]The *Fly*, a 92-ton English schooner, Captain John Wilson, first reached Honolulu on June 5 from Callao enroute to California in 1840, sailing for Monterey on July 12. It departed Santa Barbara on February 3, 1841, for Mexico. Sold in California to three co-owners, it was renamed the *Juan Diego* and returned to Monterey on May 7, 1841; sailed from San Diego on October 25, bound again for Mexico. Again it was resold, Juan B. Leandry of Los Angeles becoming the owner with Hugo Reid as captain. On May 1, 1842, it weighed anchor at Mazatlán and reached San Pedro on May 31. June 7 it sailed for Honolulu, reaching that port on June 30. Ogden, "Trading Vessels on the California Coast," pp. 917, 971, 1026.

surprise the fire within a quarter of a mile of our house—two or three straw houses all in a blaze, while the streets were lined with natives running to and fro—did not seem to know or do anything, while the residents were working the engines, and exerting all their strength, and faculty to stay its progress, and keep watch of the straw huts, which catch as easily as tinder, there being but two engines in the place, and water scarce—came twice and filled from our pump—in short, it was soon got under and nothing was seen but a dense smoke—did not get much sleep. However, I have been to church today—kept S[abbath] School—shall sleep soundly tonight, for I hear there is to be a watch and when the wind blows, the crier goes round in the eve crying take care of your fires.

19. Have finished my white dress. This evening shall wear it to Miss Piper's wedding, the lady I told you not long since was engaged to Mr. Ricker.[63] It is so uncommon to have a *Yankee* wedding in this part of the world, that it has produced quite an excitement—ten o'clock, just returned from the wedding and a still time it was—by the way, was not invited until the ceremony was performed—cake and wine was then handed round—a little promenading with social conversation. We passed the evening not a little gratified that I had been to a wedding in the S[andwich] Islands.

20. Have commenced writing[64] by the *Victoria*, Capt. S[pring], which sails in a few days for America.[65] Had quite a company to tea this evening.

---

[63]Ricker was from Salem, Massachusetts, and Miss Sarah W. Piper from Newburyport. The ceremony was performed by Rev. Samuel C. Damon. *The Friend*, 1 (Jan. 1843), 7. The couple made a round trip to Oregon and California on the Swedish brig *Bull*, Captain Wrengren, in 1845. Serving as supercargo, Ricker and his wife sailed on April 7, 1845, and left the Columbia in September 4, making Honolulu on September 27 after a brief stop at Monterey. *Ibid.*, 3 (April 15, 1845), 62; (Oct. 1, 1845), 149–150; (Nov. 15, 1845), 175.

[64]From the second copy of her journal, Mrs. Nye writes here: "Today I have been very busy in making a couple of coral baskets of sealing wax."

[65]An American ship, the *Victoria*, 600 tons, Captain Spring, arrived in Valparaíso after a passage of 120 days from New York on July 11, carrying a cargo for Alsop & Co. It sailed August 10. Valparaíso *Mercurio*, July 13, p. 3., cl. 3; Aug. 11, 1842, p. 3., cl. 3.

21. Today I have been very busy in making a couple of coral baskets of sealing wax. This afternoon attended the funeral of a young man (a sailor I suppose) and a stranger in a strange land, away from friends and home. No mother to shed a tear over the lifeless remains of perhaps an only son, or brother. It is the first funeral I have witnessed since I have been here, and it seemed to strike my mind with unusual solemnity.

22. The anniversary of our Pilgrim Fathers! A day which reminds me much of my dear home and friends. Last year at this hour I was in the Gothic church, listening to an eloquent address—surrounded by those who were near and dear to me, not aware! before the return of the next anniversary I should be so far from the land of my nativity—confined to a foreign country—where a parent's voice I no longer hear; to soothe and quiet my feelings in a lonely hour. But the return of evening has dissipated the gloom. I have been to the Thursday evening meeting as usual—returned with a heart disposed to acquiescence in the allotments of Providence. The objects which now occupy so large a portion of my thoughts will shortly lose their importance, as every day convinces me more and more of the uncertainty of earthly enjoyments.

23. Took tea to Mrs. Damon's. On looking around I could but exclaim! See what a company of Yankees! twenty or more—had a pleasant sing.

24. Have finished my letters to E. and I. which I send by the *Victoria*, which sails on Monday.

25. A Christmas sermon this morning from Mr. D[amon]; this evening Mr. Alexander from Molokai preached.[66] Sab-

[66]Born near Paris, Kentucky, July 25, 1805, William Patterson Alexander attended Centre College and completed his theological training at Princeton Seminary in 1831, with ordination following on October 13. He took Mary Ann McKinney as his wife on October 25. Together they sailed for Hawaii as members of the fifth company of missionaries. Shortly after his arrival, Rev. Alexander visited the Marquesas Islands in 1832 and again in 1833. He was stationed at Waioli from 1834–1843, then at Lahainaluna until 1857. Two years after completing his

(*continued on next page*)

bath school looks prosperous, about eighty scholars, fourteen teachers.

26. Have just returned from a dinner party to Mrs. Dudevoit [Dudoit], or I should have said a Christmas dinner—about twenty-five ladies and gentlemen. Sat down at three, rose at five—had ten courses—one would suppose it would take that time to do the dinner justice.

27. I have taken my pen to record the adventures of the day, but can think of nothing worthy of notice—ah! a pleasant ride on horseback! Often, should I delight to sit down and pour forth the feelings of my heart to dear absent ones in my native land, if there was a means of conveyance. 'Tis true, I improve every opportunity, but then they are few and far between, and should I go on the coast, the chances to write will still be less. But my friends try to comfort me by saying, when I have been from home a few years, I shall not feel so anxious to write. Not so! It will ever be one of my most pleasurable enjoyments.

28. Last week I purchased a beautiful London print. Today I have set about making it—how often I have wished there was a dress-maker here; that I need not be obliged to puzzle my brains so, but in the end, I shall not regret having learned the art of *mantua* making. The natives, too, have been very busy in setting out trees on each side of every street, should they grow, it will be a great improvement to the town. But I should not like even to think I should ever see them fully grown for it will be many, many years!!

29. News today that the volcano in Owyhee, which has not been burning for sometime, has again burst and is now sending forth streams of lava, the light of which can be seen the

---

(*continued from previous page*)
last tour of duty at Wailuku, he died in Oakland, California, August 13, 1884. His wife, born in Wilmington, Delaware, January 5, 1810, died at Haiku, Maui, June 29, 1888. *Protestant Missionary Portraits,* pp. 33–34; James M. Alexander, *Mission Life in Hawaii: Memoir of Rev. William P. Alexander* (Oakland, 1888), *passim.*

distance of forty or fifty miles.[67] Those of my acquaintance, who have visited this great volcano heretofore, say it is one of the greatest and most terrific natural curiosities on the earth. It is the opinion of some that these entire islands were originally thrown up from the bed of the ocean by the action of subterraneous fires.

30. One would suppose here, on the distant Isl[and], we lived rather a monotonous life, far otherwise. The old fashioned quietude of domestic life, here, seems much interrupted by continual excitement. You cannot imagine what a bustle an arrival produces—or any trifling affair—I do feel it injurious to anyone who lives upon excitement. It is an artificial stimulus, giving vivacity and cheerfulness to the depressed and lonely; however, it is the order of the day, and I do not consider myself free from its influence. This evening attended a preparatory lecture at the house of Mr. Damon.

31. It is now the last night and almost the last minute of the year. I have been reading and meditating until this last hour, thinking probably my dear brother and sister were at the same time lifting their voices in prayer and praise, as they were wont to do, at the close of the year. The thought that I shall be remembered by them, calms my agitated feelings. Never, during my life, have I experienced a year so fraught with changes. In pursuit of happiness, I have torn myself from the arms of a fond mother, brothers and sisters dear—have been a resident in a foreign land for many months, yet my expectations are not realized, and may not be, for months to come. For all this, I do not murmur; that wise Being who has all events under his control, will order all things aright, while he assures us the greater our afflictions here, if sanctified, the more intense will our joy hereafter.

---

[67]This would be Mauna Kea, the highest peak in the archipelago, on the island of Hawaii. Mrs. Nye's journal entry provides an earlier date for the recorded eruption, which usually is given on January 10, 1843. Charles H. Hitchcock, *Hawaii and Its Volcanos* (Honolulu, 1911), pp. 84–85.

January 1, 1843. This is the first Sabbath of the New Year. Allow me to wish you all a happy New Year! Could I control events, not a sorrow should disturb you, but each moment should bear upon its wings peace and pleasures to your bosoms. But our heavenly Father loves you more ardently and wisely than I do. To Him, my dear brother and sister, I commend you, in *his* favor may you have life and joy. This morning heard an excellent sermon, from the 2nd chapt. of Haggai. This evening the Lord's supper was administered. The dear church of which I am still a member, without doubt, came around the sacramental board this day. I often bring before my imagination the appearance of that little Flock among whom I have so often sat, and where now, had I the "wings of a dove," I would so be found.

2. Perusing an old number of the *Polynesian* (1840) to my surprise I read thus: In *this* place, on the 11th inst. by Rev. John Diell, Mr. Gamaliel Drew to Miss Abigail Elwell.[68] A cousin of mine, I do believe! Upon inquiry find Mr. D[rew] is on the coast—shall not make myself acquainted with my new cousin until he arrives.[69]

3. Had a large dinner company today; among the persons invited was the couple lately married—by the way, I have heretofore given an account of the wedding. In the evening card playing was introduced (which I detest). Sorry to say it is the chief amusement of this place. I alone am left to amuse myself the best way I can in pouring over books and looking at the pictures, and maybe I sometimes get into a tete-a-tete

[68]The first English language newspaper in the Hawaiian Islands appeared on January 21, 1837, the *Sandwich Island Gazette and Journal of Commerce,* edited by Stephen D. Mackintosh. *The Polynesian,* published by James J. Jarves, made its debut on June 6, 1840, and survived for one calendar year. It was revived on May 18, 1844, by the same editor. Helen P. Hoyt, "Hawaii's First English Newspaper and Its Editor," *Sixty-Third Annual Report of the Hawaiian Historical Society* (Honolulu, 1954), pp. 5–18.

The marriage Mrs. Nye refers to was performed on August 11, 1840. *The Polynesian,* 1 (Aug. 15, 1840), 3.

[69]There is no indication that Drew visited California. More likely he was either on the Mexican or South American coasts.

with some *odd* person who may be wishing all the while I was his partner in a game of *whist*! Work! I must not, that would not be etiquette. Ha! ha! ha!

4. Today I have been very busy in making a loose dress [*muu-muu*]. This eve. company to tea.

5. While busy at my work this afternoon, a note was sent me saying, did you know the *Bolivar*! was in sight? I ran up on the look out, and sure enough there was a brig coming round Diamond Head, under full sail, bearing rapidly for the shore. Soon a boat set off from her. In the meantime several called to congratulate me, while I began to feel somehow that it might be the *Bolivar* for there was no other brig expected; however, I sent a messenger to the wharf to meet the boat when it came ashore—to my surprise and disappointment, up walked Capt. Doane, who reported the brig to be the *Sarah Abigail* twenty days from Mazatlan, and bound to China, called at this place to obtain a little more freight.[70] At any other moment I should have considered it quite a treat to have seen the Capt. and even the vessel that had borne me safely to these distant Isles.

6. Feel almost sick today after the excitement of yesterday. However, I have spent a social afternoon with Mrs. Dimond, a missionary. Mr. Dimond came out as a bookbinder for the mission in 1833.[71]

---

[70]The *Sarah Abigail* left Mazatlán on December 18, 1842, anchoring at Oahu on January 5, 1843. Sailing on January 8, it had $150,000 in specie on board, bound for China. Paty's Harbormaster Records.

[71]Henry Dimond, who came to Hawaii as a bookbinder for the A.B.C.F.M., was born September 17, 1808, in Fairfield, Connecticut. He married Ann Maria Anner, a native of New York City, November 3, 1834. Together they came to the Islands in the seventh missionary company on board the ship *Hellespont*, Captain Henry. Sailing from Boston, December 5, 1834, the vessel reached Honolulu, June 6, 1835. Stationed in Honolulu, Dimond was released from his missionary publication duties in 1850. Turning to mercantile affairs, he prospered. He died at Honolulu, January 3, 1895. His wife, born May 19, 1808, had preceded him, dying November 20, 1893. *Protestant Missionary Portraits*, p. 49, 52; *Missionary Album*, pp. 82–83.

7. Capt. D[oane] dines with us today—will sail in a few days for China, thence to the U[nited] States. I wrote by him when he left before, and as I have not anything new to communicate—will take the same to you, promising to deliver them himself, which I know will be a pleasure to you to converse with one who has so recently seen me. This afternoon we rode horseback; called on Mr. and Mrs. Cook [Cooke], who keep a family school, for the children of the chiefs, about eleven in number.[72] The house is built of adobies, with a thatched roof, containing seventeen rooms, to the expense of about two thousand dollars. In front is a large plot filled with verdure and shade which affords a spacious and pleasant playground for the pupils. They are also allowed to walk and ride daily with their teachers, to which they are much attached. They are making rapid progress in their studies and their pleasing manners would do credit to a boarding school of the first class in the U[nited] States.

8. Sermon this morning from Mr. D[amon]—text, God is a spirit—found my S[abbath] S[chool] Scholars more than usually interesting. They seemed quite delighted to find such "sweet stories," as they call them, in the Bible. They commit to memory four or five verses from Matthew—even in those few verses, they evince more perseverance than those whom I have had the pleasure of instructing in America.

9. This morning rose with the sun, took a ride on horseback with Capt. D[oane] returned with a fine appetite for breakfast—this afternoon called on my scholars and invited

[72]Amos Starr Cooke, a teacher by profession, reached the Islands in the eighth mission band on the barque *Mary Frazier*, Captain Charles Sumner, April 9, 1837, after a passage of 116 days. Born in Danbury, Connecticut, December 1, 1810, he took as his wife Juliette Montague, November 24, 1836. Mrs. Cooke, a native of Sunderland, Massachusetts (born March 10, 1812), played an active part in Hawaiian mission education as well. Mr. Cooke, after obtaining his release from mission service, entered business, forming a partnership with Samuel N. Castle in 1851. He died at Honolulu, March 20, 1871. His widow survived until August 11, 1896. *Ibid.*, pp. 74–75; *Protestant Missionary Portraits*, pp. 54, 58, 60.

them to go to the S[abbath] S[chool] concert this eve, said they would like to go, but their dancing master (Mr. Reynolds) would be angry with them.[73] However, they ventured to attend—the consequence was, Mr. R[eynolds] turned them away—that is to say, if you go to S[abbath] School, you shall not come to my dancing school!!

10. The *Sarah Abigail* sailed early this morning. On going up to the look out, to take one more look at the vessel that had been my home for months, found her gone! For a while I could not but feel sad at the thought that I was left, while the vessel would return to my own dear land. However, during the day I received a letter from one of my fellow passengers, Mrs. Rowell. In the eve. I took tea to Mrs. Paty's.

11. Dined to Mrs. P[aty] this afternoon; visited the Charity School, taught by Mr. and Mrs. Johnstone, 90 scholars or more of both sexes.[74] By request I am learning them to sing some

---

[73]Stephen Reynolds, a brilliant but somewhat eccentric seafaring New Englander, settled in Honolulu in 1823 as a trader and merchant. For various reasons he developed a pronounced antipathy for the missionaries, some of which brought him into a confrontation with Mrs. Nye. His dancing school seems to have been the first effort to prepare *hapa-haole* (Hawaiian *hapa*-half; *haole*-foreigner, hence white person, meaning half caste) children for polite island society. This probably was not a wholly disinterested gesture on his part, since his own wife, the former Susan Jackson, was *hapa-haole*, and at least some of his five children must have attended his dancing school.

Descendant of a Revolutionary War veteran, Reynolds was born at Andover, Massachusetts, November 18, 1782. In 1810, at the age of twenty-eight he shipped on the brig *New Hazard* for a three-year cruise to the Northwest Coast, Hawaii, and China. He returned to the Pacific on the *Ida* in 1817 and touched at Hawaii on the *Emma* in 1822, the year before he permanently settled there. By 1829, he was in business for himself. Married that same year, he fathered five children and served as a sometime lawyer, harbormaster, and pilot in Honolulu. Returning to New England in 1855, he died two years later, on July 17, at West Roxford, Massachusetts. Frederic W. Howay, ed., *The Voyage of the New Hazard* (Salem, 1938), introduction; Richard Charlton to George Canning, June 30, 1818, F.O. 58/5, fo. 11, PRO; *The Friend*, new series, 6 (Sept. 26, 1857), 72.

[74]Johnstone, a British subject, and his wife came to the Islands under the auspices of the A.B.C.F.M. in 1831 as assistant to Levi Chamberlain, secular agent for the Sandwich Islands Mission, with permission to devote a part of his time to the spiritual welfare of seamen who frequented Honolulu. Through the young son of the captain of a British whaling ship, Johnstone made contact with the group of *hapa-haole* children who were growing up in the streets of Honolulu, untrained and uncared for by anyone. The abandoned youth begged Johnstone to teach them to read, so Johnstone began giving private instruction in his home.

(*continued on next page*)

On August 20, 1832, a meeting was held by local luminaries to consider the possibility of a school. As a result, Johnstone, through public subscription largely donated by local merchants and sea captains whose ships were in port, secured funds for the erection of a stone school house, thirty-six by twenty-six feet, at a site purchased for $100. Erected at a cost of $1,800, the building was built of coral stone and was "fitted with a handsome desk, benches and other conveniences for a school room," the structure was completed on December 28, 1832. John C. Jones, Jr., U.S. consul, presented a bell which was hung in the cupola.

The first board of trustees consisted of Jones, Richard Charlton, the British consul; Alexander Adams, James Robinson, Captain Eliab Grimes, Henry A. Peirce, secretary, and Captain George Ward Cole, treasurer. The school was formally dedicated January 10, 1833, in a gala ceremony. At an annual salary of $500, the Johnstones were appointed teachers. However, Johnstone continued to serve in the mission until 1836 when he resigned to devote his full attention to the school. Stephen Reynolds Journal, 1823–1842, Typescript, pp. 17–20, 23, HSA; Ray J. Baker, *Honolulu in 1853* (N.p., n.d.), p. 15.

Not long after this, the board of trustees supplied the Johnstones with a residence situated at the corner of King and Alapai streets, of sufficient size as to enable them to accept boarding students from the West Coast. Since the Oahu Charity School was the only one west of the Rocky Mountains whose classes were conducted in English and whose admissions policy was not restricted but open to all, it attracted students from the entire Pacific slope. Enrollment included children from the Russian settlements in Unalaska, including an Indian boy from that region, and more notably a large representation from California. Among the latter were two sons of Thomas O. Larkin, U.S. consul at Monterey, and the son of his brother-in-law, Captain Juan Bautista Rogers Cooper; the sons of David Spence and James Watson, British subjects, and fellow merchants. Captain Henry Delano Fitch, New England trader-merchant, all who had permanently settled in California, married native women (other than Larkin), and become naturalized Mexican citizens; the son and daughter of George Kinloch, Scottish-born carpenter living in Monterey, as well as the sons of Rafael Gómez and Romualdo Pacheco, Mexican merchant and Mexican official respectively. This opportunity for education was important for California children since Sir George Simpson accurately observed during his 1842 visit that "very few individuals of any age can either read or write." *Narrative of a Voyage Round the World* (2 vols.; London, 1847), I:350.

Thus while missionary families at great personal sacrifice sent their children back home to New England to be educated in order to protect them from the "barbarian" influence of island life, Californians were sending their children to Honolulu to escape the illiterate environment of Alta California where educational institutions for the young were unknown.

Twenty-eight years later, after attending Oahu Charity School from 1838–1843, young Romualdo Pacheco was destined to be elected lieutenant governor of California, and on February 12, 1875, to become the twelfth governor of the state—the first native-born Californian to hold that office, serving until the following December as successor to Newton Booth, who had been elected to the U.S. Senate.

In connection with the later history of Oahu Charity School, it is interesting to note that it was the parent institution from which came modern McKinley High School, a school that has played such an important role in the educational life of Hawaii. *Sandwich Island Gazette*, Nov. 17. 1838, p. [3]; W. D. Alexander, "The Oahu Charity School," *Sixteenth Annual Report of the Hawaiian Hist. Soc.* (Honolulu, 1908) pp. 20–38; Hammond, ed., *Larkin Letters*, I: 154; II: 83, 120, 151; III: 295; Hittell, *History of California*, IV: 534–535; Ronald Genini and Richard Hitchman, *Romualdo Pacheco: A Californian in Two Eras* (San Francisco, 1985), pp. 19–22, 129 *et seq.*

few juvenile pieces. Heretofore, Mrs. Hooper has taught them, but is now engaged in giving the young Chiefesses lessons on the piano. Have been up to Mount Zion to a meeting—a name given to the missionary neighborhood.

12. Spent the day to Mrs. Hall's; was much interested in hearing Mr. H[all] speak of improvements which have taken place within a few years.[75] There are two Protestant churches, Rev. L. Smith's new church, a neat and large building of adobes, capable of accommodating two thousand persons. Rev. Mr. Hiram Bingham's stone church is an imposing structure, with columns in front, which will accommodate upwards of three thousand individuals. Likewise a new stone chapel for the Catholics is now building a few rods from us—to be one hundred and fifteen feet long, by fifty in breadth, and of a chaste style of architecture—one seaman's Bethel, one stone school house, reading rooms for seamen, American and British hospitals. A stone fort mounting sixty guns—Battery on Punch Bowl Hill—fourteen forty-two pounders—Printing office and Bindery, with many other public buildings.[76]

13. A ship telegraphed from Punch Bowl Hill!![77] For the future a signal will be hoisted for all vessels which will be fine—as I need not go on the look out to watch for sail ho! I

---

[75]Edward Oscar Hall, a printer by trade, came to Hawaii in the seventh mission band, which reached its destination on June 6, 1835. Born in Walpole, New Hampshire, October 21, 1810, he was one of Hawaii's earliest printers. Released in 1850, he became editor of *The Polynesian* and manager of the government printing office, 1850–1852. Turning to mercantile pursuits, he became an important Hawaiian business figure. His first wife, Sarah Lyons Williams, whom he married on November 3, 1834, was born in Elizabeth, New Jersey, October 27, 1812. She died at Honolulu, August 15, 1876. Two years later, having returned to the States, Hall married Mary Lyon Dame, who survived him. He died at Falmouth, Maine, September 19, 1883. *Protestant Missionary Portraits*, p. 53.

[76]Refer to the map illustration of Honolulu as it appeared in 1845. An excellent description is found in Gorham D. Gilman, "1848—Honolulu As It Is," edited by Jean S. Sharpless and Richard Greer, *The Hawaiian Journal of History*, IV (1970), 105–156.

[77]William Paty's Harbormaster Records do not indicate a vessel arrival for January 13. The 355-ton whaleship *Bartholomew Gosnold*, Captain Russell, from Falmouth, reached Oahu on January 10. The next entry lists the same vessel's return from Kauai, January 27. (See *note* 81, *post.*)

can see the signal from my chamber. As one would suppose, I have learned the signal for a brig. A fine ride on horseback this afternoon, with Mr. and Mrs. B[rewer].

14. Have been very much engaged today with my sewing. I have no time to be *idle*, one wants a great many changes in this climate—though I must take time to go to singing school, to prepare for the Sabbath. How much it reminds me of my *youthful* days when I used to sing in the old church in my dear native land.[78]

15. This is the eve of my birthday. Another year has commenced with me under circumstances of which at the beginning of the last I had not the slightest anticipation. The Providence of God has directed me to this distant land, surrounded me with blessing innumerable, of which I am truly grateful. Should my expectations be realized, my dwelling for years to come will be far from the Guardian of my youth, and the companions of my playful years, whose society rendered my life cheerful and happy. Amid thoughts like these, I often find my heart desponding, and looking back with longing desires toward "my sweet home." But God, Who has said his grace shall be sufficient for his children, gives me resolution and fresh supplies of strength which enables me to persevere in the path of duty. Have been to church today—this eve listened to a temperance address, the first I have heard since I have left America.

16. Today all the family [i.e., those resident in Captain Brewer's home] went on board the *William Gray* to dine, the ship Mr. B[rewer] came out in, to which they seem much attached indeed! She was the bearer of my *first* letter from

[78]From the second copy of her journal, Mrs. Nye concludes this entry as follows: "And now dear brothers and sisters I *must* bid you adieu as my paper is exhausted. Hope you will not be wearied with the perusal. In return I only ask as long a letter from each of you. Shall continue my Journal, commencing the 14th Jan[uary] and send next to Sister E. for you see by my dates I write a little every day. With love to *all*, I remain, your Affectionate Sister, Lydia."

home. Is waiting for the *Bolivar* to arrive with hides which she will take to the U[nited] States. Got home about four, took a short ride on horseback.

17. Spend the day to Mrs. Carter's.

18. Mrs. B[rewer] and I philopeened Mr. B[rewer] who gave each of us a pretty, pretty, blue silk apron, which I have today busied myself in making.[79]

19 & 20. Two stormy days, more so than any I have experienced since I have been here—high winds, with heavy rain. Last night, I awoke and lay thinking it may be my husband is near the Isl[and]s. And at this moment in imminent danger—for a while I looked on the dark side of everything—but today I feel better—it is wrong to indulge such feelings—I know that anxiety will not lessen the evil of anything.

21. Four months today since arrived—storm continues.

22. How pleasant again to behold the sun! Been to meeting—Mr. Leslie preached temperance this eve.

23. A temperance paper came out today, edited by Rev. S. C. Damon.[80] Spent the eve to Mrs. Paty's.

24. Rode on Punch Bowl Hill (battery) with Mr. Brewer and Mrs. More [Moore]—this eve had a sweet time to Mrs. Hooper's. It being unusually cold, we set the steward to making candy.

25. Visited the Charity School, gave the scholars a few lessons in singing, then rode to Wikta [Waikiki] with Mr. and Mrs. Damon.

---

[79]Defined as: "A social game in which each of two persons eat one of the twin kernels of a nut (usually an almond), and one pays a forfeit to the other if first saluted with the word 'philopena' or other specified conditions. . . ."

[80]This was *The Temperance Advocate and Seaman's Friend*, edited and published by the Reverend Samuel C. Damon, with the cooperation of the Sandwich Island Mission Press. The first issue appeared in January 1843. It was intended primarily for sailors, and in addition to its other features, carried vital statistics, ship arrivals and departures, and other news of the Port of Honolulu. Within a year's time, its somewhat unwieldy name had shifted to *The Friend of Temperance and Seamen*, and finally to that of *The Friend*, under which title it still persists as a publication of the United Church of Christ.

26. Wrote on till time to dress for dinner, when I saw a flag on the telegraph, thought it must be the *Bolivar*—proved to be a whale ship.[81] After tea rode horseback—heard the volcano at Owyhee had burst in a new place, the light of which is seen 40 miles off.

27. Rode about six miles this morning with Mr. Grimes and lady, which gave me a fine appetite for breakfast. Wrote the remainder of the day—when weary, I would go out on the verandah and watch the natives as they passed—just saw one with nothing but a vest on, another with an umbrella open, no clothing excepting a marrow [*malo*].

28. Called on the bride, Mrs. Russel [Russell] from Koloa.[82] Met again this evening to Mrs. Hooper's where we had a fine sing.

29. The first thought when I arise in the morning is to look on Punch Bowl Hill, and sure enough there is a brig telegraphed! but not in sight to us—Can I go to meeting? I went—kept S[abbath] School—on my return found it to be Capt. John Dominis from the Coast,[83] bringing me a letter from my husband, saying he should make all possible exertion to get here, which he thought would be by the last of February.

30. Mr. Locke, brother-in-law to Mrs. Rowell, my fellow passenger, called and persisted in my going home (to Waialua) with him as Mrs. R[owell] was very much out of health—was

[81]The Falmouth-based whaler, *Bartholomew Gosnold*, returning from Kauai, anchored at Oahu for a second time on January 27. It would make three more appearances. Paty's Harbormaster Records.

[82]Captain Abraham B. Russell, of New Bedford, Massachusetts, master of the whaleship *Bartholomew Gosnold*, married Miss Susan Holder, of Hillsborough, New Hampshire, at Koloa, island of Kauai, January 30, 1843. The Reverend Cochran Forbes performed the ceremony. On April 1, the *Bartholomew Gosnold* anchored at Honolulu, departing the next day. It sailed for its home port after a forty-two-month cruise on August 2. *The Friend*, 1 (Feb. 1843), 1; (April 1843), 18; (July 27, 1843), 34; (Aug. 11, 1843), 42.

[83]The *Joseph Peabody*, a Salem-owned brig, 224 tons, Captain John Dominis, master, sailed from Mazatlán on January 18, and anchored at Oahu, January 29. It sailed for China on April 10, 1843, with five Chinese passengers on board. Paty's Harbormaster Records; *The Friend*, 1 (Feb. 1843), 8; (May 20, 1843), 26. (Also, see *note* 26, *ante.*)

very desirous to see me.[84] Heretofore, I dare not venture, thinking the next hour would bring my husband—but by his letter, another month! must run its rounds before we meet—however, to pass away the time, I complied with her request, doubting whether I should be able to take such a ride on horseback (30 miles), the road not passable for a carriage. However, I rode as far as Ewa (twelve miles) and stopped the night.

31. Was going to start at sunrise, but O! how it rains—I see no alternative, but that I must spend the day.

February 1. The sun again shines—started at 10 A.M. got to W[aialua] between three and four—how glad Mr. and Mrs. R[owell] were to see me.

2 & 3. It is a rather pleasant place—but no society. There is only one family, Rev. A. B. Smith, who preaches to the natives.[85] I do not so much wonder Mrs. Rowell being sick and lonely.

[84]Edwin Locke, born January 18, 1813, at Fitzwilliam, New Hampshire, sailed for Hawaii on December 14, 1836, with his wife, the former Martha L. Rowell (born in Cornish, New Hampshire, November 9, 1812). Reaching their destination on April 9, 1837, they took up their station at Waialua. There they labored until their deaths. Mrs. Locke died on October 9, 1842, and her husband a year later, October 28. *Missionary Album*, pp. 138–139; *The Friend*, (Nov. 4, 1843), 65, for his obituary.

[85]Asa Bowen Smith and his wife arrived in Honolulu from Vancouver on January 25, 1842, after a thirty-five-day passage. They came in hopes of finding a climate more conducive to Mrs. Smith's precarious health. Born in Williamstown, Vermont, July 15, 1809, Smith graduated from Middlebury College in 1834, and studied at the Andover and Yale Seminary at New Haven. Ordained on November 1, 1837, he volunteered for the Oregon missions. His wife, Sarah Gilbert White, born in West Brookfield, Massachusetts, September 14, 1813, became his spouse on March 15, 1838. Joining the second Oregon-bound American Board mission party, composed of the Reverends William Gray, Cushing Eells, and Elkanah B. Walker and wives, Smith reached his missionary station after a four-month trek overland on horseback. In Hawaii, Smith served at Waialau until 1845. With his wife and three adopted children, Lucy, Martha, and Mary, the orphaned daughters of Edwin Locke, he took leave of the Islands on October 15, 1845, on the *Leland*, returning to the United States via Hong Kong and the Cape of Good Hope, which was safely reached on May 5, 1846. Settling first at Amherst, Massachusetts, as pastor of a Congregational church, the family moved two years later to Buckland. It was there that frail Sarah died "of consumption" on May 27, 1855. A year or so later Smith remarried. He continued his pastoral work in New England for several more decades. He died at Sherwood, Tennessee, February 10, 1886. Clifford M. Drury, ed., *First White Woman Over the Rockies* (3 vols.; Glendale, Calif., 1963–1966), I: 273–280; III: 225–229. *Protestant Missionary Portraits*, p. 80, contains erroneous biographical data.

It being nine months today since I sailed, my thoughts have rested upon my home and friends.

4. My visit is not half made, but I feel as though I ought to be at home in case of an arrival. Started very early—rode 18 miles, stopped to Rev. Bishop's and dined.[86] Mr. Rowell and I finally concluded to pass the night, but hearing a brig had arrived during my absence, I felt that promise void. I whipped my horse, and got home—a brig had come, but not the *Bolivar*!

5. Not so much fatigued as I expected—been to church, heard Mr. Hitchcock this morning.[87] Mr. R[owell] dined with me, and waited on me to the native church. Heard Mr. Smith this eve. Mr. Damon's text "Holy, holy, holy! is the Lord of hosts"—did not expect to hear such a variety of clergymen at the S[andwich] Islands.

6. Three English gentlemen to dine with us—took tea to Mrs. Damon's—two old whalers in sight.

7. My S[abbath] S[chool] class met in my room at eleven o'clock—took tea to Rev. L. Smith, Missionary.

8. Spent the day to Mrs. [Richard] Armstrong's (missionary). Visited the printing office and book-bindery—saw the

[86]A recruit in the ranks of the second missionary company to be sent to Hawaii, Artemas Bishop and his wife landed at Honolulu, April 27, 1823, from the ship *Thames*, Captain Clasby, 158 days out of New Haven, Connecticut. Ordained September 12, 1822, Reverend Bishop attended Union College and Princeton Seminary. His first wife, Elizabeth Edwards, born in Marlborough, Massachusetts, June 17, 1796, whom he married in November 1822, lived only five years after reaching Hawaii, dying at Kailua, February 28, 1828. On the following December 1, Bishop married the teacher-missionary Miss Della Stone, who arrived in the third party, March 30, 1828. Born in Bloomfield, New York, May 26, 1800, she died in Honolulu, April 13, 1875. Bishop was stationed first at Kailua, then Ewa, and finally Honolulu, where he died, December 18, 1872. During his residence at Kailua, he translated portions of the Bible into Hawaiian. *Missionary Album*, pp. 46–47.

[87]With his wife, Rebecca Howard, who was born at Owasco, New York, December 2, 1808, and whom he married on August 26, 1831, the Reverend Harvey Rexford Hitchcock arrived at Honolulu, May 17, 1832, in the fifth missionary contingent after a 172-day passage from New Bedford on the whaleship *Averick*. Ordained on September 20, 1831, he was a graduate of Williams College and Auburn Seminary. Born in Barrington, Massachusetts, March 13, 1800, he was stationed at Kaluaaha until 1853. A two-year furlough to the United States found him back at his station on Molokai. There he died on August 29, 1855. His widow continued to live at Hilo where she passed away on April 10, 1890. *Ibid.*, p. 39.

natives printing the Bible and other books. Mr. A[rmstrong] gave me an Hawaiian Bible with the promise I would send it to my minister.[88] In the eve went to Mrs. Chamberlain's to meeting.

9. Was obliged to be my own dress-maker, ah! milliner too! have whitened my bonnet—how nice it looks too—been to Mrs. Johnstone's school and gave her scholars a lesson in singing; on my return found lots of company to tea.

10. A bad headache attends me.[89] Went to ride—could not drive it away—English Frigate [*Craysfort*], Lord Poullett [Paulet] in sight.

11. Feel quite sick, took medicine—no better—called on Doct. Judd—a letter from Mrs. Rowell.

12. Feel some better—first time I have been detained from church—very rainy.

---

[88]The first band of American missionaries brought with them a printer, Elisha Loomis, along with a press and several fonts of type. However, the first printing was not done by him until two years later in 1822. Although portions of the Old and New Testament were published in excerpted form, the first complete Bible in the Hawaiian language was printed in Honolulu by 1839. Howard M. Ballou and George R. Carter, "The History of the Hawaiian Mission Press, with a Bibliography of the Earlier Publications," *Papers of the Hawaiian Historical Society*, No. 14 (Honolulu, 1908), 9–44.

[89]William Paty's journal, which covers this period, suggest a possible reason for Mrs. Nye's headache and subsequent illness. His attempt to disguise the names of the principals is obviously transparent. He writes on February 8, 1843:

> Today we have had one of those little occurrences which so often cause excitement and scandal in Honolulu, in the absence of more important matters. It seems that Mrs. N-e (either today or within a few days) has been at the O[ahu] C[harity] School teaching the children to sing, doubtless believing that in so doing she was doing them an act of kindness, but certain wiseacres in the abundance of their wisdom considered it as an awful violation of the rules and regulations of the School. And Mr. R-y--lds, who is the "big gun" in such cases, felt himself called upon to pay a visit to the School and give vent to his bile against Mrs. N-e over the shoulders of the School teacher Mrs. J---e.
>
> The consequence is that Mr. B[rewer] viewing the affair (as most of the residents do) as being a blackguard and outrageous transaction, has addressed a note to the Board of Trustees informing them that in consequence of an insult offered to one of his family he, for himself and partner [Henry A. Peirce of the firm of Peirce & Brewer], withdraw from the list of annual subscribers to the O.C. School.
>
> Thus did Stephen Reynolds exact his revenge upon Mrs. Nye for corrupting the pupils of his dancing school by luring them to attend a Sunday School prayer meeting!

13. Had a very sick night. Diahrea [*sic*]—pain in my head—back, etc. Mrs. B[rewer] sent for a physician who gave me a dose of medicine—leaving me something to take, in case I was in too much pain.[90] Which I was careful not to touch. Sail ho! a ship telegraphed. Thought to be the *Fama* from the Coast. It is possible my husband may be a passenger, and here I am sick—two o'clock and not dressed—with a little exertion I arose, expecting a letter, of course, when lo! and behold! it proved to be an American sloop-of-war.[91]

14. Medicine had a good effect—rested much better. Salutes were exchanged this morning between the Sloop of war, Capt. Long, and the Fort. There is not a very good feeling existing between the English and Americans, or rather this government. A schooner was dispatched for the King immediately on the arrival of the English Frigate, Lord George [Paulet].[92]

---

[90]The physician was probably Dr. Judd who attended Mrs. Nye on several occasions.

[91]The U.S. ship-of-war *Boston* arrived in Honolulu from China on February 13 under the command of Captain John C. Long. The vessel and its 203-member crew remained at Oahu until March 17. *The Friend*, 1 (March 1843), 12.

[92]Richard Carlton, British consul in Honolulu, was jealous of American influence in the Islands and determined, if possible, to forestall attempts of the three Hawaiian commissioners—Timoteo Ha'alilio, Reverend William Richards, and Sir George Simpson—to secure guarantees of island independence abroad. He had forwarded a series of alleged grievances of British subjects against the Hawaiian Kingdom to Admiral Richard Thomas, commander of the British naval squadron in the Pacific, before departing in haste for the Court of St. James. It is said that in transit, he conferred in Mexico with Lord George Paulet, whom Admiral Thomas, then in South American waters, had ordered to visit Honolulu in the interests of the complaining British subjects.

Kuykendall, in his *Hawaiian Kingdom, 1778–1854*, pp. 212–219, summarizes Paulet's actual orders from Admiral Thomas. He was to give support to the British consul in case he required it in protecting the interests of British subjects; he was to express to the king the satisfaction of Admiral Thomas upon learning that a Hawaiian embassy had been sent to London; he was to investigate the seizing of Charlton's property as reported by acting British consul Alexander Simpson, and if found to be correct, was to demand its immediate restoration and to deliver a reprimand to the island government for this want of respect shown Queen Victoria.

Alexander Simpson, a former employee of the Hudson's Bay Company, was carrying on a personal feud with his relative, Sir George Simpson, then Governor General of HBC's land and activities in Prince Rupert's Land (western Canada), because he had been refused a company appointment that he coveted. Much of his hatred against the Hawaiian government

(*continued on next page*)

15. Feel much better, but rather weak—the Doct. called, says I must keep quiet—the Capt. of the *Boston* called—there seems to be quite an excitement yet. In short, ought we not to rejoice at the arrival of an American man of war? Isolated as we are from "Father Land" placed on a speck of terra firma in the midst of the ocean, we greet with more than heartfelt welcome, the extended hand of protection from our civilized home—a Chilian brig in sight.[93]

16. Went downstairs today, which I have not done before a week. Was introduced to Capt. Long (of the Frigate *Boston*) who dines with us tomorrow.[94] Capt. Grimes took me out to ride in his gig this afternoon.

(*continued from previous page*)
stemmed from this source, since Sir George was an ardent advocate both of the Kamehameha dynasty and Hawaiian independence. He also was suffering a personal pique because Governor Kekuanaoa and the king had refused him recognition as acting British consul. Simpson, *The Sandwich Islands*, pp. 68–89, presents documentary evidence, as does Bingham, *A Residence of Twenty-One Years in the Sandwich Islands*, pp. 592–607.

Meeting in lengthy conferences with Alexander Simpson and Paulet daily from February 20 to 23, it became increasingly clear to the king that their aim was not justice for aggrieved British subjects as averred, but destruction of the Hawaiian Kingdom. Simpson's demands were beyond reason. Not only did he demand the surrender of the land claimed by Charlton, but acceptance by the king of a 299-year lease of the tract, in addition to reversal of certain court decisions that were impossible to grant without revision of Hawaiian laws—for which he refused to wait—and cash indemnities for alleged wrongs, which would have set up a sort of chain reaction that would have cost the Royal Treasury over $100,000. The latter was an impossibility since there was always an acute shortage of actual money in supply both in Hawaii and in West Coast settlements as well—a fact with which Alexander Simpson was completely familiar. Kuykendall, *Hawaiian Kingdom, 1778–1854*, p. 216.

Contemplating his unhappy dilemma, Kamehameha III at first was inclined to cede his kingdom provisionally and jointly to France and the United States, but finally decided to cede it instead to Great Britain under protest on February 25, 1843, for in spite of all that had transpired, he still had faith in her basic sense of fairness and justice, which time vindicated. King's proclamation and Paulet's response printed in *The Friend*, 1 (March 1843), 14.

[93]A 125-ton brig, the *Malek Adhel*, also spelled *Makel Adel*, from Valparaíso, enroute from San Blas to China, reached Oahu on February 14, sailing westward on February 16. Paty's Harbormaster Records; *The Friend*, 1 (March 1843), 12.

[94]The *U.S.S. Boston*, seven hundred tons, was not a frigate but a sloop-of-war. It carried a crew of 190 men and was armed with four 8-inch guns and sixteen 33-pounders. Built at the Boston Naval Yard in 1826, the vessel, having seen duty in the East Indies, 1841–1843, was

(*continued on next page*)

17. Have been writing, which you know I use to do, when getting better. The King has arrived—cannons are now roaring from the Fort—three hundred troops escorted him to the Governor's house, but I do not feel able or spirited enough to go out to see them. A large company dines here today, and I am very glad to get excused from going down, it is so tiresome to sit at the table two or three hours. A ship and brig telegraphed, it is now sundown. Shall not know tonight who they are.

18. This day will be remembered by me, as long as recollection exists. As soon as the King arrived, Lord George Poullett, Commander of the English frigate, sent a note to him, demanding a private interview immediately. The King replied he was not ready. Lord George next sent in his demands, saying if the government did not accede to them, viz., acknowledge Mr. Simpson, English Consul—and other requests, which I am not able to state, he would fire upon the town at four P.M.[95] In the meantime an English brig took all the English families on board, and went outside the reef, while the Lord hauled his frigate opposite the Fort, guns all

---

(*continued from previous page*)

enroute to its new station off the coast of Brazil when it reached Honolulu on February 13, 1843. During the Mexican War the vessel was ordered to join the Home Squadron commanded by Commodore David Conners in blockading the Mexican east coast. Sailing from the U.S. to that duty, it was wrecked on Eluethran Island, Bahamas, in a severe squall on November 15, 1846. A total loss, fortunately "all hands were saved." K. Jack Baur, *Surfboats and Horse Marines: U.S. Naval Operations in the Mexican War, 1846–48* (Annapolis, MD, 1969), p. 254; *Dictionary of American Naval Fighting Ships,* comp. by the Navy Department, Naval History Division (8 vols., Washington, D.C., 1959–1981), 1: 143–144.

John C. Long, commanding the *Boston,* was a naval career officer. He became a midshipman on June 18, 1812; lieutenant, March 5, 1817, and was promoted to commander, February 25, 1838. However, he did not make captain until March 2, 1849. Shortly after the onset of the Civil War, he was placed on the reserve list, July 16, 1862, with the rank of commander. He died September 2, 1865. Edward W. Callahan, comp., *List of Officers of the Navy of the United States and the Marine Corps from 1775 to 1900* (New York, 1901), p. 37.

[95]To round cut the picture of this day, the journal of William Paty provides details. See Appendix II.

on the broadside—ready to fire! As soon as Capt. Long, of the American sloop of war, received the message, he sent a note to the Americans, offering them protection on board his ship. Of course, we had no other refuge to flee to—Supposing the houses would be plundered and the town set on fire. In short, I filled a trunk with my most valuables and at two P.M. Mr. Brewer was to call for us—as we were about bidding adieu to our peaceful abode (the natives running into the valleys for safety). When we heard them singing out, it is all pow [pau] (the native word for peace). The King has come to some terms. I know not what, but peace was announced! and glad was I when salutes were exchanged between the English and the Fort. I could not help thinking of Grandma. You know she never felt friendly towards the English. I suppose the coming week will be one of continual excitement. I do not feel very fearful. I am almost glad my husband is not here, I should feel alarmed for his safety—while I am sure of the protection from the Americans who are true to their country. The ship which was in sight last night, proved the *Fama*.[96] Mr. A. B. Thompson came passenger.[97] Immediately called on me with a letter, from Gorham, saying he might possible arrive before the letter, for he should sail on the 18th of January for Mazatlan—take the mail, then come direct to the Islands. Owing to the contrary winds, Mr. T[hompson] says he will not be here these two weeks.

---

[96]The 362-ton ship *Fama*, Captain Cornelius Hoyer, arrived directly from California. *The Friend*, 1 (March 1843), 12. The vessel had wintered along the California coast and left Santa Barbara in January for Oahu with a cargo of horses. Bancroft, *California*; V:565*n*.

[97]Alpheus B. Thompson, born in Topsham, Maine, in 1797, voyaged to Canton, China, in 1821. From there he sailed to Oahu in 1825 to undertake the management of his uncle's business, and subsequently acted as supercargo on several vessels engaged in the California-Hawaiian trade. In 1834, at Santa Barbara, he married Francisca, daughter of Carlos Carrillo. He was to grow rich on his trading ventures. Survived by two daughters and four sons, he died in Los Angeles, February 29, 1869. D. Mackenzie Brown, ed., *China Trade Days in California: Selected Letters From the Thompson Papers* (Berkeley and Los Angeles, 1947), p. 3; [Thompson and West], *History of Santa Barbara County* (Oakland, 1883), p. 467; Los Angeles *Star*, March 1, 1869.

19. Morning has again dawned upon us and no harm has befallen our persons or property. Under the shadow of the Almighty we have been secure from the "terror by night"; everything seems quite but as this is the evening of the Sabbath, it will be more appropriate to recall the events of the day. Went to church this morning—Sabbath School after service—find it very pleasant—yet I feel the responsibility of my situation that an opportunity is given to me to promote the eternal interest of my scholars. Oh may I not be found wanting when called upon to render an account of the manner in which I have instructed them.

20 & 21. Dined with Capt. Grimes. In the afternoon went on board the ship *Boston*. Last night [I] watched.

22. Washington's birthday! The cannon are firing; a public ball this eve which I shall spend to Mrs. Damon's. How many invitations to go to the ball—but I refused. Gorham sent me a fine horse by the *Fama*.

23. There is still great excitement—the English have demanded 80,000 Dols. from the government.[98]

24. Went to the sewing circle to Mrs. Hooper's, had a large society in the evening, gentlemen and ladies.

25. At three P.M. the Hawaiian flag was struck, the English flag is now waving over these Isles.[99] A salute from the fort was given, returned by the English. Fortunate for the Americans, the sloop of war, Capt. Long, will remain as long as it is necessary.

---

[98]At no time was such a monetary ultimatum submitted to the Hawaiian government. Paulet had, in his original demands, sought restitution of property seized from Richard Charlton, former British consul, and fair settlement of other pending financial disputes involving British subjects. But no more. However, settlement of pending claims could have totaled $100,000.

[99]The deed of cession is published in Kuykendall, *Hawaiian Kingdom, 1778–1854*, p. 216*n*. The outline of the government to be established under British rule is found in Simpson, *The Sandwich Islands*, pp. 84–87.

The affair would be ended when Admiral Thomas arrived at Oahu. On July 31, the Hawaiian flag would be restored. Kuykendall, *Hawaiian Kingdom, 1778–1854*, p. 220. The *Carysfort* sailed on August 25. *The Friend*, 1 (Sept. 16, 1843), 50.

26. This morning sermon from Mr. Dole, while Mr. D[amon] preached on board the *Boston.*

27. Just received a note from the Capt. and officers of the ward room to a ball on board the *Boston* to which I declined as usual—the ladies all went (Mrs. D[amon] with myself excepted). It was said they had a nice time.

28. Very busy sewing—however took a short ride.

March 1. Two officers to dine—very rainy after dinner which spoilt our ride, went to bed tired and sleepy.

2. Sewing circle to Mrs. Paty's—this evening a comet made its appearance.[100] *Where is* the *Bolivar*?

3 & 4. Do not feel well—called in Doct. Judd—ordered me to put on flannels—ride, take all the exercise I could—left me some powders to take—took one, went to bed, and dreamt of home and friends.

5. No wind for the *B*[*olivar*]—been to meeting all day and eve. Text, Hebrews, 2 Chapt. "How shall we escape if we neglect so great salvation?"

6. Engaged making a ruffled cape, often run in to Mrs. M[artha] Paty's (a neighbor to us) and pass the evening but could not do much more than watch the comet.

7. It must seem strange to anyone to think of a sewing circle meeting on board a ship—but queer things happen in this part of the world. We met on board the *Boston*, had tea handed to us—in the evening music and singing—got home about ten.

8. Spent the day to Mrs. Grimes—rode with the Capt.

9. Wrote most of the day to send across land by Mr. Marshall, bearer of dispatches—to the states and elsewhere—he

---

[100]In *The Friend*, 1 (March 1843), 12, Samuel Damon says: "On the 7th [March] at 7 P.M. (the moon shining bright), the Comet was distinctly visible, of a pale red color, having a diameter of several seconds. No stars could be seen near it, owing to its nearness to the horizon, but at the hour of 7 P.M., it seemed to be between the constellations Ceti and Pegasi, the train extending more than 40° towards Canis Major . . . from Observations taken on Board the *Boston.*"

has long been an inmate of our family.[101] I have requested

[101]William Paty records in his journal for Saturday, March 11: "Schooner Albert [late *Ho'oikaika*] sailed for St. Blas and Mazatlán. She went outside just at sundown and anchored, and finally got under way at about 12 o'clock midnight. This vessel is the property of the S[andwich] I[sland] Government but has been taken possession of by the Right HONORABLE Lord Geo. Paulet for the use of Queen Victoria and now goes to San Blas to carry Mr. Alexander Simpson (late Acting Br. consul here) on his way to England. Mr. J.F.B. Marshall also goes as passenger in her on his way to England as bearer of dispatches for the S.I. Government. On the result of this expedition will depend the fate of the S.I. Government."

James F. B. Marshall, a young American, had been employed by Dr. Judd in the Royal Treasury as a clerk whose principal duty was the copying of government documents, but soon joined the firm of Peirce & Brewer. (See Marshall's testimony in *Report of the Proceedings and Evidence in the Arbitration Between the King and Government of the Hawaiian Islands and Messrs. Ladd & Co., Before Messrs. Stephen H. Williams & James F.B. Marshall*... (Honolulu, 1846), pp. 248–249.) At this time Peter Brinsmade, one of the partners of Ladd & Co., was in Europe attempting to negotiate a contract with a group of Belgian businessmen to take over the extensive lease of crown lands held by his company, for the purpose of developing sugar plantations on them. He was believed to be enroute to the Islands from Belgium with a substantial down payment to close the transaction, which was vitally necessary to keep Ladd & Co. from bankruptcy. (*Ibid.*, pp. 249–254.) Accordingly, the company had chartered the king's vessel, *Ho'oikaika*, to meet him in San Blas. In the event he had sent the money instead of bringing it in person, a company representative was to go on the vessel to receive it and bring it to Honolulu.

Alexander Simpson and Lord Paulet were in agreement that it was imperative for Simpson to get to England as quickly as possible to have the cession confirmed before the three Hawaiian Commissioners had persuaded the British government to guarantee the independence of the Hawaiian Kingdom, and also before news of the British take-over could reach the rest of the world. Accordingly, both the *Ho'oikaika* and the *Piia*, vessels belonging to the king, were commandeered by the British "for the use of Queen Victoria." Ladd & Co. protested vehemently because the former was already under charter to them, and were given the right of sending a representative on her to San Blas—where Simpson was bound with all possible haste—to secure and return the expected funds, and to hold the vessel there fifteen days if necessary to contact Peter Brinsmade, who would have to cross Mexico by mule.

The scheme to send Marshall, ostensibly as representative of Ladd & Co. but actually as Commissioner of the Hawaiian Government to England, was hatched at the ball on board the *Boston*, which Mrs. Nye and Mrs. Damon declined to attend, and to which none of the British had been invited. Marshall gives details of this in his "An Unpublished Chapter in Hawaiian History," *Harper's*, XLVII (Sept. 1883), 511–520. With permission of his prospective employers, Peirce & Brewer, who were competitors of Ladd & Co., Marshall was named representative of the latter in order to get him on his way as royal commissioner to the Court of St. James.

Since there was no lawyer in the Sandwich Islands, Marshall's papers, he says, were "copied verbatim from an old Bluebook containing the credentials of John Adams as the first American Minister to England" were prepared "by Doctor Judd and a confidential clerk" working late at night "in the royal tomb (then adjoining the Palace grounds in Honolulu)

(*continued on next page*)

him to call and see you, which he promises to do—no arrivals—O for a trade wind!

10 & 11. Invited to Mrs. Carter's to a large party, did not feel like going. Mr. Marshall sailed.[102] Took a letter across land to A[rmstrong]—Rode about four miles today.

12. Have been to meeting morning and eve, another Sunday, no arrival.

13. Finished my letters to send by the *Boston.*[103] Was spending the afternoon to Mrs. Doct. Judd's—a brig came in

---

(*continued from previous page*)
with a king's coffin for a table. . . . The papers prepared, a canoe with picked crew of *Kanaka* was dispatched from a distant point of the island to summon his majesty and suite to a midnight council." Returning, "they landed on the shores of Waikiki . . . and in its coconut grove by the light of torches, my credentials received the signature and seal of the king and *kuhina nui*—"great minister"—Kekauluohi, the 'big-mouthed queen,' then the king and his attendants returned to his mountains without Lord Paulet having a suspicion they had ever left them."

Marshall, ostensibly official representative of Ladd & Co., but carrying dispatches to Washington, D.C., from William Hooper, American consul at Honolulu, and protests of the American residents against the act of Lord Paulet, in addition to his own commission, traveled in company with Alexander Simpson to San Blas, H.M.S. tender *Albert*, commanded by a midshipman from H.M.S. *Carysfort*, which was reached April 10, and thence by muleback across Mexico. Arriving May 1 at Vera Cruz, Simpson embarked for England via Havana, while Marshall was delayed until May 10 awaiting a ship to New Orleans. Further delays in the United States brought him to England a week later than Simpson who arrived in London June 18. But even with the added advantage of being able to present his side of the case first to Foreign Office officials, Simpson failed in his efforts to add the Sandwich Islands to the possessions of Great Britain. Marshall, "An Unpublished Chapter in Hawaiian History," p. 514; Simpson, *The Sandwich Islands*, p. 89.

Marshall, working in conjunction with the three Hawaiian commissioners and Peter Brinsmade, whom he found still in Europe where news of the British occupation had stalled his Belgian deal, on August 17, 1843, received the personal assurance of Lord Aberdeen, British Minister of Foreign Affairs, that the Sandwich Islands had been misrepresented by Charlton and Simpson, and that Great Britain would render justice. Leaving his associates to receive the formal announcement, Marshall hastened to Boston and his waiting fiancee. He states the total cost of his embassy was $1,995.95. This was paid by the American merchants of Honolulu who had financed it, and by the king in the form of firewood for use on ships, since this was one of the few resources that had been left him by the British occupation. Simpson, *The Sandwich Islands*, p. 89; Marshall, "An Unpublished Chapter in Hawaiian History," pp. 511–520.

[102]Marshall sailed on H.M.S. tender *Albert,* commanded by a midshipman from H.M.S. *Carysfort*, on March 11. The vessel reached San Blas on April 10, and from there Marshall traveled overland to the east coast of Mexico to take ship to Washington, D.C. "An Unpublished Chapter in Hawaiian History," p. 514.

[103]The *Boston* sailed on March 17. *The Friend*, 1 (April 1843), 18.

sight; supposed it to be the long expected one—got in a carriage, rode home all in a hurry—when lo! it was the *Lama*, who reported the *B*[*olivar*] to be off Diamond Head.[104]

14. Rose with the sun, went up on the look out. Saw to my surprise! my expectations were soon to be realized. The *Bolivar* had come. Yes, that long desired vessel was in full view, riding proudly over the blue waves, of the yet heaving ocean—then a favoring breeze bore her rapidly onward, and before ten o'clock, was safely anchored.[105] Soon I heard a well known step approaching my room—the next moment, I was in the arms of my husband. Congratulate me my dear friends! that I am in the presence of that dear one for whom I have crossed the stormy ocean. I can hardly realize! In short, I find

---

[104]The *Lama*, a 144-ton brig, Captain Owen Jones, a Honolulu-owned vessel (Peirce & Brewer), had been at sea fourteen months. En route to Valparaíso, it departed on April 8, 1843. Paty's Harbormaster Records; *The Friend*, 1 (April 1843), 18; (May 20, 1843), 26. Bancroft, *California*, IV: 567*n*, gives tonnage of 208 tons.

[105]A Salem-owned brig, the 212-ton *Bolivar Liberator* first sailed along the California coast 1832. On this voyage it had touched at Mazatlán en route to Oahu. In later years it became the prison ship for Sacramento and was rechristened the *La Grange*. Eventually, a group of Chinese purchased the rotting hull and by 1873, the once proud vessel lay on the bottom of the Sacramento River. Paty's Harbormaster Records; Hammond, ed., *Larkin Papers*, I:4; Sacramento *Union*, Nov. 19, 1857; Feb. 1, 1873.

Sir George Simpson explains in his *Narrative of a Journey Round the World*, I:429, 432, when a ship arrived off Diamond Head in the evening, as the *Bolivar Liberator* did, it often had to spend the night outside. He says:

> As the entrance of the basin is too intricate to be attempted with anything but a fair wind, we were reluctantly obliged to wait for the sea-breeze, which generally blows in the morning, from a little before sunrise to about nine o'clock; and we accordingly anchored for the night in the outer roads....
>
> On entering the channel, whose breadth did not exceed twice the length of the Cowlitz, we could almost have touched with an oar a crowd of natives who were elbowing each other on the reef up to their middles in water, all the while jabbering, and shouting.... On our handing out a hawser to these fellows, who, if sufficiently numerous, could, I verify believe, tow a vessel swimming, we were speedily hauled close to the wharf....

Alakea Street in downtown Honolulu is derived from *ala*—path, road trail—and *kea*—white. White coral stones from the sea were used to pave a tow path on which shore laborers could tow vessels into the harbor of Honolulu. This area was later filled in, thus the name survives to remind the present of the use of the path in the past. Clarice B. Taylor in collaboration with George Mirairda, "Tales from Hawaii: Honolulu Street Names—4," Honolulu *Star-Bulletin*, Jan. 30, 1956, p. 20, cls. 3–4.

in him the same kindness and affection which were so natural to him—I only lament Mrs. Brewer's giving a dancing party this evening, thirty couple, or more, but there is no alternative—we must go.

15. Company stayed late, did not get much rest, everything passed off pleasantly—but I don't enjoy parties.

16. Sail ho! The *Bherings*, from the States—what an excitement—a great number of passengers. Mrs. Dominis—Mr. Calkin and lady—Mr. Johnson, from Charlestown, etc,[106] and no letters for me—how disappointed! By the *Boston* this morning, I sent several.

17 & 18. Gorham sent up his things today. I have passed it every pleasantly in looking them over; shall find enough to do to get things in readiness for the Sabbath.

19. Been to church morning and evening with my husband too! Many years have elapsed since we walked to the house of God in company. Twelve years since the Hymenial torch was lighted by the altar of love—yet it burns with unabated fervor. Old Ocean has not quenched it nor time smothered it in our bosoms.

20 & 21. This afternoon has a pleasant ride in a carriage—in the evening went to the seaman's concert prayer meeting—on my return found Mr. Drew and Mr. Southward.[107]

22. Sewing society met at our house this afternoon—our

---

[106]The Boston-owned 275-ton bark *Bherings*, Captain Snow, master, after a voyage of 134 days, anchored on March 17. Among its passengers were: "Mrs. John and Master Dominis; Mr. & Mrs. [Samuel N.] and Miss Castle; Miss Sarah A. Goodale; Mr. & Mrs. [Milo] Calkins; Mr. Johnson & Mr. [Stephen A.] Reynolds." The vessel sailed on April 24 for Kamkchatka. Paty's Harbormaster Records; Paty's Journal, [March] 17, 1843 (punctuation supplied); *The Friend*, 1 (April 1843), 18.

[107]Drew was a relative, a cousin. (See *note* 69, *ante*.) Eli Southward, native of Massachusetts, first appeared in the Pacific along the California coast in 1838 on the *Don Quixote*, possibly earlier (1833–1835) on the *Loriot*. As a business partner of John Paty's, he was in San Francisco, 1843–1845, where he clerked for William Heath Davis. Later he entered the lumbering business and from 1853 lived with Davis at San Leandro until his death in 1857. Bancroft, *California*, V:729; *Sandwich Island Gazette*, May 26, p. [3]; Nov. 17, 1838, p. [3]; Davis, *Seventy-Five Years*, pp. 253–255.

object is to clothe a destitute family with four children—mother sick—have traveled from the states—now bound to Oregon, Columbia River.

23. By the *Bherings* came out some silver plate from some institution in the States to be presented to the Governor for some noble act of his.[108] At eleven o'clock, a table was spread; after partaking of a collection, Mr. Brewer presented it to his Excellency, who received it very gratefully.

24 & 25. Yesterday went on board the *Peabody*[109] and the *Bolivar*, where we spent most of the day—and where my husband had spent many years. Returned in time to take tea to Mrs. Damon's.

26. Been to church—kept S[abbath] School. Was taking a little rest when a servant knocked at my door telling me two gentlemen from Plymouth wished to see me. I made all possible haste down. Whom should I meet but Wilm. Carver [and] Mr. Finney (brother of Mrs. C[arver]). They were extremely glad to hear so direct from home; the next day was to sail on another cruise.[110] I sent them all the newspapers I brought from Plymouth.

---

[108]According to a column under the pen-name "Herodotus" in the Honolulu *Advertiser*, July 28, 1926, p. 14, cl. 3, this story is reported in retrospect:

> On the third of December, 1841, the American ship "CALIFORNIA" appeared at the entrance of the Harbor of Honolulu in distress. She had struck and become fixed on the coral rocks at that entrance. After having remained a short time, she keeled so much that her situation was apparent from the town as desperate. Lieutenant R.E. Johnson of the United States Navy was among the first to reach the ship, where he found all was confusion.

Apparently Johnson took command and was able to save the day. Subsequently ten presidents of the American insurance companies sent a letter of commendation for Johnson's "self-possession, good judgment, and promptness" to the Secretary of the Navy. These same gentlemen also expressed comparable appreciation to Mateo Kekuanaoa, governor of Oahu, for his assistance in the rescue effort which included help from the local populace. In recognition of the governor's invaluable aid, the insurance companies sent him a silver service.

[109]Captain John Dominis' vessel, the *Joseph Peabody*. See *note* 83, *ante*.

[110]These sailor visitors were probably from the ship *Helvitia,* Captain Rice, out of New London, Connecticut. It reached Honolulu March 25, having been at sea eight months on a whaling expedition. It sailed on March 26. *The Friend*, 1 (April 1843), 18.(*Helvitia* is possibly *Helvetia.*)

27. The drums are beating—preparing for a sham fight, on the Plains, between the English frigate and the natives—Sham enough too! The Americans are so indignant, they did not take notice of it.

28. Gorham is very busy unloading—I have been up to Mount Zion to make calls on the missionaries—at five o'clock rode—find G[orham] a fine horseman.

29. Wrote to Koala [Koloa], to Mrs. Doct. Smith—Dined to Capt. Grimes'—met with the sewing circle to Mrs. D[amon]'s.

30. This may as well pass for a rainy day. Mrs. H[ooper] came to pass the day with us, was called to Mrs. M[artha] Paty's who gave birth to fine daughter.[111]

31. Just finished a grass cloth collar, think I shall send it to Ma. Shall leave Gorham writing while I go to the preparatory lecture. Mr. Johnson came to pass the eve, was taken spitting blood.[112]

April 1. I was sitting very quietly writing to Mrs. Rowell, when Gorham came in to tell me he had left the *Bolivar*, was going to sail in three weeks for Oregon in the ship *Fama.* Would you like to go? O yes! I would like to visit the Columbia River, then it is but a few days sail to the Coast from the river. There had been several families waiting for a vessel to take them to C[olumbia River] besides a large freight for the missionaries at Wilhamet [Willamette] Falls[113]—a voyage of three months, we shall then get on the coast in season to take what hides we can, then back to the Isl[and].

[111]This was Captain John Paty's first daughter. His wife, Mary Ann Jefferson (1813–1891), whom he had married on August 31, 1831, had given birth to a son, John, in 1840. However, this child died in late February 1844. See Epilogue, *note* 1, *post*, and Green, ed., "Captain John Paty's Journal," p. 38 (although the date of birth there is erroneously reported as 1844).

[112]This would be the Mr. Johnson from Charleston, Massachusetts, who came on the *Bherings*, March 17. *The Friend*, 1 (April 1843), 18. (The Reverend Edward Johnson, Hawaiian missionary, died in 1867.) No doubt, this new arrival was suffering from tuberculosis.

[113]Since there was no scheduled transport between the Islands and the Pacific coast, it was customary for both personnel and supplies for the Oregon missions to be accumulated in Honolulu awaiting trans-shipment to their destination. For the missionary band sailing, see *note* 118, *post*.

2. Went to church this morning. Kept S[abbath] School. This afternoon to the native Church. This eve the Lord's supper was administered. Yes, my enjoyment this day has far exceeded my expectations. I had felt as this was probably the last Sabbath I should spend with my Christian friends for many, many months, the sensation might be painful; far otherwise while meditating of the goodness God in restoring to me my husband who is ever kind, does not oppose me in the "one thing needful," but is pleased to accompany me at any time and listen to the truths of the Gospel.

3 & 4. This morning Gorham, Mrs. More [Moore] and I rode horseback before breakfast, which gave us a fine appetite. At two o'clock went to dine to Mr. & Mrs. Hoopers, the American Consul. Got home about four. Accepted of an invitation to tea to Mrs. Diamonds [Dimonds] (Missionaries). Last evening the monthly concert was unusually interesting.

5 & 6. Have commenced writing by the *Wil[lia]m Gray.*[114] Must sew a little, however. Took tea to Mrs. Knapp's where I found a letter from Mrs. Rowell.

7. A note this morning from Mrs. Doct. Wood, to tea this eve—you may think strange that I can find time to go so often—'tis true I have visited them all many times, but not with my husband before.

8. Gorham has gone to the Masonic meeting, so I shall spend the evening in writing if I can find any idea.[115] My first

---

[114]The Boston-owned *William Gray,* a ship of 293 tons, anchored at Oahu on November 19, 1842, with a cargo of goods assigned to Peirce & Brewer. Captain Stickney departed for his home port on April 18, 1843. Paty's Harbormaster Records; *The Friend,* 1 (May 20, 1843), 26.

[115]The Masonic Order first came to Hawaii under French auspices. From the journal of William Paty, under date of April 11, 1843, it states: "This evening joined the Masonic Lodge ["Lodge le Progres de l'Oceanie," No. 124] just established here by Captain Le Tellier. My brother John, F. W. Thompson, and R. Davis, were taken in at the same time." Ten in all were inducted, including John Meek. Captain Le Tellier, master of the 398-ton French ship *Ajax,* out of Le Havre, anchored at Oahu, March 30, 1843. The vessel's ten-month voyage was resumed on May 3. Paty's Harbormaster Records; *The Friend,* new series, 24 (Feb. 1, 1875), [10].

thought—It is sister E. birthday; how old? Dare not think! By the way Capt. Dominis sailed for China today (one of our family).[116] Gorham sent by him to get me a light brown satin that I may look as I used to in my juvenile days. Still will not own that I have changed.

9. Sermon today from Mr. Leslie who takes passage to Oregon with us—Text, "Let me die the death of the righteous, and let my last end be like his." Very good Methodist sermon.

10. Made a mosquito net for my bedstead and a poncho for Gorham, which has kept me busy.

11 & 12. Yesterday I wrote all day. Should you get my letters by the *Wil[lia]m Gray*, you will say it time and patience both. Today went on board the ship to see my accommodations—found my room papered and carpeted, bedstead set up, etc. In short, I can set all the furniture in my room I took out with me, and I assure you it looks nice. I found it reminded me too much of home.

13. Have been packing all day—shall sail in a week.

14. March winds still prevail—recd many calls.

15. Sent part of our things on board—stopped and dined, it already seems like home, but ah! how different when on the broad ocean—but time enough to enjoy that a week hence—thought we should have one more pleasant ride on horseback; but find the rain will prevent. In fine, I dislike to ride Saturdays; I will tell you why. There are few scenes more novel and interesting to a stranger, than that to be witnessed here on Saturday afternoon. But it is losing its originality, and becoming tempered by civilization. It was formerly a gala day for all classes, now by the natives only. Picture to yourself on the wide plain east of the town, all of the natives assembled, from the tiniest urchin, to the portly adult, who have been so fortunate as to find four legs besides their own beneath them.

[116]Captain John Dominis sailed his ship, the *Joseph Peabody*, for China on April 10, as reported in *The Friend*, 1 (May 20, 1843), 26.

Of saddles some have none, the bridles are as various and primitive as the rest of the equipment, a rope, or nothing—on goes this cavalcade, hilter skilter, their loose kapers [*tapas*] streaming in the wind—bareheaded, away they scamper, enveloped in a cloud of dust. In striking contrast to this, is a little group of urchins, who have succeeded in ensnaring, some stray donkey—such fun; two and even three, are mounted upon this diminutive animal, their companions whipping and pushing to get him ahead, till the poor beast can endure no longer—he makes a sudden start, and with a jerk, leaves his riders sprawling in the dust. Neither is this riding confined to the kanackars [*kanakas*] alone, the wihenas [*wahines*] are equally as fond of it—condemning alike beaus, side saddles, and all the garniture so much esteemed by the civilized. It is not an uncommon sight to see two astride of the same animal—careless alike of looks. Their dress consists of bright colored calico loose gowns, with a *kihei*,[117] or piece of red, green, or yellow silk, or something less costly, wrapped tightly around their waist, and encircling their nether members in loose and graceful folds. Wreaths of flowers or feathers deck their brows; and necklaces of the odoriferous hala-nut,[118] while their eyes sparkle with triumph as they look down upon the staring pedestrian. Add to this the brilliant uniform of naval officers that may be in port; and the neat costume of the residents, some on horseback, other sporting gigs. In short, it is a mixture of rude barbarism—here are people of all tongues and nations, gathered together for one purpose—pleasure; and the chiefest [*sic*] pleasure is to gaze on them.

16. We have attended meeting today, but this evening have been writing and indeed, until late at night—have finished and sealed our letters, expecting to sail tomorrow. Yes, I leave these Islands to live the remembrance of them over again in

---

[117]This should be *pa'u*, a shirt.

[118]The lower sections of the ripe, orange hala fruit.

memory's blissful domains. Five months of my existence passing so rapidly away.

17. Went on board this morning, most of the ladies accompanied me. At eleven o'clock, the steward set out some ham, tongue, salad, etc., with which we refreshed ourselves. Capt. Grimes officiated. However, the wind not being favorable, did not sail. Capt. Grimes would have us go on shore with him to tea and pass the evening. Came off about ten o'clock and I think slept much more soundly than I shall the ensuing night.

18. This morning a large company of gentlemen came on board to bid us farewell—set sail about 10 o'clock, with a fair wind—twenty-one passengers, six children.[119] The ship *Wil[lia]m Gray*, Capt. Stickney, sailed the same time.

---

[119]Passengers on board included the Reverend David Leslie; Mr. and Mrs. Francis W. Pettygrove and child; Mr. and Mrs. Philip Foster and four children; Mr. and Mrs. Peter H. Hatch and child; and Nathan P. Mack, all destined for Oregon. *The Friend*, 1 (May 20, 1843), 26, provides the last names of the aforementioned, but no others are given.

Pettygrove would become one of the founders of the city of Portland. His would be a career of mercantile activity. Born in Calais, Maine, 1812, he died at Port Townsend, October 5, 1887. Lewis A. McArthur, "Oregon Geographic Names," *Oregon Historical Quarterly*, XXVIII (March 1927), 72.

Foster first settled at Oregon City, then subsequently moved to farm at Eagle Creek. His wife, Mary Charlotte, was Pettygrove's sister. Born in Augusta, Maine, January 29, 1805, Foster died on March 17, 1884. His wife preceded him in death in 1879. McArthur, "Oregon Geographic Names," *ibid.*, XXVII (March 1926), 184–185.

Hatch reached the Sandwich Islands as a blacksmith on a whaling expedition. On reaching Oregon, he settled in Oregon City, moving to Salem in 1863. On the death of his first wife, he married Sarah Cornelia Locey, February 9, 1847. Born in Parsonville, Maine, December 26, 1810, Hatch died at Salem, August 25, 1898. E. Ruth Rockwood, ed., "Diary of Reverend George H. Atkinson, D.D.," *Oregon Historical Quarterly*, XL (June 1939), 186*n;* Charles H. Carey, ed., "Diary of Reverend George Gary-IV," *ibid.*, XXIV (Dec. 1923), 390 and *note*; Howard M. Corning, *Dictionary of Oregon History* (Portland, 1956), p. 108.

Mack, from Massachusetts, had been for several years in the Pacific as a trader and whaler. A carpenter by trade, he practiced his vocation in Oregon City, later settling on a farm about ten miles east of that city until he relocated in Salem. Bancroft, *Oregon*, I:423.

Chapter III

To Oregon

Tuesday 3 o'clock, May 2, 1843. Ship *Fama* at sea: Lat. 41°32'. My journal for the last two weeks has been treated with entire neglect; ill health (or rather sea-sickness) must plead in my behalf and be my apology for allowing the pleasantness of the last two weeks to lay unregistered in black and white.

The return of this day must bring with it recollections most painful and interesting—taking a last farewell of friends and country, home—that dearest, sweetest spot—was exceedingly trying. A year this morning since I sailed from Boston; now bound to Oregon, thence to the Coast of California. How rapidly the time has flown. Why? How soon three years will pass away could I but know I should then return to my native land. Nearly six years since, I humbly trust, I committed my all to God willing that he should dispose of me as he saw best. What but the light of God's countenance could make me happy in my own land, and what but that can delight my soul in a far distant country?

For me remains nor time, nor space,
My country is in every place;
I can be calm and free from care
On any shore, since God is there.

3 & 4. These last two days have felt much better; have been able to do a little sewing for the Capt.

5. Fair wind, sailing eight knots—not sick today.

6. Heavy swell, with a high wind, lay to for a few hours—while breakfasting, the ship rocked violently—the table upset—each one caught something, then took to our rooms—

placing myself in the bed with things to support me (like a child just beginning to sit alone). I finished my breakfast which was not a very light one.

7. So rough Mr. Leslie thinks he shall not be able to preach, however, prayers this morning and evening.

8. Eighteen days out; made land at nine o'clock A.M. At two P.M. made the bar—breakers were such did not like to pass over, back to sea.[1]

9. Made another attempt this morning, did not fetch. Many vessels have been ship-wrecked here! May that God, who has hitherto been our protector, still stand by us. At four P.M. succeeded in getting over the bar safely—now the only difficulty, the wind is not fair to carry us to Baker's Bay, the only safe anchorage.[2] However, at nine in the evening, dropped anchor; there was not an alternative, we must either cross the bar and put to sea again, or lie at anchor in this uncomfortable place.

10. Morning has again dawned—the sound of yo heave ho! awakened me; but sorry to learn cannot make the harbor. The Capt. with myself passed a sleepless night—took but little breakfast—went on deck, tried to raise a breeze, set the children to crying, the dogs to barking—but all to no purpose. Several beautiful birds flew on board, indeed, the scenery is

---

[1]The entrance to the Columbia River was always a hazardous venture. Sandbars, currents, weather, these were the handicaps to be mastered for safety. Many a vessel foundered here and was lost.

Reverend Gustavas Hines, who was connected with the Methodist Mission in Willamette Valley for a time in the 1840s, states: "The channel across the bar is five fathoms deep and half a mile wide.... When the wind is high from the south and west, the waves of the Pacific and the torrents of the Columbia meet upon this bar with the most terrific violence, producing a line of breakers, often extending from one point to the other...." Gustavus Hines, *Oregon: His History, Condition and Prossfact.* (Buffalo, 1851), p. 330.

[2]Baker Bay, named by Lieutenant William R. Broughton of the British-sponsored George Vancouver expedition in 1792, had previously been named by the American captain of the *Lady Washington*, Robert Gray, who also discovered the Columbia River. The new name was derived from James Baker, the captain of the American schooner *Jenny*, which Broughton found anchored in the bay. It usually is written as Baker's Bay. Edmond S. Meany, "Washington Geographic Names," *Washington Historical Quarterly*, VIII (Oct. 1917), 277.

very romantic, lofty pine trees which grow by the water's edge with the green hills all around is rather an imposing sight. Add to this Cape Disappointment just before us (rightfully named I think).[3] However, about 12 o'clock got under weigh; soon found we were aground. During the time were visited by several canoes with Indians—did not stop long—before we floated they paddled off, while we came safely to an anchor.

11. This morning several canoes alongside, with fish and Indian baskets to trade, by them Mr. Leslie learned his two daughters and son-in-law were drowned passing Wilhamette Falls a few months since.[4] Sad intelligence—I had often heard him speak of them while on the passage. About eleven A.M. were visited by Mr. Birnie[5] and Mr. Raymond[6]

[3]Cape Disappointment is one of the oldest geographical names in Washington. On August 17, 1775, Bruno Heceta, the Spanish explorer, found a bay with indications of a river. The bay he called "Bahía de la Asunción," the northern cape he called "San Roque," and the southern "Cabo Frondoso." Later, the Spaniards called the bay "Ensenada de Heceta" in honor of its discoverer. John Meares, an English explorer, knew of the Spanish charts and on Sunday, July 6, 1788, he rounded the cape and looked for the "river which was surmised by the Spaniards." Thwarted in that effort, he changed the name to Cape Disappointment, which has remained. *Ibid.*, IX (Jan. 1918), 35.

[4]The report of the drowning tragedy is found in a letter written by David Leslie to Reverend Samuel C. Damon, dated Willamette Falls, August 2, 1843. The sad event occurred on February 2, and the victims included Mr. and Mrs. Cornelius Rogers; the latter's little sister, Aurelia; Nathaniel Crocker, from Langsville, Tompkins County, New York; and two Clatsop Indians. Rogers, a former Presbyterian missionary who came overland to Oregon with the 1838 missionary party, married Leslie's eldest daughter, fifteen-year-old Satira, on board the *Chenamus*, at anchor in Baker's Bay, Dr. John P. Richmond, missionary, performing the nuptial shortly before the brig sailed on September 1, 1842, for the Hawaiian Islands with Leslie and two other daughters on board. He entrusted two other small daughters to the newlyweds. *The Friend*, I (Oct. 28, 1843), 57–58; Hines, *Oregon*, pp. 134–138; Bancroft, *Oregon*, I:199–200.

[5]James Birnie, an employee of the Hudson's Bay Company, was born in Paisley, County Renfrew, Scotland, 1800. He emigrated to Canada in 1816 and two years later joined the North West Fur Company as an apprentice. Stationed at Fort George at the mouth of the Columbia, formerly Fort Astoria, in 1821 he was retained by the HBC when it merged with the Nor'westers that year. He was returned to Fort George on a permanent basis in 1839. Retiring from company service in 1845, he settled at Cathlamet, Washington Territory, where he died, December 21, 1864. Married to a daughter of a Frenchman Bianlien, he had thirteen children. Elwood Evans, *History of the Pacific Northwest: Oregon and Washington* (2 vols.; Portland, 1889), II:213.

[6]William W. Raymond reached Oregon on the *Lausanne* with his wife. He was entered

(*continued on next page*)

from Fort George, or rather Astoria.[7] After dinner, the Capt. and his lady went ashore, stopped but a few hours, then returned to our home.

12. Very foggy—a boat from Astoria, with Mr. B[irnie] and Mr. and Mrs. Raymond, who dined with us. At two P.M. got under weigh, at night came to an anchor—dangerous sailing in this place in the dark. Several of the passengers have gone to the Clatsop Plains to get some butter and milk, and other good things.[8]

13. Two o'clock and here we lay around again! However, the passengers have just returned bringing with them butter, cheese, etc. from Mrs. R[aymond] for which we feel very grateful; eleven P.M. once more afloat.

14. Again tried to cross the channel, but have not succeeded. However, this has been a pleasant day. All assembled in the cabin and listened to the precious truths of the Gospel from the Rev. D. Leslie; after prayers, the eve was spent in singing.

15. Four A.M. all hands on deck! got under weigh; was making rapid progress, tow men heaving the lead constantly—

(*continued from previous page*)
as a farmer. In 1842, he and his family were settled at Clatsop at the newly established mission farm. On May 23, 1842, his wife delivered a child. Later, on the death of his first wife, Raymond married Miss Elmira Phillips, also a *Lausanne* missionary passenger, who resided with his family at Clatsop. Henry B. Brewer, "Log of the *Lausanne*-V," edited by John M. Canse, *Oregon Historical Quarterly,* XXX (March 29, 1929), 116; Bancroft, *Oregon*, I:177, 187; Hines, *Oregon*, p. 193.

[7]Fort Astoria was originally built by the Pacific Fur Company, the property of John Jacob Astor, on the south bank of the Columbia near the mouth of the river, some twelve miles up stream. Founded in March 1811, it was one of the victims of the War of 1812 when it was sold to the North West Fur Company shortly before H.M.S. *Raccoon* anchored nearby. Rechristened Fort George in honor of the British monarch, it remained a Hudson's Bay Company property until restored to the United States. The fact that a fort was built there led to the development of a permanent settlement which bears it historic name, Astoria. E. E. Rich, ed., *Simpson's 1828 Journey to the Columbia* (London, 1947), pp. 149–150, 163–164.

[8]The missionaries had established a farm at Clatsop and it was prospering under William W. Raymond's charge. Commenced in February 1841, two years later it was highly productive. One guest recorded dining there in June 1843 on "beef, pork, potatoes, bread, butter, pie, cake, and raspberry preserves. . . ." Hines, *Oregon*, p. 194.

The water is shallow and of a dirty light green—surrounded by shoals—one we lightly touched, where we must lie the remainder of the day. An Indian came alongside and presented us with two fresh salmon; at night, I made a most delicious meal. Their superstition will not let them sell salmon until the strawberries are ripe, which are very abundant. From our short stay we shall not be able to judge of their quality.

16. After many unsuccessful attempts, we have at length succeeded in crossing Tongue Point Channel, and are now sailing up the river with a fine breeze.[9] Were it in my power, how gladly would I describe the scenery around us. How venerable is the aspect of those gigantic oaks, upon which we are now grazing, planted upon either bank; and how black is the entrance of the dark vistas—a long sweep of forest is before them, while the stately trees are festooned with wreaths of moss. Some Indians are seen bathing, others fishing; others sitting at their ease on the banks, with little tawny children around them. We anchor in the river tonight.

17. Have had a pleasant run up the river, are quite near the place of our destination. Hark! I hear the pilot say the ship is aground. The canoes come frequently to our vessel, and the Indians chatter, the Capt. does not allow them on board, for it is thought best not to take much notice of them. Many of them are naked, except a blanket over their brawny shoulders, while decked with ornaments. Their hair is black and very long, floating loosely over their shoulders—some have it shaved off the forepart of the head, and tied in a bunch behind. They are of a dark copper colour, some of them with quite interesting countenances appear active, and as though they were capable of acquiring knowledge.

---

[9]Tongue Point was named by Lieutenant William R. Broughton, a member of the George Vancouver expedition, October 21, 1792. Lewis and Clark also camped there in November 1805. The point is on the south side of the Columbia. Lewis A. MacArthur, *Oregon Geographic Names* (Portland, 1953), p. 605.

18. Having lightened the ship of but little of her cargo, she again floated, and at eight o'clock in the eve. were safely moored at Ft. Vancouver.[10]

19. Passengers left the ship early this morning. Doct. McLoughlin (agent of the Hudson Bay Company) called on us, invited us to stop at his house while we were in port.[11] It was for me to decide, however; went on shore—spent the afternoon, returned at sundown—found there was no place like home, notwithstanding had a pleasant visit.

---

[10]In 1824, the Hudson's Bay Company, having merged with the North West Fur Company and having established the Columbia District, decided to abandon Fort George at the mouth of the Columbia, formerly Fort Astoria, which dated back to 1811, and seek a new location upstream. A site was chosen on the northern bank opposite the confluence of the Columbia and Willamette rivers. Construction commenced in late November or early December 1825, and by early 1826, matters had progressed satisfactorily. On March 19, 1826, it was formally dedicated and christened. John A. Hussey, *The History of Fort Vancouver and Its Physical Structure* (Portland, 1957), pp. 36–45.

Hines described Fort Vancouver as Mrs. Nye must have seen it:

> The fort . . . consisted of a stockade, inclosing a space of ground about eight hundred feet long, and five hundred broad, with a bastion at one corner, with three gates in front . . . and one in the rear. In addition to the artillery mounted in the bastion, there were two eighteen-pounders and two swivels planted in front of the residence of the chief factor, and commanding the principal entrance to the fort.
>
> Within this enclosure were situated some thirty buildings, serving as dwelling-houses, stores, magazines, and work-shops. Near the fort was the building occupied by the servants, as also a hospital, barns and a large boathouse. In the rear of the fort the company have a splendid garden in the highest state of cultivation which produces all kinds of fruit for which the climate is adapted, such as apples, peaches, pears, and grapes. Here is also cultivated a large farm of some three thousand acres, producing wheat, barley, oats, peas, potatoes, etc., in great abundance; and herds of many thousands of cattle are supported on the adjacent plain.
>
> Connected with the fort and about four miles distant, up the Columbia, are a flouring-mill and a saw-mill, which have been in operation for several years.

Gustavus Hines, *Wild Life in Oregon* (New York, 1881), pp. 388–389.

[11]John McLoughlin, the "Father of Oregon," was born in the parish of Riviere de Loup, Quebec, October 19, 1784. Educated in medicine in Scotland, a brief practice in Montreal ensued before he launched a distinguished career in the fur trade. When that firm merged with the Hudson's Bay Company in 1821, he was appointed chief factor for the Columbia District. After his arrival, it was under his direction that Fort Vancouver was built and designated headquarters for the Columbia District. He concluded his company service in 1846, preferring to remain in Oregon rather than relocate to British Columbia when the firm concluded Fort Vancouver operations. He became an American citizen in 1849. About 1812 he married Marguerite Wadin McKay, by whom he had four children. He died at Oregon City, September 3, 1857. *Dictionary of American Biography*, edited by Allen Johnson and Dumas Malone (20 vols.; New York, 1928–1936), XII:134–135.

20. A beautiful morning—the birds are singing, the Indians are paddling their canoes—while all hands are at work, hoisting out cargo. At the same time two English ships are discharging very near.[12] After the heat had a little subsided, the Doct., myself, and husband rode horseback about three miles on the plains. Came directly to the shore, dismounted—a boat was in readiness—was soon on board, where I found Rev. Jason Lee,[13] with four others of the Oregon Mission, who came to receive their goods, in short, they very rapidly accepted the invitation to pass the night.

21. Sunday—Today for company we have Rev. J[ason] Lee, Rev. E. Frost,[14] Mr. Abernathey,[15] Mr. Robb, a native

---

[12]As will be pointed out later (see *notes* 20 and 21, *post*), the two vessels were the *Columbia* and *Vancouver*, Hudson's Bay Company barks.

[13]Jason Lee was born June 28, 1803, in the vicinity of "Stanstead, Quebec (County), then considered a part of Vermont." A religious vocation took him to Wilbraham Academy in Massachusetts for training. In 1830, he began his ministerial career in the Stanstead area. Three years later he was chosen to head the first Protestant missionary effort in Oregon. He traveled overland, reaching his destination in 1834. The second band brought him a bride, Anna Maria Pittman, whom he married on July 16, 1837. While making an 1838 return trip overland to the east, he learned of her death on June 26, along with his infant son. He took as his second wife Lucy Thompson the following year and sailed for Oregon on the *Lausanne*. He lost his second wife in 1842. To blunt criticism of his handling of his mission, he again returned east, via a combination of sea and overland travel, Hawaii-Mexico-New Orleans-New York, in 1844. Successfully clearing his name with governing mission authorities, his health failed in August. Returning to his birthplace, he died there on March 12, 1845. *Dictionary of American Biography*, XI:111–112.

[14]The Reverend Joseph H. Frost, with his wife and one child, reached Oregon on the *Lausanne* in 1840. Born in Rochester, New York, March 25, 1805, his Oregon service was short-lived. In February 1843, he was granted permission to leave because of a "disease of the throat which unfitted him for exposure...." His wife was also "much broken down and discouraged." They sailed for California, then Honolulu, on the bark *Diamond*, Captain Fowler, of Scarborough, England, on August 14, 1843. The *Diamond* reached Honolulu September 16 with additional passengers including two other Oregon missionaries, wives, and children, along with three additional passengers picked up in California. Passage to the United States was resumed on the *Bhering*, Captain Snow, for Frost and one of his fellow missionary colleagues on November 18. The following year Frost and Daniel Lee (his fellow passenger) authored *Ten Years in Oregon* (New York, 1844). He died in 1865. *The Friend*, I (Oct. 28, 1843), 62; (Nov. 4, 1843), 65; (Nov. 18, 1843), 69; (Dec. 2, 1843), 76; Bancroft, *Oregon*, I:188; Corning, *Dictionary of Oregon History*, p. 94.

[15]George Abernathy was born in the city of New York, October 7, 1807, and was educated there in commerce. He married Anne Pope, January 21, 1830, and sailed to Oregon

(*continued on next page*)

teacher,[16] Mr. Campbell.[17] From Mr. Lee a fine sermon this afternoon; which I shall ever recollect with peculiar sensations—the singing was melodious.

22. All hands are at work on deck, while I with my boys are doing some necessary work in the cabin. Doct. M[cLoughlin] sends us new butter and milk and warm bread every morning. Rather early for vegetables.

23. Today dined to Mrs. McLoughlin's, her two daughters, which are married,[18] board with her (the only family in the

(*continued from previous page*)
with his wife and two children on the *Lausanne* in 1839, arriving June 1, 1840. He worked closely with the missions, operating their principal store on the Willamette. On June 3, 1845, he was elected governor for the provisional Oregon government, serving two terms until March 3, 1849. He maintained his business affairs in Oregon City until 1861 when a disastrous flood brought ruin to him. Living in modest circumstances, he died in Portland, May 2, 1877. *Dictionary of American Biography*, I:29–30.

[16]James R. Robb, native of Butler County, Pennsylvania, was born August 21, 1816. A carpenter by trade, he traveled overland to Oregon in the 1842 immigration and settled at Oregon City. One of the framers of the provisional government, he helped build the first Protestant church in the West and served as one of the original trustees for the Oregon Institute, later Willamette University. He married Elizabeth Parrish, an 1844 immigrant, April 6, 1845. Lured to California by the gold discovery in 1849, he returned to Oregon and became a member in a firm of commission merchants, later becoming a partner of George Abernathy in Oregon CIty until 1855. On the death of his first wife, he married her widowed sister, Mrs. Rebecca S. May. He died in Portland, November 22, 1890. Caroline C. Dobbs, *Men of Champoeg*, (Portland, 1932), pp. 172–173.

[17]Hamilton Campbell, like the aforementioned, arrived on the *Lausanne* in 1840. Born in Kanawha County, Virginia, June 12, 1812, his parents subsequently migrated to Ohio, then Sangamon County, Illinois, where he was educated. There on February 5, 1835, he married Harriet B. Biddle (born Amherst Court House, Virginia, February 2, 1817). After marriage the couple settled in Springfield until 1839 when they responded to the Oregon mission call. A skilled artisan, he built the parsonage near Salem, and later had charge of the Mission Indian School. Another of his responsibilities was the mission's stock, which won him the nickname "Cow." With the closing of the mission, he took up land in Chehulpum Valley, but failed to prosper. Moving to Corvallis in 1854, he commenced a photographic business. In 1859, he moved his large family (he had eight children) to San Francisco where he continued his business. Offered the position of superintendent of mines in Guaymas, Mexico, he resettled his family in Portland and assumed his duties in 1862. He perished at the hands of Mexican bandits, June 12, 1863. Harvey K. Hines, *An Illustrated History of Oregon* (Chicago, 1873), p. 624.

[18]Mrs. McLoughlin had formerly been married to Alexander McKay of the Astorian party. A half-breed Indian lady, she married her second husband about 1812, the year following McKay's death. Her two daughters were Maria Elizabeth (birth date unknown) and

(*continued on next page*)

place to visit); after tea we all rode horseback. On our return to the ship, found Mr. Leslie, Mr. Lee, Doct. Wil[l]son,[19] so we have quite a Methodist Society.

24 & 25. Yesterday, Mr. M[cLoughlin] and lady dined with us. Today we dined on board the ship *Columbia*, Capt. Humphreys, from London.[20] After dinner visited the ship *Vancouver*, Capt. Duncan, from England.[21] Returned in season to fulfill an engagement I had made to ride with Doct. M[cLoughlin] as the Capt. could not leave the ship—very busy.

26 & 27. Cargo all bought, are getting ready to sail on the coming week—been on shore and took tea—bought some English worsted—began a pair of stockings for G[orham].

(*continued from previous page*)
Maria Eloisa (born in 1818). Eliza married (date unknown) a British army officer named Epps. They subsequently resided for a time in Quebec, then moved to England. Eloisa married William G. Rae, one of the Hudson's Bay Company officers, a native of the Orkney Islands, in 1838, who committed suicide in San Francisco. Widowed in 1845, she remarried in 1850, taking Daniel Harvey, one of her father's employees, as her second husband. Richard G. Montgomery, *The White-Headed Eagle: John McLoughlin, Builder of an Empire* (New York, 1935), pp. 182, 242.

[19]William H. Willson came to Oregon as a layman in the first reinforcements for the Methodist Mission on the brig *Diana*, May 18, 1837. Born in New Hampshire, April 14, 1805, he had experience as a whaler on several voyages. En route to Oregon he "read" medicine under Dr. Elijah White. He practiced medicine and carpentry for the mission establishment, besides being licensed as a local preacher. In 1840, he married Chloe Clark, a newly arrived overland immigrant. The founder of Salem, he played an active part in numerous aspects of Oregon history. He died on April 17, 1856. Dobbs, *Men of Champoeg*, pp. 56–59. (The year of birth is taken from Corning, *Dictionary of Oregon History*, p. 271, since Dobbs states the date was 1801. Harvey W. Scott, *History of the Oregon Country* (6 vols.; New York, 1924), II:231, gives 1805.)

[20]The bark *Columbia*, Captain Charles Humphreys, sailed from London in September 1842 for the Northwest Coast. It anchored at Honolulu on March 23 and entered the Columbia River on May 12, 1843. *The Friend*, 1 (April 1843), 18; E. E. Rich, ed., *McLoughlin's Fort Vancouver Letters, Second Series, 1839–44* (London, 1943), pp. 105, 392.

[21]The *Vancouver*, 303-ton bark, had been built in London in 1838. It reached Honolulu from London on January 5, 1843. From there, under the command of Captain Alexander Duncan, it sailed for California, calling at Monterey and San Francisco in February, before departing for the Columbia River. It entered the river on May 12. *The Friend*, 1 (Feb. 1843), 8; Rich, ed., *McLoughlin Letters, 1839–44*, pp. 5*n*, 105; *Lloyd's Register, July 1, 1842–June 30, 1843* (London, 1842), Entry No. V12; Bancroft, *California*, V:569*n*.

28. Went on shore to meeting, but no preaching—the Episcopal services were read only.[22]

29. This morning the ladies came on board to bid us good-bye, three of whom stopped and dined.

30. I did not think of going on shore again, but the Doct. [McLoughlin] has come to invite us to tea once more. His kindness I never can forget nor his venerable looks, his hair is wholly grey (white)—of noble stature, and I'll assure you makes a very dignified appearance. After tea, all escorted us to the ship, when we bade each other farewell! perhaps never to meet again.

---

[22]At this time, there was no resident Episcopal clergyman at Fort Vancouver, or in Oregon for that matter. The first to arrive, Herbert J. Beaver, who was appointed chaplain to the Hudson's Bay Company, reached his post on September 7, 1836. Married, he was accompanied by his wife. Thirty-six years old, a native of Ash, Surrey, England, Beaver was a graduate of Queen's College, Oxford. Ordained in 1823, he spent eight years on St. Lucia, British West Indies, as a chaplain. However, his HBC chaplaincy proved a stormy one. He clashed repeatedly with McLoughlin, and in the end left for England in November 1838 to prefer charges against the chief factor. His effort was for naught. The company severed its ties with Beaver and thereafter steered clear of further ministerial involvement. Thomas E. Jessett, ed., *Reports and Letters of Herbert Beaver, 1836–1838* (Portland, 1949), pp. xii–xiii.

Chapter IV

To California

May 31, 1843. Five o'clock this morning sailed from Vancouver with a fair wind; a light rain, however.

June 1. For passengers Rev. J. H. Frost and lady and son for Astoria, generally speaking, Fort George.[1]

2. Got along finely down the river, half way perhaps. Hope the Indian pilot will be sure and not get the ship aground.

3. I find Mrs. F[rost] to be very pleasant society, and such pleasant sailing too! no motion whatever, like sailing in our harbor. Then such fine living. O if you could but just take tea with us tonight, you would like this fresh salmon, I know, it is so very nice.

4. This is the first Sabbath since we have left Oahu that we have not had worship in the cabin. Mr. Frost is not able to preach, on account of his health; will return to the States very soon.[2]

5 & 6. Yesterday lay aground but a few hours only in Tongue Point Channel. This morning anchored at Fort George. Mr. Birnie, the only English resident, came off.[3] A storm arose—stopped the night.

7. The storm has subsided. The sun seems to shine with unusual brightness after a "storm at sea." Went on shore with Mr. B[irnie]; walked out in the green fields, picked a few berries, took tea, came off at sundown somewhat fatigued.

---

[1]This would be the Reverend Joseph H. Frost, his wife and son, who would depart the Oregon Mission in August for a return to the United States. See Chapter III, *note* 14, *ante*.

[2]He had a throat illness. Bancroft, *Oregon*, I:188.

[3]For James Birnie, see Chapter III, *note* 5, *ante*.

8. Three of Mr. B[irnie]'s daughters came on board and spent the day with me. One of them presented me with a canary bird (cage likewise) which I very gratefully accepted.

9 & 10. Not a fair wind to sail. The men have gone into the woods to cut some spars, while we have spent the day to Mrs. B[irnie]'s. Partook of a nice dinner, though rather wild. Elk and beaver was the two principal dishes, bread, butter and cheese, vegetables, fruit, etc., all the produce of the country.

11. It being unusually calm Mrs. B[irnie] made a call. Shall be obliged to stop another day. No wind and no preaching—which makes it rather dull.

12. Before the sun had gilded the horizon, we left Ft. George, and with outspread sails, were wending our way. Mr. B[irnie] with his two eldest daughters accompany us as far as Baker's Bay.

13. Anchored last night in B[aker's] Bay; this morning went ashore at Cape Disappointment. I did not think of ascending the hill, but followed on until I found myself on the very pinnacle of the mountain near the observatory which the men of the squadron had erected on their exploring expedition.[4] (It is supposed no foreign lady had ever ascended before.) Feeling some weary, we proposed resting ourselves under the shade of an old tree, while the gentleman in the meantime were in pursuit of some potatoes which they had ascertained were growing in a field close by. Of which they dug not a few, and set them to boiling, for we had a nice fire. At two P.M. a nice dinner was sent us from the ship. The steward spreading a mat on the ground, placed the contents before us. Seating ourselves

---

[4]The allusion to "exploring expedition" is the United States' naval expedition under the command of Lieutenant Charles Wilkes. This major scientific expedition visited the Columbia River and the Willamette Valley from May to October 1841. The observatory was one of the first chores executed at Astoria. One of the expedition's vessels, the *Peacock*, was lost at the mouth of the Columbia. The survivors (there were no fatalities in the wreck) built a temporary encampment at Astoria. David B. Tyler, *The Wilkes Expedition* . . . (Philadelphia, 1968), pp. 285–308; Charles Wilkes, *Narrative of the United States Exploring Expedition* . . . (6 vols.; Philadelphia, 1845), IV:306.

on the grass (native style), we partook, not very sparingly, however. A few rods from us were a group of Indians trying to conquer their unsatiable appetites with some roasted salmon which they had just taken from the burning coals.

16. This is the third day of wind and rain; very fortunate for me to have such pleasant company. However, this afternoon at four o'clock, it cleared off very pleasant, when Mr. B[irnie] with his two daughters took leave—wind not fair.

17. A ship in sight! Supposed to be Capt. D[uncan] from Ft. Vancouver. If so, shall have company over the bar.[5]

18. Often vessels lay two and even three weeks waiting for a fair wind to cross the bar. At this season it is rather uncommon, however; it is to be our misfortune. It seems more like November than the lovely month of June.

19 & 20. A week yesterday since we anchored here; however, there is a ship along side which is company for us, another just crossing the bar. Supposed to be an English vessel.[6] Think we shall sail tomorrow; the weather looks more favorable.

21. Again we are blessed with a favorable wind. At nine

---

[5]The *Vancouver* left Fort Vancouver on June 10 "with supplies for the trade of the North West Coast, and with the cargo of the *Valleyfield* belonging to the Russian American Company . . . she was first to proceed to Sitka. . . ." At Fort Simpson, Captain Duncan switched his command to the steamer *Vancouver*, while Captain William Brotchie took over the bark *Vancouver*. Rich, ed., *McLoughlin Letters, 1839–44*, p. 131.

[6]This was most likely the 249-ton bark *Diamond*, Captain Bartholomew Fowler in command. Chartered from the firm of Carter & Bonus, Leadenhall Street, London, it sailed for the Columbia at the end of December 1842. It reached Fort Vancouver on June 30, having been ordered to proceed there directly "without touching at the Sandwich Islands or any other Port. . . ." On leaving the Columbia, the vessel stopped at San Francisco where it disembarked a group of Californians in the employ of Jacob P. Leese who had driven "between four and five hundred cows and about the same number of sheep [to Fort Vancouver], all which he sold. . . ." Other passengers bound for Oahu included the Reverends Frost and Lee and Dr. [Ira John] Babcock, "with their wives and five children." In San Francisco three additional passengers came aboard, Dr. Sandal, Mr. Teal, and Mr. Titcomb. The *Diamond* made Honolulu on September 15, departing for Sydney on November 25, with Dr. Sandal as passenger. Rich, ed., *McLoughlin Letters, 1839–44*, pp. 108 and *note*, 136, 295; *The Friend*, 1 (Oct. 28, 1843), 62; (Nov. 4, 1843), 65; (Dec. 2, 1843), [76]. Also, consult Chapter III, *notes* 13 and 14, *ante*, and *notes* 28 and 33 in this chapter.

A.M. weighed anchor. Sailed for Monterey in company with the ship *Vancouver*. In a short time we were safely over the bar, and glad am I once more to be on the broad ocean. Give me sea room enough and I do not feel fearful.

22 & 23. Strong wind, going ten knots an hour, think I am sea-sick a little; more moderate today.

24. Two P.M. are within ten miles of Monterey, but a thick fog will prevent getting in tonight. Must lay to.

25. At eleven A.M. anchored in Monterey. While we were entering the harbor, passed three sails going out; [so] that now we are the only remaining vessel. You are well aware Monterey is the port of entry, therefore, all vessels must enter here or are liable to pay five hundred dollars bond.[7] The boarding officers came off as soon as we dropt anchor. It being Sunday, they could not pass examination, accordingly sealed up the hatches, and left an officer to remain until morning. To me it seemed quite laughable to have such restrictions used where there was not the least cargo to enter—hold full of ballast; in short, we had but very few stores, but as is customary. The officers came the ensuing morning and passed examination (my room only excepted).

26. Went on shore. Made a few calls. Dined to Mrs. Spence's.[8] Came off on board not much pleased with Mon-

[7]Governor Manuel Victoria, February 9, 1831, declared Monterey "the only legal port, at which exclusively foreign vessels must discharge their cargoes and pay duties. . . ." In January 1841, Governor Juan B. Alvarado, under a newly enacted Mexican law, reiterated this position. Bancroft, *California*, III: 367; IV: 206.

On Nye's first voyage to California from Honolulu as captain of the *Loriot* in 1833, he ran afoul of Victoria's proclamation, by anchoring first at Yerba Buena (San Francisco). As a result, the cargo was seized "upon the presumption that full duties had not been paid." In the bargain, the supercargo, Alpheus B. Thompson, who resisted arrest to no avail, was imprisoned. The ship's sails "were unbent and taken away" as well. Finally, the matter was sorted out. Thompson was released and the cargo restored, but in a badly deteriorated condition which produced a sizeable loss for the voyage. Davis, *Seventy-Five Years*, pp. 195–196.

[8]David Spence, a Scotsman, resided several years in Lima, Peru, before reaching California on the *Pizarro* in 1824. Baptized a Catholic at Santa Cruz in 1828, the following year he married Adelaida, the daughter of Mariano Estrada. She survived him only by a month after his death in 1875. Their only son, David, born in 1830, was educated in Honolulu. Bancroft, *California*, IV: 730–731.

terey. It is very still and quiet, rather barren, not having been any rain for the past two years, the foliage is yellow and sear, more like autumn than June.[9] In the evening being quietly seated around the table, Gorham says, would you like to hear from home? I replied, nothing would give me greater pleasure. Then taking a letter from his pocket, which I soon learned was from Eliza, I questioned him to know if that was all. Giving me rather an evasive answer, I still persisted in my inquiries. After teasing me for half an hour or more, gave me another! from brother Wil[lia]m. Finding my mother and friends were well and reading of the many incidents that had transpired, gave me sensations wholly unknown before. Those only who have visited foreign lands know the welcome sound of a letter from home after a year's absence.

---

[9]By referring to Simpson's *Narrative of a Journey Round the World*, I:344–345, Mrs. Nye's feeling regarding the appearance of Monterey can be better understood.

> The town occupies a very plain, which slopes toward the north and terminates to the southward in a tolerably loft ridge. It is a mere collection of buildings, scattered as loosely on the surface as if they were so many bullocks at pasture, so that the most expert surveyor could not possibly classify them even into crooked streets. What a curious dictionary of circumlocutions a Monterey directory would be! The dwellings, some of them attain the dignity of a second story, are all built of adobe, being sheltered on every side from the sun by overhanging eaves, while towards the rainy quarter of the southeast they enjoy the additional protection of boughs of trees, resting like so many ladders on the roof. In order to resist the action of the elements, the walls . . . are remarkably thick, though this peculiarity is here partly intended to guard against the shocks of earthquakes, which are so frequent that a hundred and twenty of them were felt during two successive months of the last summer. This average, however, of two earthquakes a day is not so frightful as it looks, the shocks being seldom severe, and often so slight . . . as to escape notice of the uninitiated stranger.
>
> Externally, the habitations have a cheerless aspect, in consequence of the paucity of windows, which are almost unattainable luxuries. Glass is rendered ruinously dear by the exorbitant duties, while parchment, surely a better substitute than a cubic yard of adobe, is clearly inadmissible in California . . . perhaps the Californians do not feel the privation of light to be an evil. While it certainly makes the rooms cooler, it cannot by any possibility interfere with the occupations of those who do nothing, and, even for the purpose of ventilation, windows are hardly needed, inasmuch as the bedding, the only thing that requires fresh air, is daily exposed to the sun and wind.

27. Passed the day very pleasantly to Mrs. Watson's.[10] Having Gorham for an interpreter, I got along finally in talking with the Spanish ladies. The only American lady in Monterey is Mrs. Larkin from Boston, on whom we called.[11] Found her quite sick. Each of these families have a son at Oahu attending school; they were much pleased to hear from them so recently.[12]

28. Last night Gorham was taken sick; I feel very much afraid of the cramp. Does not seem any better, otherwise than that the vomiting has subsided. I think there is yet an obstruction.

29. Today [Mr. Nye] has sweat profusely. The medicines have acted favorable; think I feel encouraged. Several gentlemen came off to see him, thought he had an excellent nurse.

30. Well, as my fears are in a measure subsided, Gorham is so much better as to talk of getting his papers from the Custom house to be ready to sail on the morrow.

July 1. Not yet had the sun gilded the horizon ere we were on our way to Santa Cruz, but a few hours sail. Should a thick fog make its appearance, perhaps it would be several days.

---

[10]There were two men by the name of Watson then residing in Monterey who had wives. Both men were English and had married California women. Edward Watson, born in 1805, settled in Monterey in 1828. In 1833, he became a convert to the Catholic Church, taking the name José Eduardo María. He married María Guadalupe Castillo and became a Mexican citizen in 1841. James (or David) Watson, having jumped ship from a whaler, also settled in Monterey, probably in 1824. He married Mariana Escamilla in 1834, raised a family, and grew prosperous. Mrs. Nye is referring to one of these two women. Bancroft, *California*, V:769.

[11]Mrs. Rachel Hobson Holmes had been a fellow passenger with Thomas Larkin on his outbound voyage to California on the *Newcastle*. Reaching Monterey, April 13, 1832, the couple were married June 10, 1833. It was in Monterey, where she expected to join her sea-captain husband, that Mrs. Holmes learned of his death from fever in Lima, Peru. Since both were non-Catholic, the marriage took place at sea off the coast of Santa Barbara on the ship *Volunteer*, and the master of the vessel, John Coffin Jones, Jr., who was also U.S. consul to the Hawaiian Islands, performed the rite. She was the first American lady to reside in California and her son had the distinction of being the first American child born in California. She lived until 1873. Hammond, ed., *Larkin Papers*, I:vii–viii.

[12]It became a common practice for Californians to send their children for education to the Oahu Charity School in Honolulu, the nearest boarding school available. See Chapter II, *note* 74, *ante*.

2. Fortunate, indeed, we have been. Here we are anchored in Santa Cruz, ready to take in lumber on the morrow, shall probably lie here some time.[13] I can give no description of the place until I have been on shore. The view from the harbor is not very favorable, though rather romantic. I see but two houses, though I am told there is a Catholic mission here.[14] O! how I would like to be with my dear friends—especially those who on this holy day will come around the table of the Lord and partake of the blood and body of Christ. Though denied of that blessed privilege, and many of the means of grace, I can even here hold sweet communion with my Heavenly Father.

3. One would suppose it was rather monotonous to be on board ship, with no female companion, but the society of my husband fills all vacancy. It is true I think of home and its endearments. This evening in particular, I would like to attend the Monthly Concert. Perhaps I think more of it being in the unenlightened land.

4. The 4th of July! has again come around, how differently I am situated from the last. Then was I on the mighty ocean in Lat. 40°16', Long. 47°4'. Had not passed Cape Horn, nothing to be seen but the sky above, and the foaming billows

---

[13]Santa Cruz was the lumbering center at that time. Sherwood D. Burgess, "Lumbering in Hispanic California," *California Historical Society Quarterly,* XLI (Sept. 1962), 237–248.

Thomas Oliver Larkin was the first to exploit effectively California redwood timber, so abundant in supply. He had, at the time, a contract with the "sawyers" who carried on a crude mill operation, for redwood lumber delivered on the beach. Larkin became the dominant lumber retailer. The Hawaiian Islands were one of the ready markets for Santa Cruz redwood lumber. Reuben L. Underhill, *From Cowhides to Golden Fleece* (Stanford, Calif., 1946), pp. 52–53.

[14]"At the northeast corner of the [Monterey] bay is a green gorge, down which flows a small stream of pure water. Near its mouth, on a snug little plain, stand the mission of Santa Cruz, with its chapel and adobe Indian huts. Around it are some fields, on which the Indians raise grains, vegetables and grapes. Beyond this, to the northward, the country swells away into lofty hills, covered with grass and sprinkled with copse of pine and oak." Thomas J. Farnham, *Life and Adventures in California* (New York, 1846), p. 51. The mission was founded August 28, 1791, by Fray Fermín Francisco de Lausén. H[enry] A. Van Coenen Trochiana, *Story of the Mission Santa Cruz* (San Francisco, 1933), pp. 176–179.

beneath. But the object I had in view kept me from despondency. I had dreamt there was happier days for me and was it a dream? No! It has in a measure become a reality.

5. Dined today on green peas and roast beef which is the only kind of meat on the Coast. Some fowls, however, but beef and beans always sure to see on the table (a kind of bean one does not get tired of, in jest called free-holders),[15] then you know beef is the most nutritious meat, so I can but give credit for my good keeping. All kinds of vegetables; are much earlier than at home.

6. Well, sometimes I think I shall obliged to give up writing *every day* for want of matter. There is much sameness from day to day. I fear it will not be interesting. Perhaps if I did not write every day I should not write at all. However, I find enough to busy myself about, to be sure I have the Captain's clothes to look after, with my own, then again I am not so industrious as formerly. I take time to read and sleep too!

7. The last few days have been discharging ballast, today the men have brought from the beach one raft of lumber, now all hands are busy stowing it, while the Capt. is looking on and giving orders. When I get tired of the cabin, I go on deck, or between decks (which is a large spacious room), sometimes in the trade room. Gorham laughs and says I find him in every place, should he wish to get rid of me, would have to take to the mast head. Ha! Ha!

8. A week today since we dropt anchor in Santa Cruz. Lay about three quarters of a mile from shore. It is rather slow work getting off lumber, shall probably stop two weeks or more.[16]

9. Welcome delightful morn! Thou day of sacred rest. The boat is going ashore with the second and third officers to visit

---

[15] *Frijoles* (beans).

[16] For a brief resume of lumbering in the Santa Cruz area, see Burgess, "Lumbering in Hispanic California," *passim.*

the mission, with that exception, it is as quiet and still as any private family. Though we have no place of worship to go to, the day is set apart as a holy day. All secular employment is laid aside, with exception of the cook and steward, who perform their usual round in the galley, for fasting on board ship cannot be brought about very easily.

10. Washing day at home and on board ship too! One of the men (a native from the Islands) does our washing, while I look after him, so he does nicely. But I usually feel some fatigue but not so much so. Were I in my native land, I should attend S[abbath] School Concert, which, if as usual, will be on this evening.

11. Today it has been very foggy and damp, too much so, to have a walk on the deck, which I usually take once or twice a day. The Capt. does not complain of lonely walks as heretofore.

12 & 13. Having some business at the sawmill some distance from the beach,[17] Gorham has left me quite alone. Could I have obtained a quiet horse, I [would have] accompanied him. However, this evening has been telling me of a tree which he saw 200 ft. high, 54 ft. in circumference, had the curiosity to measure it.

14. I believe I have told you heretofore when in Oregon I had a canary bird given me, which has never sung a note yet! but as the old saying is, poor company is better than none; for it is pleasant to see it hop and skip about. Then there is three dogs on board. A large watch dog, which keeps all vexatious intruders away. If a boat comes near the ship, Glen is the first to make it known. When in Columbia [Oregon], could not bear the sight of an Indian, had to keep him chained while the pilot was on board, but was very affectionate to those belonging to the ship. Then we have a little dog named Polly

---

[17]The small mill had been built in 1841 by Peter Lassen on Zayante Creek. He sold it to Isaac Graham in 1843. *Ibid.*, p. 244.

(How much it reminds me of one we had named Jewel); she is seven or eight years old.

15. Another week gone! You may think they seem tedious; far otherwise, they pass rapidly away. Every Saturday night have a bullock killed, sometimes it does not last us through the week. Our ship's company number twenty-five, two passengers we took from Vancouver for San Francisco, one an orphan girl about nine years old who is some company. Her mother, a native of Columbia, her father, Mr. Black (from Boston) who was shot by an Indian, had accumulated a handsome property, was preparing to go home and take his children.[18]

16. The day on which Christ arose from the dead has again returned. How shall I spend it? Far from the happy land where salvation is proclaimed, my thoughts have wandered over stormy seas, and rested with those dear friends who are

[18]Samuel Black was born in the Parish of Pitsligo, County Aberdeen, Scotland, May 3, 1780. He immigrated to Canada in 1802, having been recruited as a clerk for the X.Y.Company, and engaged in the fur trade. When the company was reorganized and became part of the North West Company, he continued service with them. He had a wide variety of trade experience in western Canada, especially in and around Lake Athabaska and the Peace River. He was retained as an employee by the Hudson's Bay Company in 1821 when that firm merged the North West Company. He returned from England to accept the post. Because of his strength, coolness, and suspicious nature, he was "admirably adapted for the Service of the North West coast where the Natives [were] so treacherous. . . ." He was assigned the exploration of the Finlay River expedition in the summer of 1824. Subsequently, he was appointed to Fort Colville in the Department of the Columbia in 1825, thereafter serving at "the important post of Walla Walla or Nez Perces." In 1830 or 1831, he took over Fort Thompson. His lengthy service there in the Kamloops area ended tragically: he was slain at his post by an Indian on February 8, 1841. Although he never officially married, it is known that he had fathered eight children. During his tenure at Fort Thompson, four of these children were born. At his death, a girl of about "five years," called King King, was one of his survivors. As indicated by Mrs. Nye, the girl may have been older. And, there is no question but that Black was anticipating concluding his Hudson's Bay Company service and had been planning to return to Britain. E. E. Rich and A. M. Johnson, eds., *A Journal of a Voyage From Rocky Mountain Portage in Peace River to the Sources of Finlays Branch and North West Ward in Summer 1824* (London, 1955), pp. xvii–xlviii, ixxxi–c.

It would appear that the young daughter of Black may well have been returned to Oregon from San Francisco since available evidence indicated she became a dependent of James Keith because Black's will made no provision for her or her younger brother. *Ibid.*, pp. xcix–c.

sitting under the gospel light and listening to the sound of a Saviour's love.

17. Now if you could look in upon us this evening, you would think we were enjoying ourselves. The ship lies very quiet, all hands have retired, and we are left quite alone. While Gorham sits reading, I am busying myself with my patchwork, which you know is a favorite amusement of mine. I have a valence around my bedstead, which makes my bed quilts quite too large, so I have commenced a smaller one.

18 & 19. Finished taking in lumber today; one hundred thousand ft. boards, 150 thousand shingles. And I have got my quilt in the bars.[19] My room now is pretty well filled, though I could manage very well to have Ma and Aunt S. to quilting. Though small, it seems quite an undertaking, then I have somebody who helps a little. Shall sail tomorrow for Monterey, weather permitting.

20. Have been trying to persuade the Capt. to remain another day, but he says no! Never stops for anything when the ship is ready for sea, much less for a quilting. However, sailed at twelve. In three hours were safely moored in the harbor of Monterey. Came so fast, I was obliged to turn in (as the sailors say). I was soon in the arms Morpheus; was awakened by the talking of the boarding officers, who came off thinking we were a new comer. When we were here before, the ship was very light, which made her look very different on the water.

21. The *California*, Capt. Arthur (Clapp, supercargo), arrived this morning. Been trading on the coast about two years.[20] They immediately called on us, took tea, spent the evening. Capt. A[rthur] supposes his wife is on her passage

---

[19]Quilting frame.

[20]The 422-ton ship *California*, James P. Arther, master, and Curtis Clap, supercargo, arrived from Boston at Monterey in February 1842. Sailing up and down the coast, it is recorded as having been in Monterey in October 1843; thereafter there is no other record of the vessel until the spring of 1845 when it returned with a new cargo of goods from Boston. Bancroft, *California*, V:564*n*.

out.[21] Gorham says I draw a great deal of company, every one has a curiosity.

22. Saturday night, I as usual talk about home and think of the large baked pudding and beans, and brown bread, too, which I have not tasted since I left the States. The flour is very poor in this part of the world.[22] I have done eating bread and took to eating Irish potatoes, which are very nice here.

23. Even here a sail in sight produces quite an excitement. About five P.M. a barque hove insight. Being very foggy, could just discern her. As she approached, found it to be the *Don Quixote*, Capt. J[ohn] Paty, who came on board and spent the evening with us.[23]

24. How I wish I could write home, have not had a chance since we left the Isl[and]s, which is three months or more. You will probably hear from us by the *Wil[lia]m Gray* in Sept.[24] After that it will be some time before you hear, but I assure you it will not be a heavier trial to you, than to me, who would gladly write every week, could I have an opportunity.

25. Been here near a week, and have not been on shore; the Capt. has just pulled off. But I have been rather busy. When in port, I am quite industrious. On the passages, not a little indolent; however, have promised to go on shore in the morning.

26. Spent a very pleasant day to Mrs. Watson's. Feel some

---

[21]There is no evidence available which indicates Mrs. Arthur ever joined her husband.

[22]A decade later another American lady was not so dissatisfied. She observed: "We could get no flour, and use California flour, which is very dark but sweet." Mrs. Benjamin Hayes to a sister, Los Angeles, March 13, 1852. *Pioneer Notes From the Diaries of Judge Benjamin Hayes, 1849–1875*, edited by Marjorie T. Wolcott (Los Angeles, 1929), p. 89.

[23]The American bark *Don Quixote,* some 270 tons, first touched California in 1833, John Meek, master. It returned in 1836 under the same command. A third voyage followed in 1838, under the name of the *Plymouth*, John Paty, master, as one of the owners of the vessel. Sold in 1836 to the Hawaiian government, John, with his brother William, bought the bark for $9,500. After a return voyage to Boston, the ship was once again along the California coast by April 1840. She continued round trips between the coast and Honolulu in the ensuing five years. It was sold in March 1847 at Honolulu for its original purchase price to Theodore Shillaber. Green, ed., "Journal of Captain John Paty," pp. 316–329; Bancroft, *California,* IV:103*n*; V:565*n*.

[24]The vessel had sailed for Boston on April 18, 1843, from Honolulu. See Chapter II, *note* 113, *ante*.

tired tonight. Gorham says, if I would go on shore oftener, it would not fatigue me so much. Tonight it looks very much like rain, or rather, as it used to at home when we had fine showers.—But no ! The people say it often looks so, but there is not been rain for more than two years. The country is completely burned up with the sun and the fires in the woods. Took a walk in the woods after tea, was astonished to find anything green. By the way, I saw a rattlesnake, and often a squirrel would cross our path.

27. Took tea to Mrs. Larkin's. Had a fine sail off and on to the ship, but I must say a day on shore seems much longer than on board. If called a city, it is a very quiet one. I cannot see much to interest me. Tomorrow we leave for San Francisco; the *Quixote* and *California* for St. Barbara.

28. This morning [Doña] Ocio, a Spanish lady, sent me a valuable present, as she supposed.[25] An old fashioned Tuscan bonnet, such as used to be worn say ten years ago, some cake likewise. But I don't like the Spanish dishes as yet, there is too much fixings for me altogether.[26] Yesterday, at Mrs. Watson's,

[25]Antonio María Osio, a native of Baja California, married Delores Argüello, daughter of the last colonial governor of Lower California, José Dorio Argüello, at San José del Cabo in 1822. He and his wife migrated to Upper California subsequently, and by 1827 his name appears in local records. He had a varied career in government service. At this time he was in charge of revenues at Monterey, having been appointed by Governor Juan Bautista Alvarado. He subsequently took his family and resettled in Baja California. Pablo L. Martínez, *Guia Familiar de Baja California, 1700–1900* (Mexico, 1965), pp. 13, 38; Bancroft, *California,* III:761–762. (The name is sometimes spelled Ozio.)

[26]What Mrs. Nye refers to as "too much fixings" undoubtedly included the super-abundance of garlic and pepper in California cooking which Sir George Simpson found so distasteful during his visit to California in 1842. He describes a meal at which he was a guest in the home of General Mariano Guadalupe Vallejo at Sonoma, which consisted of five dishes, "two kinds of stewed beef, rice, fowls, and beans . . . every mouthful was poisoned with the everlasting compound of pepper and garlicky. . . ." This he characterizes as an aristocratic repast, adding that "elsewhere we more than once saw in one and the same dish, beef, and tongue, and pumpkin, and garlicky, and potatoes in their jackets, and cabbage, and onions, and tomato, and pepper, and Heaven knows what besides,—this last definite ingredient being something more than a mere figure of speech, considering that all the cookery . . . is the work of native drudges, unwashed and uncombed." To this he add, "bad tea and worse wine, and the reader has picked up a perfect idea of California breakfast, California dinner, and California supper." Simpson, *Narrative of a Journey Round the World,* I:311–312.

they had one very dainty dish on the table. Upon inquiry I found it was roasted beef chopped, seasoned with spices, and made into balls, put into the skin of an onion, then dropped into an egg and fried. Dainty, I think! Well, it is now about 12 A.M. I hear the crew heaving up the anchor. In a few minutes more, shall be on our way to St. Francisco.

29. At half past twelve yesterday, I left Monterey. The wind is now blowing from the northwest; if it continues hope to get to [San] F[rancisco] in three days.

30. Can go down in half that time; going up have to beat, which is not very pleasant sailing. This going about so often makes me light-headed, so I find the bed is the most comfortable place.

31. A very thick fog this morning. The Capt. says keep quiet, I can feel the way through; in a few hours you'll be in the Bay of [San] Francisco. Sure enough, about two o'clock, I heard the anchor drop; now we are safely moored, for many weeks I suppose.

August 1. I have taken my pen with the intention of noting down the gentlemen that have called on us today, but in truth, I did not see all. Early in the morning Mr. Ray came off and invited us to stop at his house while in port. He married Doct. M[cLoughlin]'s daughter of C[olumbia]River. While there I often heard the Doct. speak of Mrs. Ray, so I feel quite in a hurry to see her.[27] Mr. Spear gave us a similar invitation. Finally it was left for me to decide, which I should not like to do until I have been on shore. This afternoon, Doct. San-

[27]William Glen Rae was "a large, handsome man, educated at Edinburgh," who was a native of the Orkney Islands. He was employed as a trader at different Hudson's Bay Company posts from 1834–1837, when he was appointed head clerk at Fort Vancouver. The following year, 1838, he married Dr. John McLoughlin's youngest of two daughters, Maria Eloisa, and shortly after was promoted to chief trader. In 1841, he was sent to San Francisco to open a company post, which proved a failure. Supposedly "discouraged over business affairs at his post," he took his life in 1845. At his death, Mrs. Rae had three children when she returned to Oregon, a son and two daughters. The son died early, but the two daughters married and resided in Portland. Bancroft, *Oregon*, I:36–37.

dall,[28] Capt. Hatch,[29] Lardsdorf[30] with six others; many more sent their respects to me. There has been but few American ladies on the Coast; Gorham says those were not a fair specimen.

2. One very disagreeable fault in this place is the high winds, which are constantly blowing. Prepared myself to go on shore, when the wind breezed up, so shall be obliged to defer it until tomorrow; while the Capt. has gone and left me quite alone—scarcely ever returns without bringing one or more to dine or take tea with us.

3. Supper being over, Gorham has taken a book, while I have taken my pen to record the adventures of the day. Dined to Mrs. Ray's, whom I find to be a very pleasant lady. As regards the place, I am not able to give a very minute description. There are but two foreign families residing here.[31] The houses stand on an eminence, with the harbor in front, trees and shrubbery back. Hides are the staple article of the place, and they are as scarce as may be. To be sure I did see some Indians drawing a few in a hand-cart, while I felt just enough interest to wish they were going on board the ship *Fama*. By the way, I saw a bullock, hoisted from a launch (which had

---

[28]Dr. Gustavus M. W. A. Sandals (also spelled Sandels, Sandalls), a Swedish scientist, came to California from Mexico on the schooner *California*. The vessel anchored at Monterey on June 2, 1842. He sailed on the *Diamond* for Honolulu, reaching that port on September 16, 1843, and continued on the vessel which sailed for Sydney, Australia, November 25. For his own account of his travels, see G. W. Waseurtz af Sandels, *A Sojourn in California by the King's Orphan* (San Francisco, 1945), *passim*; Bancroft, *California*, IV:711; *The Friend*, 1 (Oct. 28, 1843), 62; (Nov. 4, 1843), 64; (Dec. 2, 1843), 76.

[29]Captain James B. Hatch, master of the *Barnstable*, 1842–1845. Bancroft, *California*, II:779.

[30]From 1842 to 1845, William A. Leidesdorff, a native of the Danish West Indies, was master of the *Julia Ann*, a 106-ton American schooner. Born in 1810, Leidesdorff became Larkin's vice consul in San Francisco where he amassed a fair fortune prior to his premature death in May 1848. Bancroft, *California*, IV:711.

[31]The two families would be that of Mr. and Mrs. William G. Rae and Mr. and Mrs. Jacob P. Leese. The latter had journeyed overland to California by late 1833, settling in San Francisco, then called Yerba Buena, in 1836. He married a sister of Mariano Guadalupe Vallejo, Rosalia. *Ibid.*, III:709–710; IV:710.

just returned from a cruise up the Bay) and splash it went into the water; while a Spaniard on shore (horseback) had a rope around the neck of the poor beast. So he set his horse a running which made the animal scamper out of the water, and away they went, John Gilpin like.[32] In fact those poor creatures are treated with little or no respect. The hide is the only object in view, which they frequently take off and leave the body lying by the roadside. I think it time to draw my story to a close for hides and tallow may not be so interesting to you as to those who are trying to make their fortune for the hides of those poor creatures.

4. From what I wrote last evening, you will very readily come to the conclusion that I shall not like living on shore. My room in which I am now writing, with everything convenient, "servientos" at my call, is far more preferable. Besides I have the society of my husband more on board. As the old saying is, home is home, if it is ever so homely. Just had a crate of pears sent me by a friend, I know not whom. But this I know, they are very acceptable.

5. This is a very busy day at home. I find it similar on board ship. I have many pieces of work about which I like to finish on Saturday. You may wonder what I find to do, but it is about with me as at home, always in a hurry.

6. Again has the Sabbath returned, but seemingly no Sabbath has it brought to me. I endeavor to bear without murmuring this privation. God has graciously promised, "All things shall work together for good to those that love him." But do I love him? O search me by thy spirit and lead me in the ways of eternal life.

---

[32]The reference to "John Gilpin like" is based on a poem by William Cowper, "The Diverting History of John Gilpin," published in 1785. To celebrate his twentieth wedding anniversary, Gilpin borrowed a horse and a chaise; he loses control of them and a headlong ride ensues. See Paul Harvey, *The Oxford Companion to English Literature* (Oxford, 1967), p. 432.

7. Just finished a pair of worsted hose (for Gorham), which I commenced at Vancouver. When any foreigner saw me knitting, he would exclaim, Well, I have not seen anything since I left home, which reminds me so much of my Mother! To the Spanish it seems almost incredible—never saw the like before.

Again has the time arrived for the monthly concert, which scarcely ever passed unobserved by me. The teacher's meeting, not be held at any stated period, I can only remember as a means of grace which I am deprived of, one that was ever dear to me. How was I pleased when I read in sister's letter the full meeting at our house and the way it was brought about. I think it was asking in a very polite way for sister to be more punctual.

8. This morning, Gorham went on shore, as I supposed to stop the forenoon, I was sitting very quietly when Glen gave an alarm. Immediately two gentlemen was ushered into the cabin, and introduced as Mr. Teal and Mr. Titcomb from New York.[33] Gorham had but just got on shore, when they in a polite way, asked to be made acquainted with Mrs. Nye. An *American lady* always excites attention. However, they stopped and dined, we then went on shore, found Mrs. Ray preparing to go across the Bay with her husband to collect

[33]Hiram Teal, a native of New England, reached California from Mazatlán with a stock of some $20,000 in goods and opened a store in San Francisco in 1841. Rufus Titcomb, a fellow New Englander, came with him and served as his clerk. The business prospered and in two years he had disposed of his goods, "such as silk and cotton *rebozos*, serapes, ponchos, *mangas*, costly and ordinary; silver-mounted and gilt spurs; saddles, ornamented and ordinary; *armas de pelo*, or riding robes for protecting the legs and body up to the waist; silver headstalls for horses, hair bridle reins, and other fancy and ornamental goods; an assortment of Mexican products." He had had earlier experience in mercantile trade having launched his career in Santa Fé, New Mexico, out of St. Louis.

In 1843, the two sailed to Honolulu on the *Diamond* en route to Mexico, and a return to New Mexico. The two reached Oahu on September 16, but nothing is known of their departure date. Davis, *Seventy-Five Years*, pp. 124–125; Bancroft, *California,* IV:744, 746; *The Friend*, 1 (Oct. 28, 1843), 62; (Nov. 4, 1843), 65.

hides. Gorham thinks of going soon, think I shall make the tour with him.

9. This morning early went on board the *Julia Ann* to see Mrs. Ray and her family off.[34] On my return was taken prisoner. What do you say? Taken prisoner!! By whom? By my husband to be sure. Got in the boat to come to the ship as I supposed, when Gorham says to me, it is a beautiful morning, don't you want to go ashore? I exclaimed no ! no! for I was in my morning dress, blue cloak and hood. But you are most there. Stopped to Mrs. Spear's and dined. Came off about three o'clock. Must say I have not enjoyed myself better at any time. Gorham says it was because I was not afraid of the fog taking the starch out of my ruffles, not having any on. Ha! Ha!

10 & 11. Today the ship *George and Henry* sailed for Saint Barbara.[35] Now the *Barnstable*[36] and *Julia Ann* are lying at anchor, while the ship *Fama* lies so snugly moored. I cannot say when we shall have sails unbent, are preparing to paint.

12. I know Ma was afraid it would be injurious to my health to have hides on board. I think her worry will be useless. As yet, have not one, except the bullock we have eaten. It is a very

---

[34]The 106-ton schooner *Julia Ann*, Captain William A. Leidesdorff, appeared at Monterey for the first time on June 22, 1841, from New York. After a round trip to Honolulu, it spent the years 1842–1843 along the coast, calling at many ports. Bancroft, *California*, V:566*n*.

[35]Bancroft and Davis lists this vessel, the *George and Henry*, as an American bark of 344 tons, commanded by Captain Stephen Smith, master and owner, with a crew of nineteen. On board also was Mrs. Smith and her mother. It sailed from Baltimore, Maryland, via Payta, reaching Monterey in May 1843. It brought the first steam engine, which was set up at Bodega, as well as the first pianos to California. It was anchored at Sausalito in January 1844. Bancroft, *California*, V:565–566*n*; Davis, *Seventy-Five Years*, p. 278; E. D. Holden, "California's First Pianos," *California Historical Society Quarterly*, XIII (March 1934), 34–37.

[36]The *Barnstable*, 373 tons, James B. Hatch, master, arrived at Monterey from Boston on July 7, 1842. It spent two winters along the California coast, and sailed for its home port, Boston, on December 17, 1844. There is no record of the vessel touching Honolulu on its return voyage. Bancroft, *California*, V:563*n*; Ogden, "Trading Vessels on the California Coast," pp. 1000–1004.

bad season. Nobody kills when it is so dry.[37] How I would like to see it rain.

13. The starboard watch has liberty to go on shore today, which greatly diminishes our number. The day has passed quietly and pleasantly. This evening have had a fine sing. "The Power of Prayer" sounds as well here as in America.

14. Well, I really did not think of taking a trip around the Bay so soon, when I spoke of it last week. As Gorham is going to send a launch after wood, hides, and lumber, thinks I had better go, otherwise he will not. The launch has a nice little cabin, is about thirty-five ton.[38] The steward is preparing fowls, pies, and everything good to take with us.

15. At nine A.M. set sail for Napper [Napa]. At four P.M. the wind being unfavorable, put in at Peola [Pinole], where Capt. Hin[c]kley (formerly of Hingham) resides, having married Don Marteniou's daughter.[39] As soon as her brother heard of our arrival (Capt. H[inckley] not being at home), he came with horses to take us to their house, which was three miles or

---

[37]Refusal to slaughter during a drouth arose from two reasons, both valid; first, because the layer of fat that normally exists between hide and carcass is essential to preserve the hide from damage during the skinning process; and second, because thin cattle, as all were at this time, yield no tallow—one of the two major products of the industry.

[38]From the description given, this was probably the schooner *Susannah*, which had been built in Napa Creek in 1841. It sailed to Mazatlán in November 1843 and was sold there. Sometimes the vessel is called the *Rosalia*. Bancroft, *California*, V:568*n*.

[39]William S. Hinckley began his career as an Hawaiian-California trader in 1830. In 1834, he was master of the *Avon*, his first command. Later he was master of the *Kamamalu* (formerly the *Diana*). Subsequently, he became a partner with Nathan Spear and Jacob Leese in the San Francisco Bay area. He died in June 1846, age thirty-nine. His first wife had sailed with him on at least one recorded voyage. In the latter part of April 1837, Captain Hinckley sailed from Honolulu with an Oregon-bound missionary party headed by Jason Lee on the *Diana*. After the return voyage to Oahu, Mrs. Hinckley took passage on the *California*, Captain James Arther, for Boston, leaving Honolulu on October 8, 1837. As to when she died, nothing is presently known. However, Hinckley took as his second wife, Susana Martínez, daughter of Ignacio Martínez, in 1840. She survived him on his death. *Ibid.*, II: 785–786; IV:101*n*; Bancroft, *Oregon*, I:154–158; Frank Soulé, *et al.*, *Annals of San Francisco* (New York and San Francisco, 1855), pp. 167–169; John H. Brown, *Reminiscences and Incidents of the Early Days of San Francisco* (San Francisco, [1886]), pp. 17–21.

more. Not liking to mount a stranger, I took a seat beside Don Vacenta (not astride) California style.[40] Soon arrived at the rancho or farm, where the old folks were extremely glad to see us, children likewise, eleven in number. As is customary, a cup of tea and some tortelius (a kind of pastry) was served;[41] at nine o'clock, a hearty supper.

16. This morning inquired how we had rested, did the fleas trouble you? It may seem vulgar to you, indeed, it did to me at first, but it is a common question to ask. They are very numerous on the Coast. The houses are not kept very neat, most of them built of adobe, mud, and O how comical they are funished. Don Marteniu is what we should call a rich farmer.[42] Owns 6,000 head of cattle, 300 horses, 500 sheep. His farm is very extensive.[43] As we were about ready to start, up rode Capt. H[inckley] and Doct. Sandal, so we stopped and dined. Got to the launch at 3 P.M., when we again set sail. Arrived at Nappa Creek ten o'clock at night.

17. Slept pretty soundly after the fatigue of yesterday. By the way, we did not come exactly for hides, but to get timber

---

[40]Vincente José Martínez, born in 1818, was the son of Ignacio Martínez. Vincente was still living in 1882. Bancroft, *California*, III: 733–734.

[41]It was the custom during the summer to take "a cup of cha, as tea was called by the Californians." Usually served with it was some sweet. In most cases this was *niscoyote*, a thick corn tortilla, with a small quantity of fat added to it, together with sugar, *panocha* (brown coarse sugar), or honey to sweeten it. Hubert H. Bancroft, *California Pastoral* (San Francisco, 1888), pp. 363–365.

[42]Ignacio Martínez, born in Mexico City in 1774, settled in California in 1800. He was to have a long and useful career in both the military and civil service of the province, including a term as alcalde of San Francisco in 1837. For his service, he was awarded the Rancho Pinole, situated in present-day Contra Costa County, in 1829, reconfirmed in 1842. His wife, Martina Arellanes, was fifty-four years of age when Mrs. Nye met her. At the rancho also lived several daughters and sons. He died sometime before 1852. Bancroft, *California*, III:733.

[43]The Rancho Pinole, Contra Costa County, stretched from Pinole to Martinez. Originally four leagues in size, when the title was confirmed to Martínez's daughter, María Antonia Martínez de Richardson (she had married William Richardson, an Englishman), the patent was issued for 17,761 acres. Cowan, *Ranchos of California*, p. 61. "Pinole is derived from the Aztec *pinolli*, designating ground and parched or toasted grain or seeds." Martínez was named after Ignacio. Edwin G. Gudde, *California Place Names* (Rev. ed., Berkeley and Los Angeles, 1969), pp. 149–247.

for new railings to the ship. While the carpenters are in the country cutting it, the crew are chopping wood, so we shall return with a full cargo at all events. After all had gone to their several employments, finding it rather warm on board, Gorham pitched his tent (which he always takes with him) under a large oak tree, and here we are quite to ourselves, having everything comfortable. There is one family on the opposite side of the creek who owns an extensive farm.[44] I can see a great many Indians at work and hear them too! Most of them without clothing, their hair long; they look at me with surprise! but I do not feel the least fear of them.

18. Received an invitation from Mr. Yaunts to pass a day or two on his farm, about fifteen miles.[45] The questions was, how shall I get there? To ride those California horses I dare not. The only alternative is to ride as other ladies do, not exactly in a team, for the carriage has two wheels and drawn by two yoke of oxen. After breakfast, the barouche was tackled, the tent spread over the top for an awning, mattress and cushions for seats.[46] When ready, we placed ourselves in the easiest position, and away we rode with two Indians for drivers. Pretty

[44]Although Mrs. Nye's reference is vague, it is probable that the "extensive farm" was the combined land grants conferred on Nicolas Higuera in 1836. He obtained the Rancho Carneros and the Rancho Entre Napa. Those lands were situated south of present-day Napa. Cowan, *Ranchos of California*, pp. 23, 34.

[45]George C. Yount was born in North Carolina in 1794. In 1804, his family moved to Missouri. After several years working as a trapper in the transmontane west, he emigrated to California in February 1831. In 1836, he settled permanently in the Napa Valley. He died at the age of seventy-one at his Caymus Ranch, October 5, 1865. He was not a bachelor as Mrs. Nye mistakenly suggests later in her journal. His family joined him later in 1843. Mrs. E. H. Day, "Sketches of Early California Settlers: George C. Yount," *The Hesperian*, II (March 1859), 1–6; Charles L. Camp, ed., "The Chronicles of George C. Yount, California Pioneer of 1836," *California Historical Society Quarterly*, II (April 1923), 3–66; San Francisco *Alta California*, Oct. 7, 1865.

Yount had obtained two land grants in what today is Napa County, the Rancho Caymus, two leagues, in 1836, and the Rancho Jota, one league, situated in and around Angwin, in 1843. Cowan, *Ranchos of California*, pp. 25, 42.

[46]This vehicle was a *carreta* or Mexican cart with high wooden wheels. The fact that two yoke of oxen were required to draw it is attributable, at least in part, to the traditional California custom of yoking oxen across their horns instead of across their necks. This placed the strain on their heads and necks instead of across their shoulders and thus made it impossible for them to draw very heavy loads.

good representation of a family moving to Ohio. In the meantime a boy led a horse (saddled) in case it should be too jolting for me; Gorham would take me on the horse beside him. But I found it very comfortable. Arrived about the hour for dinner. Sat down. Saw a large teapot, cups and saucers to each plate. Began to think how nice a cup of tea would taste after our ride, when lo! instead of tea, pure cold water came streaming from the nose. Necessity is the mother of inventions. No pitcher nor tumblers in the house, which was built of mud, though hard as any granite, but I have not time to give a description of all. Suffice it to say everything corresponds to an iota. Now this gentleman is an old bachelor I believe, a miser anyhow worth a handsome property. Offered us anything we would like that was on his farm. But O the heat was intolerable. I could not walk out until sundown.

By the way, I heard there was three families of emigrants that had traveled by land from the States to Oregon. Did not like it, so kept on traveling 'til they at least stopped here. We had a great curiosity to see them. Upon inquiry, found the other two families had not found a resting place yet. In short Mrs. Bennett and daughter soon called on us, dressed in their best attire, which if I should describe, would cause you to laugh, and that I would not do myself.[47] Meanwhile, Gorham

---

[47]The family of Vardamon and Mary Bennett, comprising eight children, came overland the hard way. Setting out from Arkansas, they heeded the call of Langsford W. Hastings to immigrate westward. In May 1842, a company led by Hastings departed Independence, Missouri, and struck out for Oregon. Reaching that initial destination, those who looked to California as their home spent the winter at Salem. In that same year, 1842, Elijah White led a large party of Oregon-bound immigrants. In May 1843, Hastings led a party of fifty-three southward to the promised land. Encountering Indian difficulties in the Rogue River Valley, the light-of-heart turned back to the Oregon settlements, reducing the party to thirty-four, the Bennett family among them. The other known family in the party was that of Thomas Shadden. Mr. Bennett settled his family in San Francisco. Three years before his death, his wife separated from him and moved to Santa Cruz. Her subsequent life was mercurial, to say the least. Mabel D. Early, "Biographical Narrative of Bennett Family," *The Pony Express*, XVII (Sept. 1950), 8–9, 13, 15; (Nov. 1950), 9–10.

Mrs. Bennett's maiden name was McSwain. Of Irish descent, she probably was born in Virginia, lived and married in Georgia, resided in Tennessee and Arkansas before heading for California.

went to see the carpenters who were cutting timber close by, which left us to ourselves. And sure enough they gave me a history of their journey, which to me seemed almost incredible. In the evening we returned the call, saw her husband and eight children—hearty as pine knots. They left with property but their expenses had taken it all. But what is more strange, they were packing to start Sunday morning to go seventy miles further where her daughter was going to marry Mr. Sinclair, and where they too thought of settling.[48] Here I saw one hundred Indians digging a canal. No work was done while the white woman was in sight—their eyes were riveted.

19. After the fatigue of yesterday, one would suppose we slept soundly. But horrid to relate, our bosom friend (the flea) kept us awake most of the night. Good morning! says Mr. Yaunts. Did the fleas trouble you? Yes! Well, they always make much of strangers. Says I to myself, they have got all of us they'll get. I should like to [have] stopped through the day, but in order to avoid the heat, must go early in the morning or late at night, which I would not like to do. When the news reached Mrs. Bennett I was going, she, with her husband and children, came over bringing her horse, which she had rode from the States, and kindly offered it to me, which I very gladly accepted. Having mounted, bade them a final farewell, leaving our serviento in care of the baggage. Got home about

[48]Mrs. Bennett had four daughters with her: Catherine, Amanda, Julia, and Samantha. Catherine later married Isaac Graham in September 1845. As to which daughter is mentioned here, there is no way of knowing at present. However, Sinclair was most likely John Sinclair, a former Hudson's Bay Company employee. A Scotsman, he served a brief time as editor of the *Sandwich Island Gazette,* then came to California in December 1839. He was associated in business with John A. Sutter, then Eliab Grimes. He occupied the latter's land grant, the Rancho Paso, situated north of present-day Sacramento, in 1842. Dr. Sandals visited him in 1843, as did John C. Fremont the following year. He died while on a steamer bound for the States in 1849. *Ibid.*, p. 15; Bancroft, *California*, V:721; Doyce B. Nunis, Jr., *The Trials of Isaac Graham* (Los Angeles, 1967), p. 62.

It must be pointed out, however, that Fremont on his meeting with Sinclair in 1844 makes no mention of a wife. Donald Jackson and Mary Lee Spence, eds., *The Expeditions of John Charles Fremont, Volume I, Travels From 1838–1844* (Urbana, Ill., 1970), pp. 652, 656–657.

nine A.M. Found Lady Pansy (the name of my horse) to be very gentle and easy. What a ride! fifteen miles before breakfast. Did not feel much fatigued. Soon the carriage arrived bringing our baggage, many kinds of vegetables, with a nice little lamb, and I assure you I did not eat very sparingly.

20. Sunday morning. Find it so warm have had the tent pitched again, under the old oak tree, and now we are quite alone with the Bible, hymn book, Memoirs of Job Scott, a Quaker.[49] I read, then sing just as loud as I like. How much it reminds me of Camp Meeting. I can almost imagine I hear the distant sound of the Preacher at the stand. When O when! will the day arrive, when the Gospel, the true Gospel, shall be preached to these people. The day has passed pleasantly, and I hope profitably.

21. The carpenters think they will not be able to get through with their work until another week. Well, I can make myself as contented here as elsewhere. Today I feel some headache. Having killed a large bullock and hung it under a large tree in order to keep it cool, the foxes or kioties [coyotes] finding they could not appease their hunger, set up a most horrible yell around it. To quell the tumult, Gorham took a gun and fired. Afterwards all was quiet.

22. Hearing Capt. Nye with his lady are here, people come from their farms every day to see us. I did think we were out of reach of company. But the Spanish ladies and gentlemen think nothing of riding fifteen or twenty miles to make a call, and what is till more strange, they never refuse a good dinner. Today sitting very quietly I heard the rattling of spurs at a great distance. I ran to see the cavalcade, and surely there was four horses, bringing a family containing seven, wishing to take passage to Peola. They finally spent the day. Then started for the Mission about twelve miles to stop until we sailed.[50]

---

[49]Mrs. Nye was probably reading the *Journal of the Life, Travels and Gospel Labors of that Faithful Minister of Christ, Job Scott*. First published in New York in 1797, it was reprinted in 1815 and 1820.

23. The crew have finished taking in wood. Have now gone after water. Have plenty of room for hides, but very few can we get owing to the dryness of the season. The cattle are not fat, therefore the farmers will not kill, so the creditors have to suffer the consequences.[51] Gorham says there has not one visited us, but that owes the firm.

24. This morning talked of going out to the Mission at Sonoma to see the General and his family,[52] but as the weather is becoming more moderate so I can walk and go out in the vessel, which lays so a few steps across a plank takes us to shore, have concluded to pass the remainder of our time on board. I have already accomplished some sewing; am never at a loss for employment.

25. Hearing the carpenters could not get through for several days, then the timber is to be carted twenty miles, Gorham thinks he cannot leave the ship any longer. Shall therefore sail tonight and send the launch immediately back. How I have enjoyed eating fruit, melons in particular; had them sent me from adjacent farms, likewise milk, which is quite a luxury.

26. At three o'clock this morning made sail. Had not sailed far before we were aground. Shall probably lay until tomorrow. The creek is narrow but not dangerous. It is very pleasant sailing. Thousands of cattle do I see grazing on the hills above us. The scenery, too, is beautiful.

27. Started again this morning with about ten passengers. Got out of the creek into the bay, found it very rough. Don

---

[50]Mission San Francisco Solano at Sonoma was founded July 4, 1823, and has the distinction of being the youngest of California missions.

[51]The hide business with the Californians normally was done on the basis of twelve months' credit—that is, the *rancheros* were supplied with goods as needed, for which payment was made once a year, after the annual round-up and slaughtering had been completed, since hides were legal tender. With anything as unforeseen as a prolonged drouth, it was necessary to extend credit beyond the customary one-year period.

[52]Mariano Guadalupe Vallejo and his family resided at the present-day city of Sonoma on the Rancho Petaluma, granted to him in 1834. The mission is situated south of his *casa*, a short distance.

Vincenti, wife and babe,[53] were very sea-sick. Be assured I *never* let a good opportunity passed unimproved. Arrived to Penola about sundown, left a few of our number, then started on our way to Yerba Buena.[54]

28. Arrived this morning about eleven o'clock, all well, after a pleasant tour of two weeks. During our absence, a ship had arrived from Vancouver (bound to Oahu) with three families on board, whom I become acquainted with while at Vancouver, two of whom were going from the Is[land]s to the States.[55] I did not stop to rest, for the vessel was to sail on the morrow, but commenced a letter to Ma, which I closed at an early hour and retired.

29. While Gorham is writing to A[lpheus Thompson], I had time to write to Mr. and Mrs. Brewer at Oahu. We then visited the ship, gave the letters to Mrs. Frost of N[ew] York, who spent a week with me while in Vancouver.

30. There is quite a fleet of vessels lying in the harbor, eight ships, two brigs; two of which are going to the States this fall, but not with a full cargo. I shall leave letters for them to take should I leave for the Isl[and]s before they sail.

31. Every day brings its work, at least I find it so. Have had the curtains taken down in the cabin and altered them to my own taste. You know I love to have things look well. The cabin is larger than our east room and very nicely furnished.

September 1. Been on shore and dined with Mrs. Ray. The day seems much longer than on board ship, and then how cold it is. Why! it seems more like March than Sept. I began to think I was not going to enjoy any warm weather, but soon found my mistake. At Nappa the heat was almost insupport-

---

[53]Probably Vincente José Martínez and his family. His first wife was Guadelupe Moraga. As to the identity of the other passengers, nothing is known. Bancroft, *California*, III:733.

[54]The earlier name applied to San Francisco, meaning good or sweet herb.

[55]This would be the *Diamond*, Captain Fowler. On board as passengers were the Reverend Joseph H. Frost, Daniel Lee, Dr. Babcock, with their wives and five children. Frost and Lee, after reaching Honolulu, continued on to Boston. *The Friend*, 1 (Oct. 28, 1843), 62. Also see Chapter III, *note* 13 and 14, *ante*, and *note* 6 in this chapter.

able. I soon sighed for the salubrious air of St. Francisco (in Spanish Yerba Buena).

2. This morning, early, Gorham went on shore and took Mrs. Ray with her family off to spend the day with me. The day was very fine, but when night came on, how boisterous! I would like to had her stop the night, but she thought it was too much of a good thing to stop with three children, two servants.

3. Have been somewhat sick today, with a slight cold I think I took coming off from shore. There is very sudden changes in the weather. One can dress in thin clothes in the morning, by night would gladly exchange for cloak and mittens. But I am generally careful. If Gorham does say, I am afraid I shall not look pretty.

4. Feel much better. Have a most excellent nurse. Mr. A. B. Thompson (partner) has just arrived.[56] Already began to consult where to go next. We have laid moored five weeks in this place—I hope to Sa. Barbara. I seem to think I shall like it there. Besides there is a Boston lady (Mrs. Stephens [*sic*])[57] boarding at Mr. T[hompson], so I shall have someone to converse with. You know, I never was very social, but now I am *obliged* to remain passive for I am no Spanish scholar yet.

5. A voyage in contemplation—something about a mill which they own in Sonoma.[58] Mr. T[hompson] says Gorham must go with him for his judgment is better than his. But how can I think of being left alone four whole days? I ought not to manifest any unwillingness—business before pleasure.

6. Not yet had the sun gilded the horizon, ere the Capt.

---

[56]John C. Jones, Jr., was Thompson's partner. Brown, ed., *China Trade Days in California*, pp. 38–44.

[57]The lady was Mrs. Stevens, wife of Captain James Stevens, as mentioned in the Prologue. See *notes* 89 and 94, *post*.

[58]George Yount had already erected "a small flouring mill, to be driven by the waters of the Napa Creek. . . ." This mill was constructed sometime between 1840–1842. Charles L. Camp, ed., *George C. Yount and His Chronicles of the West* (Denver, 1966), p. 159. It is unclear what Thompson and Nye planned.

accompanied by Mr. T[hompson] sailed for Centreville,[59] intending to take horses, or by the way to go on horseback from there to Sonoma. Pleasant places no doubt, as I had so recently returned from a tour to Nappa, I declined going, promising to make myself as happy as possible.

7. Sitting in the cabin which I now command with not eye upon me save that of my Heavenly Fathers, I have taken my pen in hand to record the adventures of the day, which has passed quietly away, nothing having disturbed my tranquillity. I have thought much of home and its endearments, and long again to hear the sound of a Mother's voice. I cannot tell you how much I wish to see you, nor how much joy a letter at this moment would give me. Neither distance nor long absence can ever wean me from my own dear country and friends.

8. Not having anything to draw my attention, I intend finishing several pieces of work, then to spend the remainder of my time in writing, which I dislike to do, unless quite alone. Now I have no excuse, I hope to improve the opportunity.

9. How rapidly the time has flown! This is the fourth day of my husband's absence. Did he not promise to be at home Saturday night? Yes! I will not think otherwise but hark! I hear the officers on deck say the boat is coming, but the Capt. is not in her! I was just removing from the dinner table to welcome his return, when I heard that last sentence. But as yet, I retain the self possession which is so natural to me. I waited to hear the next sentence, which was cheering! The boat was heavy laden with hides and tallow. The Capt. had sent a letter requesting another boat to be sent to Sausolita, (whether he had already come by land) to take him across. Would probably be here about midnight.[60] It is now about

[59]Situated in Alameda County, this may well be the present-day Centerville. Gudde, *California Place Names*, p. 59.

[60]Sausalito, meaning a "little grove of willows," was a favorite anchorage inside San Francisco Bay on the northwest entrance side (Marin County). A land grant to the adjacent area was conferred on William Richardson in 1838. *Ibid.*, p. 300.

ten o'clock. I have been walking the deck with my faithful companion (Glen) by my side, who seems to catch at every sound, as if conscious of his master's absence. All nature, animate and inanimate, seems to be buried in repose and silence. The waves lay themselves down hushingly upon the shore, as if to slumber the winds have fallen asleep to their own gentle lullaby, while the gulls, sea-mews, and other birds, which in the day time are perpetually hovering over this part of the Coast, have all betaken themselves to their hiding places and folded their wearied, sea-wet wings for the night. Moonlight, and the serenity of the elements (for there was hardly a breath of air), at last gave me to understand there was no probability of the boat's return until the next tide, so I quietly laid me down to sleep.

10. Have this day commenced reading the life of Doct. Payson.[61] How infinitely short do I fall of this holy conformity to my Maker, which he so justly describes as the property of a Christian. About four P.M. a boat was seen steering for the ship. By the aid of the spy glass I could discern the features of one whom I was most desirous to see. Soon, very soon, had the pleasure of seeing him in reality, which you must think after an absence of nearly five days, was really pleasant.

11. The fowls we have on board, furnish us with fresh eggs. The steward has been assisting me in making some cake. 'Tis true he can make a nice cake, but I thought my make would taste better.

12 & 13. These two days have had the entire company of my husband, being a little sick. Took cold, being in an open boat, is subject to a cough.

[61]Possibly Mrs. Nye had a copy of *A Memoir of the Reverend Edward Payson, D.D., Late of Portland, Maine,* by Reverend Asa Cummings (New York, [183?]). This seems likely since Payson was interested in the welfare of seamen as evidenced by *Accounts of Shipwreck and Other Disasters at Sea ... Containing Dr. Payson's Address to Seamen and a Few Prayers for Their Use* by [William Allen], printed in Brunswick, Maine, 1823, as well as a number of sermon tracts by Payson on the same theme.

14. Is much better today. Gone on shore, while I have busied myself in covering a couple of stools. Not at all sorry I tried my patience a little, they looked so nice when finished.

15. The ship is improving every day in looks, has been painted outside. Now the spars and rigging are going through their regular ordeal of tarring, splicing, etc. In a few days the carpenter commences putting on new railings.

16. The day in which the Mexicans declared themselves free and independent from the Spanish. Although the 16th of Sept., it is called by foreigners the 4th of July.[62] Early in the morning the flags were hoisted on all the ships. I went on shore and spent the day with Mrs. Hin[c]kley. About eleven o'clock a collation was given by a Spanish gentleman and I believe a dance in the evening However, we came off at sundown quite tired. Sitting so quietly all day with Mrs. H[inckley], could not converse; only when Gorham was present to interpret for me.

17. A violent headache—feel rather sick, think I must have taken cold yesterday. It was uncommon pleasant in the morning. In the afternoon it grew cold very suddenly. A person needs two changes of clothing in a day. I cannot think why it is so healthy here, the change is so great from morning to evening.

18. By taking medicine in season, have quite thrown off my cold. Feel much better. Just had three dozen musmelons sent me from a gentleman I never saw, though an intimate acquaintance of Gorham's. The dance which was to be on Saturday eve was deferred until Sunday evening.

19. Five months today since we sailed from Oahu. When I think of Oregon and the many places we have visited, the time seems short. A fast sailing ship and a good Capt. accomplished much in a short time.

---

[62]September 16, 1810, was the occasion on which Father Miguel Hidalgo y Castilla uttered his famous "*grito*," calling for Mexican Independence. However, independence from Spain was not formally declared until February 24, 1821, and recognized by the viceroy six months later.

20. One would suppose by the movements of things we were getting ready for the sea once more. Have taken in not a few bags of corn and beans, while the Capt. has gone on shore to purchase twelve cattle to be killed and salted this week.

21. I intended to have spent this day in writing, but the noise on deck is such I must defer it. The carpenters are at work putting on a new toprail. Then the men are taking in some boxes of soap. The Capt. is doing some painting, while I have run on deck to tell him to be careful and not paint his cloths. In fact it is a busy day with us all. Another addition to the fleet, a whaleship.

22. So how I can hardly recollect what I have been doing through the day, for you know woman's work is various—but I can always tell what the people's is. All hands bending sails today. Shall sail sometime next week; it is not decided where we go yet.

23. This may be called the line gale in truth. Last night I was aroused by the whistling of the wind, by the sound supposed it to be a violent storm. I made an attempt to rise, but found I had better keep quiet. The vessels in the harbor were dancing merrily. At four P.M. the wind ceased, the sun shone in cloudless splendor, the air cleared, and all nature seemed freshened. A boat with three of the crew is supposed to be out during the gale which caused some anxiety.

24. This morning my first inquiry was any news from the boat? Yes! Returned about midnight, all safe. Seeing them about the ship so much, it made me feel unpleasant!

25. From Monterey we learn by the arrival of the frigate *Constellation*[63] that Oahu is evacuated by the English and reoccupied by the Hawaiians, whose flag on being hoisted, was

[63]The U.S. man-of-war *Constellation*, thirty-six guns and a crew of 350 men, commanded by Commodore Lawrence Kearny, arrived at Honolulu on July 7 from Amoy, China. It sailed for Monterey, August 16. *The Friend*, 1 (July 27, 1843), 34; (Sept. 16, 1843), 50; A.B.C. Whipple "The Hard-Luck Frigate," *American Heritage: The Magazine of History*, 7 (Feb. 1956), 16.

saluted from Punch Bowl Hill, and from the Fort.[64] I think there must have been great rejoicing with the King and Chiefs. I feel very much in a hurry to get to Monterey thinking I may find letters as there has been an arrival from the States.

26. Have had quite a dinner party. Mr. and Mrs. Ray and family, Mr. Thompson, with several others.[65] Do you ask what we dined upon? Why! roast beef, fowls, meat's tongue—for dessert, apple and mince pies—quite a Yankee dinner.

27. Went on shore early this morning, spent the day to Mrs. Spear's, daughter of the late Mr. Holmes, formerly of Plymouth.[66] When I return to the Is[and]s, I intend to call on Mrs. H[olmes], who I should think, was very old.[67]

---

[64]According to Paty's Harbormaster Records, the *Piia* or *Victoria*, so called by the British, did not sail for Valparaíso to make contact with Admiral Thomas until March 17, a full twenty days after the cession had been made. Since the voyage, for a vessel of her size, required more than two months, Lord Paulet undoubtedly felt this would provide Alexander Simpson with sufficient time to reach London before Thomas could act.

John Meek, former harbormaster and pilot for Honolulu, was a native of Marblehead, Massachusetts, who first arrived in the Sandwich Islands in 1809 as first officer of a trading ship plying between the Northwest Coast and China. He settled in Oahu in 1812. Later he became a livestock breeder of some note. He was a firm friend of the kings and high chiefs from Kamehameha I on. He died January 29, 1875, at age eighty-three. *The Friend,* new series, 24 (Feb. 1, 1875), [10]. He made the voyage to Valparaíso apparently as a crew member or pilot, perhaps having had it in mind from the outset to communicate directly with Admiral Thomas if opportunity arose, since he obviously did not trust Paulet to render an objective report of what had transpired.

Thomas, although without specific instructions from the Foreign Office or Admiralty, abrogated the cession in light of Lord Aberdeen's policy regarding British relations with Pacific island rulers. Kuykendall, *Hawaiian Kingdom, 1778–1854*, p. 186.

Since all Hawaiian flags had been confiscated and destroyed by the British under Paulet's orders, Admiral Thomas had a new flag made on his ship, the *Dublin*, and presented it to Kamehameha III. It was embossed with an olive branch and a crown superimposed on the central area. A second Hawaiian flag used during the restoration ceremonies was made and presented to the king by Honolulu merchants Peirce and Brewer. See Appendix III for an interesting view of the Restoration.

[65]William G. Rae, Hudson's Bay Company agent in San Francisco, and his wife Eloise, daughter of John McLoughlin, had a son and two daughters. Alpheus B. Thompson, Santa Barbara merchant, was also a dinner guest.

[66]Nathan Spear, a Bostonian, born August 24, 1802, made his first trip to the Pacific, touching at the Sandwich Islands, in 1819. He returned in 1823 on the *Rover*, which called at Monterey. Returning to the Islands in 1829, the following year he married Jane Holmes, a daughter of Captain Oliver Holmes and his native wife, Mahi, and settled in California the

(*continued on next page*)

28. Have made an excellent day's work, traded 50 dollars in things I brought out, which were of no use to me. Capt. Fitch thought it was a pity I did not come out when the *Loriot* came;[68] thought I should make an excellent salesman.

29. The Capt. has gone to Sousoleta a few hours to purchase some powder, and some American pork from a whaleship.[69] During the day I have been somewhat busy preserving peaches. I hope in St. Barbara to get quinces.

30. Have quite a bad sore throat, the severest I have had since I left the States. Suppose I feel somewhat alarmed, being subject to the throat ail. Have steamed my throat, taken a dose of Smith's Elixir, applied the same on the outside. All hands busy in boating off hides from the house in which they are stored when collected.

October 1. Last night tried a new medicine. Took half an ounce of nitre, threw in some burning coals, which instantly filled the room with a dense smoke. After inhaling it for half an hour, it seemed to relieve me, so I rested very quietly.

(*continued from previous page*)
next year. He was "an enterprising businessman, honorable in his dealings, gentlemanly in his manners, and scholarly in his tastes though of limited education." William Heath Davis was his nephew. After a varied business career, he died in San Francisco at the home of his nephew, October 21, 1849. Davis, *Seventy-Five Years,* pp. 2 *et seq.*; "Yerba Buena Biographies," *California Historical Society Quarterly*, XIV (June 1935), 127–128; San Francisco *Alta California*, Oct. 25, Nov. 8, 15, 1849.

[67]Captain Oliver Holmes, a native of Plymouth, Massachusetts, was discharged on Hawaii, October 7, 1793, by Captain James Magee of the ship *Margaret*. He moved to Oahu on January 3, 1796, arriving on the *P.W. Henry*. Subsequently, he married Mahi, a native woman, and fathered five daughters. Loyal to King Kamehameha I, he served for a time as governor of Oahu. Reputedly, he was the "only white man known to have been in the service of Kalanikupule when Oahu was conquered by Kamehameha." His name sometimes appears in local records as "Homa." In 1826, Hannah, a daughter, "married" John C. Jones, Jr., who later denied the legality of the union and put her aside. As for Holmes, he died, while intoxicated, in 1825. Smith, *Yankees in Paradise*, pp. 52–53; Edward Josesting, *Hawaii, An Uncommon History* (New York, 1972), p. 80; Bruce Cartright, "Honolulu, 1809–1810," *Paradise of the Pacific*, 38 (Dec. 1925), 60; Honolulu *Advertiser*, Oct. 14, 1928, p. 3, cl. 2, and File M 66, HSA. Also, see Chapter I, *note* 11, *ante.*

[68]Captain Nye and Alpheus B. Thompson, supercargo, brought the schooner *Loriot*, seventy tons, to California for a trading venture, 1833–1835. Bancroft, *California*, IV: 383*n*.

[69]Possibly the American whaler *Caroline* or *Merrimac* anchored at Sausalito. *Ibid.*, V:564*n*, 567*n*.

2. Feel much better—appetite rather small. I can but think how nice some food would taste prepared by my Mother's hand. What we have is good still. I dream of eating from our table and often from Granma's.

3. Have been reading some late newspapers sent me from Oahu. By them I learned something of the state of things since we left. At one time there were six ships of war lying in the harbor.[70] At the time the Isl[ands] were restored there was ten days of feasting. The King gave three luaus and I should suppose not a little rejoicing among the residents.[71] All business was suspended for several days.

4. Shall not sail as soon as was expected on account of some freight just offered. 5,000 hides (from Mr. Ray) to be boated off and stowed.

5. The *Caresfort*, Hon. Lord George Poullett, arrived a few days since.[72] Has sent an invitation to the masters of the ships in port to dine with him. The *Caresfort* lay two miles or more from us, and feeling a little indignant towards Lord George for his transactions at Oahu, I did not feel inclined to go. However, Gorham went. Was treated very politely, notwithstanding his [Paulet's] treatment to the Americans while at the Isl[ands].

6. Today on shore, was much amused with the manner in which the hides were brought off. I think Dana in his book (entitled *Two Years Before the Mast*) speaks very correctly.[73] In the first place they are taken from the hide house, put in a hand cart, and drawn by Indians to the shore. The men take

---

[70]The naval vessels included the British *Carysfort, Hazard,* and *Dublin;* the American *Constellation, Cyane,* and *United States.* See ships in *The Friend* for July–August 1843.

[71]Because it is said that nothing of its nature held in the Islands has ever equalled the luau given by King Kamehameha III in honor of Admiral Thomas, that graphic description is reproduced in Appendix IV.

[72]H.M.S. *Carysfort* departed Honolulu, August 25, and remained at Monterey, October 4–21, when it sailed to Mazatlán. *The Friend,* 1 (Sept. 16, 1843), 50; Bancroft, *California,* IV:564*n.*

[73]It is interesting to note that Dana's book was published in 1841, and Mrs. Nye had read it.

two on their heads at once, wade into the water some distance, place them in the boat, which when loaded are brought to the ship and stowed.[74]

7. Today Mrs. Hin[c]kley and sister spent the day with us, though I could not talk with them much. It is pleasant to have company.[75] By the *Caresfort* I recd. a letter from Mrs. Rowell (an ocean friend) writes her health is very poor, has a babe a few months old.[76]

8. Painful indeed it is to me to record what I have heard is to take place on this holy day. About three miles from town the Declaration of Independence is to be read, a collation given—in the afternoon Bull fight. I suppose a dance in the evening. But we have had for company today Capt. Makenzie,[77] whom I saw in the whaleboat which passed through the principal streets of Boston (on that memorable day) the 10th of Sept., 1839.[78] It is about ten months since Capt. M left the States—is a fine man, appears more like some great statesman, full of politics, temperance, and religion.

---

[74]A concise description of the hide and tallow trade, penned by Sir George Simpson during his 1841 visit to Alta California, is printed in Appendix V.

[75]See *note* 39, *ante.* Mrs. Hinckley's sister, María Antonia, was the wife of William R. Richardson. Born in England in 1795, he took residence in California on leaving his ship, the *Orion,* August 2, 1822. After conversion to Catholic faith, in 1823 he married María Antonia, the daughter of Ignacio Martínez, commandant of the San Francisco Presidio. From 1829–1835, he lived near Los Angeles. In 1835, Governor José Figueroa appointed him captain of the port of San Francisco, a post he held until the latter part of 1844. He died there, April 20, 1856. [R.S. Brooke], "Alcalde Grants in the City of San Francisco," *The Pioneer,* 1 (April 1854), 193; San Francisco *Alta California,* April 23, 1856; Feb. 25, 1872; May 28, 1874; San Francisco *Bulletin,* April 23, 1896; Sacramento *Union,* May 25, 1874; Oakland *Tribune,* March 4, 1928. An excellent sketch is provided in Davis, *Seventy-Five Years,* pp. 9–15.

[76]Mrs. Rowell gave birth to a daughter who was "named Malvina Chapin Rowell." It was the first child born to the Rowells. *Missionary Portraits,* p. 167.

[77]McKenzie was master of the New Bedford whaleship *Caroline.* It was on its first year of a whaling cruise. It called at Honolulu, January 12, 1844, thirteen months out, 500 barrels of oil, and departed February 13. On December 13, 1844, it called again, reporting 450 barrels sperm oil and 1,050 barrels of whale oil. *The Friend,* 2 (Feb. 1, 1844), 16; (Feb. 14, 1844), 20; 3 (Jan. 1, 1845), 8.

[78]The occasion of this parade in Boston remains a mystery. Perhaps the date given is a lapse of memory. Local annals disclose no such affair.

9. I had quite forgotten to note down the earthquake which was felt a few nights since, several shocks, but were not sensible of it. I think it was not felt on the water. More freight offered. About 500 hides to be taken on board. Shall sail Wednesday.

10. Very glad to have so pleasant [a] passenger; Capt. Grimes has come on board to remain with us until we arrive at Oahu. Shall not go down to the Isl[ands] with a light ship. When full below, are to take horses on deck. What a stamping there will be.

11. The Capt. has returned from shore with his papers. The ship is partly unmoored. Are now waiting for the tide to turn. Shall then put to sea.

12. Last night it was a dead calm. So close [to] land, the Capt. was obliged to be on deck all night. This morning a fine breeze. Sail along very quietly.

13. Two o'clock P.M. dropt anchor in Monterey 48 hours from St. Francisco. I can hardly control my feelings so impatient am I to know if there is letters on shore for us. While Gorham was preparing to go see, a gentleman came off bringing a number of letters which came by the *Delaware*.[79] O how my heart beat. I looked at them, hesitated which to open. I had hoped to hear good news, if otherwise ordered, I prayed to be resigned.

14. Last evening passed very pleasantly in reading letters. Happy to hear our friends were well and prosperous. But must I add have not received the two boxes my dear mother was so kind to send me. The value I do not think of, so great is the disappointment. They came safe to Oahu, for Mr. B[rewer] wrote to Gorham saying he had sent me two boxes

---

[79]The 218-ton brig *Delaware*, Captain William F. Penhallow, anchored at Honolulu, July 24, 1843, after a passage of thirty-three days from Callao, Peru, outbound from Boston. It sailed for Valparaíso on August 11. The vessel that conveyed the letters to Monterey was probably the U.S.S. *Constellation*, which sailed from Hawaii on August 16 for Monterey. Paty's Harbormaster Records; *The Friend*, 1 (July 27, 1843), 34.

by the frigate *Constellation*, which left Monterey a few days since.[80] It seems they were not delivered to anyone. Had fortune favoured, we should been here in time to receive them ourselves. The *Caresfort* follows me wherever I go. Has just anchored quite near the ship. The band is now playing God save the King (the Queen too, I hope), while salutes are exchanging from the fort.

15. I feel I could walk most any distance could I but attend Church this day. But that privilege is denied me. I can but think of the Sabbaths I once enjoyed—the sermons I have heard preached. Text will often come into my mind which I supposed were forgotten, but will ever live in memories blissful domains.

16. For company to dine Don Ocio, Mr. F[itch] with two officers, belonging to the troops,[81] which prevented me from going ashore, so late when we rose from table.

17. A heavy fog this morning. At two o'clock the sun broke out in cloudless splendor. Mrs. Larkin went out with me to make calls. On my first arrival at this place I was not much pleased with its appearance.[82] But now things wear a different aspect. The general (Micheltoreno) has arrived from

[80]The United States man-of-war *Constellation*, Commodore Kearney, commanding, was from China bound for the American east coast. It stopped off at Honolulu (see *note* 63, *ante*) and visited Monterey, September 15–29, 1843. Bancroft, *California*, IV:564*n*.

[81]Don Antonio María Osio has been previously identified. (See *note* 25, *ante*.) Henry Delano Fitch, born in New Bedford, Massachusetts, May 7, 1799, first reached California in 1819. On April 14, 1829, he was baptized in San Diego and soon after married Josefa Carrillo. He led a vigorous life as sea captain and merchant-trader on the California scene for two decades. He died after a fifteen-day illness from typhoid pneumonia in San Diego, January 13, 1849. His widow survived him and died at the Rancho de Sotoyome in January 1893, at the advanced age of eighty-two. San Diego *Union*, Aug. 5, 1943; Idwal Jones, "Dona Josefa," *Westways*, 43 (May 1951), 8–9; Fitch Notebook, Serra Museum, San Diego Historical Society. Ronald L. Miller has written the first extensive biography, "Henry Delano Fitch" (Ph.D. dissertation, University of Southern California, 1972).

[82]Monterey sits in close proximity to the great San Andreas fault, whose frequent, restless movements have been responsible for most of California's numerous earthquakes. Recall the statements of Sir George Simpson in speaking of the thickness of the adobe walls of buildings in Monterey, p. 197n. Simpson visited Monterey in 1842, a year ahead of Mrs. Nye.

Mexico with three hundred troops.[83] At every corner of the street are seen groups of soldiers, dressed in uniform. Almost any time in the day can hear music. The general wears a three-cornered cap with a large white plume and dressed in splendid uniform.

18. This morning I have spent in writing over land. After dinner went on shore. The general was going to give a dance in the evening. All the masters of the ships were invited. Gorham with his acquaintances were very anxious I should go once, for it was the only place to see the manners and customs of the people. As little as I wished to go, I finally consented, but must say I was disappointed. 'Tis true we were introduced to the general; most of the gentlemen were dressed in uniform—while the music was fine, having the band from the *Caresfort*. In short, I did not enjoy it; went to gratify others, not myself.

---

[83]This was General Manuel Micheltorena, the new governor and military commandante of California, whose presence was intended to keep at bay the encroaching Americans. Because the officials at Mexico were given to laying large plans for California, but always forgetting to implement them with funds, the five hundred troops ordered to accompany the general to his new post proved to number but one hundred, and he was unhappily forced to empty jails and prisons of some of their least desirable inmates in order to secure the prescribed force of five hundred. Assembled at Tepic, it appeared that uniforms were lacking for most of them, and their number began to be decimated by disease, as many as six to eight deaths occurring daily. The convicts had been permitted to bring their womenfolk, who some felt were even less desirable characters, and when they finally embarked, officials at Mexican ports of call refused to allow any of them to land.

Captain Henry Fitch at San Diego wrote Thomas Larkin, June 10, 1842, an account of these proceedings together with warnings of what was likely to happen in Monterey when the new governor and his forces arrived. Hammond, ed., *Larkin Papers*, IV:241.

Reaching Los Angeles, the general and his troops disembarked and the latter were soon in mischief, inspired in part, no doubt, by the fact that funds were still lacking for their support. Just as the general was ready to continue his voyage to Monterey, the disquieting news arrived that the town had been seized by the Americans, the *faux pas* already mentioned, committed by Commodore Jones, so Micheltorena prudently decided to remain where he was. Subsequently Jones came to tender his official apology, and the general demanded a substantial indemnity. The matter was referred to the two respective governments for negotiation and settlement. Whether from this source or elsewhere, the general seems to have managed to finance suitable uniforms for his men by the time they were seen by Mrs. Nye, adding life and color to the drabness of Monterey. Since she speaks of only three hundred troops, perhaps the others had been returned to *calabozos* like the ones from which they had been recruited.

19. One could not help smiling to see ladies go a shopping here. Hides are called bank bills. For instance, you see a lady walking along, at a little distance, a boy, dragging a hide, which is considered the same as cash. I never had so little use for money. I see nothing worth purchasing.

20. Have spent the live long day in writing by the ship *Tasso.*[84] Indeed I have spent days and weeks in writing. Sail tomorrow for St. Barbara. Have taken on board six thous[and] hides. Mrs. Watson[85] sent me a large box of quince marmalade, which I assure you, tastes very nice; some new butter would be good. In a country like this, where there are so many cattle, you would suppose butter and milk would be had in great abundance; cannot get it but very seldom.

21. Sat[urday] twelve o'clock. Gorham says are you ready for sea? All ready. Set sail in company with two other ships, though bound to different places.

22. Again are we on the broad ocean, but not out of sight of land, with a rather light breeze. I have read and slept a little. It is now ten o'clock. The Capt. says he shall not stop below until the ship has passed Point Conception.[86]

23. Are sailing along the coast very prettily, light winds but fair. I do not mind having a little longer passage, if I can but have it smooth that I may not be deterred from my usual employment.

24. At ten o'clock last night anchored in St. Barbara after a passage of three days only. This morning I was on deck early taking a view of the town, which lies some distance from the shore. However, as far as I can discern, it has the same appearance as the other places.

---

[84]The 314-ton American bark *Tasso,* Captain Samuel J. Hastings, arrived from Boston at Monterey, June 28, 1841. It departed for its home port in late 1843. Bancroft, *California,* IV:569*n.*

[85]See *note* 10, *ante.*

[86]Point Conception, originally sited by Cabrillo, October 18, 1542, was actually named by another explorer, Vizcaíno, in 1602. He reached the point on the day of the Feast of the Immaculate Conception, December 8, thus the name. Gudde, *California Place Names,* p. 72.

25. This morning heard the report of several cannons. Upon looking through the spy glass, saw a procession moving very slowly toward the Church. During the day, Gorham went on shore, was surprised to find it to be Mrs. Burton who died the day [before]. Sister to Mr. Thompson's wife.[87]

26. Have received an invitation from Mr. and Mrs. T[hompson] to pass our time with them while here. Early this morning Mr. T[hompson] sent a carriage down to take me to his house, which is situated about a mile from the shore. Not knowing how I should like the place and the people, I made preparations only for a few days at first.

27. My sail from the ship to the shore, my ride to the town very pleasant. Was met by Mr. J. C. Jones[88] and Mr. T[hompson]. Was soon introduced likewise to Mrs. Stephens [*sic*], an American lady.[89]

28. Sunday morning, seven o'clock. The Catholic bells are now chiming. At eight services commence. If I go, I cannot understand, the sermon will be in Spanish. As it is a place of worship I will attend.[90] But how can I think of going to

[87]María Antonio Carrillo de Burton, wife of Luis Burton, died on October 24, 1843, and was buried out of Presidio Church by Father Narciso Durán, October 25. Entry No. 519, Deaths of Gente de Raxon [Razon], Presidial Burial Register, 1782–1848, Transcript, Santa Barbara Mission Archive-Library.

[88]A Bostonian and long-time Honolulu merchant, John Coffin Jones, Jr., visited California yearly between 1830–1838 as a master or supercargo on a number of vessels in which he had a commercial interest. Jones had taken as his first "wife" Hannah Holmes, who was the young widow of Captain William Heath Davis, Sr. The latter couple had two children. A son, named for his father, went on to fame as a San Francisco captain-merchant. Later, Jones took as a "wife" a daughter of Don Francisco de Paula Marin, having children by both his first and second brides. However, neither of those marriages were ever legalized. After his 1837 legal marriage to Manuela, daughter of Carlos Carrillo, the sister of Alpheus B. Thompson's wife, he terminated his Hawaiian affairs and made a visit to the east coast. On his return, he settled in Santa Barbara in 1841 and became Thompson's partner. In 1846, he returned to Boston and died there on Christmas Eve, 1862. He served in the capacity of U.S. consul in the Sandwich Islands, 1820–1838. Ross H. Gast, *Contentious Consul: A Biography of John Coffin Jones* (Los Angeles, 1976), *passim.*

[89]Mrs. Stephens would be Mrs. James Stevens who came from Boston when her husband brought the *Roger Williams* (renamed the *Joven Guipuzcoana*) which had been purchased for José Antonio Aquirre, Santa Barbara. See the Prologue for details and *note* 94, *post*.

[90]The bells would be those of Mission Santa Barbara.

church without a bonnet, which is the custom here. However, I acceded, put on my dark satin dress, shawl of the same color over my *head.* As we entered all were kneeling (there are no seats in the church). As I looked around upon the audience dressed so plain, not attempting to make the least show and all upon their bended knees, how could I but feel solemn. O that the religion that they profess was the true gospel—the religion of Jesus Christ.

29. This morning took a ride and a sail before breakfast. Got on board just as the steward was turning out coffee, and I assure you, I did not eat very sparingly. Came off very early thinking to find the beach smooth, but it was far otherwise. As I cannot go off and on to the ship, on account of the distance and continual swell in the harbor, have concluded to go on shore and remain until ready for sea.

30. At ten o'clock A.M. took my leave of the ship for about two weeks it is supposed. As we approached the shore, found there was a tremendous surf. However, one must have firmness and confidence in Him, who alone can preserve us, in order to brave the dangers of the sea. Gorham says keep quiet, I will put you on shore, and not a spray of salt water shall touch you, which to my surprise was done. The men jumped into the surf, pulled the boat to shore (tremendous weight)—set me in the carriage. Rode directly to Mr. T[hompson] who lives in a large two story house with a verandah on each side and very handsomely furnished.[91] The

[91]Sir George Simpson agrees with Mrs. Nye in this. He writes on California homes:

> The rooms in general are handsomely furnished, many of them with carpets. . . . In Santa Barbara, as elsewhere, the bed appears to be the grand point of attraction, and to embody all the skill and taste of the females of the families. . . . with its snowy sheets fringed with lace, its pile of soft pillows covered with the finest linen or the richest satin, and its well-arranged drapery of costly and tasteful curtains. Still . . . this bed is but a whited sepulcher, concealing in the interior a pestilential wood-mattress, the impregnable stronghold of millions of *las pulgas*, fleas.

He adds that the farther south one travels, the more populous and lively the fleas became. *Narrative of Journey Round the World,* I:330, 345.

houses on the Coast and at the Isl[ands] are built without chimnies.[92]

31. Most of the ladies and gentlemen called on us today. Mrs. T[hompson] has four sisters; all are married to foreigners so they understand some English, but do not like to speak it.[93] However, I think I shall pass my time very pleasantly as Mrs. Stephens [*sic*] is always ready to interpret for me.

November 1. Having learned Mrs. S[tevens] is something of a dressmaker, I fortunately purchased a piece of poor black silk at $2 per yd. and sat myself down to dressmaking the remainder of the week.

2. All the spare time for the last two days I have worked on my dress 'till it is at length finished. Gorham says I shall not confine myself to sewing, must run about for exercise. Indeed, I have become so dignified, being so many months on shipboard, that I do not feel inclined to run as in my juvenile days.

4. The family have just returned from Mass. I feel myself perfectly justified in staying home. Is it beneficial to any one to see and hear that which they do not believe? It grieves me exceedingly to see one of my country women (Mrs. Stephens [*sic*]) about to be baptized to the Catholic faith. I tried to convince her she was in error, but alas of no effect—Is decidedly a Catholic.[94] I cannot but think of the enjoyment of

---

[92]For an authentic discussion of early California dwellings, see Harold Kirker, *California's Architectural Frontier* (San Marino, Calif., 1960), Chapter I. He concludes that there was "an inherited Spanish prejudice against interior fires." Chimneys were introduced by Anglo settlers. George C. Yount and Thomas O. Larkin built the first in 1835.

[93]Five of the daughters of Carlos Carrillo married Americans: Josefa married William G. Dana, August 20, 1828; Encarnación, Thomas M. Robbins, in 1834; Manuela, John C. Jones, June 4, 1837, and María Antonia was survived by her husband, Lewis T. Burton. Bancroft, *California*, IV:744; Entry Nos. 153, 196, 216, Marriage Records, Santa Barbara Mission Archive-Library.

[94]Mrs. Stevens was sponsored for baptism by John C. Jones and Mrs. Alpheus B. Thompson. She was baptized by Father Narciso Durán, December 13, 1843, as Francisca Antonia Stevens (Estevans). Entry No. 1588, Presidio Baptismal Register, April 10, 1822–January 29, 1849, Transcript, Santa Barbara Mission Archive-Library. See *note* 89, *ante.*

those in my "native land" this day, as they come around the sacramental board—a day which is never forgotten by me, though far away.

5. Yesterday dined at Mrs. Robbins.[95] Today, have returned most of my calls. Find very pleasant society and the place decidedly preferable to any I have visited on the Coast.[96]

6. Were I to attempt to give a description of St. Barbara, it would be but a poor one. Imagine to yourself a town built wholly of adobies (that is blocks of sunburnt clay) laid in the same manner as bricks. Not one wooden or stone building. No! not as much as a stone wall to be seen. Not having any rain for months and even years, the houses, fences, and ground are of one color; not a blade of grass to be seen. When walking, clouds of dust arise, which is very annoying.

7. By the recent death of Mrs. Thompson's sister, many hearts are made sad. Had it not occurred, parties were to be given on our arrival. Man appoints but God disappoints. Instead of a house of feasting, we came to a house of mourning which Solomon says "Is far better." They may think I do not enjoy myself, but I assure them I pass my time pleasantly.

8. Last evening called on Mrs. T[hompson's] father and mother, Don Carlos and lady.[97] About as large a couple as I ever saw—and rather pretty. They have six daughters, five of

---

[95]Thomas M. Robbins, a native of Massachusetts, sailed along the coast 1823–1839. In 1830, he settled at Santa Barbara, opened a store, and maintained a vessel. In 1834, he married Encarnación Carrillo. He died in 1857, while his widow survived until 1876. Bancroft, *California*, V:697.

[96]Again, Sir George Simpson agrees with Mrs. Nye's views. In his *Narrative of a Journey Round the World*, I:379, he declared: "Santa Barbara, in most respects, being to Monterey what the parlor is to the kitchen."

[97]Carlos Antonio de Jesús Carrillo was born in Santa Barbara in 1783. After a youthful career in the military service, he entered politics. The holder of several large land grants, he was an exceedingly prosperous man, ranking next to José de la Guerra y Noriega, as one of the richest men in Alta California. His wife was Josefa Castro. He "was large and of magnificent presence; distinguished for his courteous and gentlemanly manners." He died in 1852, his widow the next year. Bancroft, *California*, II:743–44.

whom married Americans, and live close by each other.[98] Heretofore, I should think they were very lively, even now, they crack some pretty good jokes. The Spanish ladies wear no bonnets, whatever distance they may be going. They wear a sirapar [*serape*] (or mantle) over their heads. Smoking paper cigars is very fashionable. Imagine to yourself a dozen ladies and gentlemen sitting around the room smoking and talking Spanish, while I cannot understand a word that is said, only as Gorham interprets for me; he speaks excellent Spanish, the Hawaiian language likewise.

9. This morning early, Gorham went off to the ship to have her hauled in nearer, to take the horses which were already on the beach. I could not imagine how they were to be got on board, but I soon ascertained. A rope is attached to them and made fast to the boat, while they swim along at their leisure. On their arrival to the ship, instead of being drawn up in a chair, the poor creatures are hoisted up with a block and tackle, not without some kicking as one would suppose. However, I am not to see the fun, as the sailors call it; shall not go on board until the ship is ready for the sea.

10. This afternoon rode out to the mission, about a mile from town, which is rather a pretty place. Visited the Church; was shown all the different dresses [vestments] of the Priest. On entering was requested to take my bonnet off, to which I complied, left it with a servant outside. Called on the Priest,[99] who inquired of Mrs. S[tevens] what my religion was. When told, said no more, but treated us with some very

---

[98]Bancroft in his "Pioneer Index" does not list a sixth daughter. *Ibid.* However, John Wilson, a Scotsman, who was a shipmaster and trader, settled in California in 1826. He married Ramona Carrillo de Pacheco, the widow of Romualdo Pacheco (died 1831), November 9, 1835 (?). Entry No. 211, Marriage Records, Santa Barbara Mission Archive-Library; Bancroft, *California,* IV:764; V:777.

[99]At this time, the fall of 1843, there were four Franciscans in residence at Mission Santa Barbara: Antonio Jimeno, Narciso Durán, Francisco Sánchez, and José María de Jésus González Rúbio. Maynard Geiger, O.F.M., *Mission Santa Barbara, 1782–1965* (Santa Barbara, 1965), p. 249.

fine grapes. We next visited the garden, which is very spacious. It was said the Bishop had just entered. However, we did not go over half the ground, consequently did not see him; and glad was I for I would rather be excused from falling on my knees and kissing the ring on his finger, as is the custom.[100]

11. Did not think of sailing today, but by appearances, it is supposed a storm is gathering. If so, the ship would be obliged to go out to sea. Therefore, it is thought best to go for good. Many ladies and gentleman accompanied us to the shore, where we bade each other farewell! Every moment the surf was increasing. For a moment I hesitated. The seas to me look terrific. The only way to get the boat off between the rising billows, which was done so successfully, not a spray of water came upon us. Soon we were on board the ship, where I feel quite at home again. Have been gone two weeks from her.

---

[100]On April 27, 1840, Pope Gregory XVI created the Diocese of Both Californias and appointed Francisco García Diego y Moreno as the first bishop. Born at Lagos, Jalisco, Mexico, September 17, 1785, he entered the Franciscan order and was ordained a priest on November 13, 1808. After a number of important Franciscan positions in Mexico, he came to California in 1832, later returning to Mexico. It was there the he learned of his episcopal appointment. Consecrated in the basilica of Our Lady of Guadalupe, October 4, 1840, he reached his diocese on December 10, 1841, landing at San Diego. He sailed to Santa Barbara, arriving January 11, 1842. He died on April 30, 1846, having suffered a lingering and painful illness, and was buried in Mission Santa Barbara. Maynard Geiger, O.F.M., *Franciscan Missionaries in Hispanic California, 1769–1848: A Biographical Dictionary* (San Marino, Calif., 1969), pp. 98–103. Francis J. Weber was authored a biography entitled, *Francisco García Diego, California's Transition Bishop* (Los Angeles, 1971). Mission Santa Barbara was the episcopal residence at this time. The bishop's ring, a diamond, was the gift of the Pope at his consecration. Simpson, *Narrative of a Journey Round the World*, I:388–389.

Chapter V

Return to Hawaii

November 12, 1843. Yesterday at twelve A.M. loosed the sails—got under weigh with a fine breeze; this morning out of sight of land, fast wending our way towards the Isl[and] of Oahu.

16. These last three days have kept my room, indeed, the most of the time my bed! Living on shore but a short time, has quite taken me off my sea legs, and caused me to go through the ordeal of sea-sickness, which I so much detest.

17. Have taken the trade winds, so the ship sails along very quietly; it is quite amusing to go on the deck; it looks rather comical to see a farm yard on board ship. Rather than think it a joke, I will enumerate them. First there is thirty horses, which we take to the Isl[ands] to sell. Then for livestock, one bullock, a cow (and calf) which gives first rate milk—four sheep—six pigs—three dozen fowls—corn and hay to supply them. By the way, three dogs running about. Now reader do not say I have varied much from the truth in saying the ship resembled a farm yard.

19. Yesterday being the Sabbath, I did not take much exercise, no more than to read, sing, and sleep a little, today I have been very busy sewing, while Gorham has been taking my music box to pieces, and made it to play as well as ever—was surprised to find it in existence.

22. Fair winds, but rather light, and the ship being so deeply loaded, does not sail so fast [as] when making the passage to Oregon; however, having good company, the time does not hang heavily; for the passengers, Capt. Grimes—

Mr. Reynolds,[1] with two Spanish boys, going to the Isl[ands] to school.[2]

24. Alas for my poor bird! which I found dead this morning, owing to the carelessness of the steward giving it bread with grease on it. To be sure, I shall not miss its singing, for it was too young to learn the notes, but then it was very lively—besides the idea, it came from Oregon!

26. Ever since I have been an inmate of the ship, I have been begging the indulgence of having a good sea chest made. Finally I heard the Capt. giving the dimensions to the carpenter, who immediately set about it, and made me a nice chest, that will last all my going to sea, even if I go round Cape Horn several times more. What a thought!! I don't wish to go round but once more, and that only to get my "native land."

28. This morning while walking on the deck, I tried to ascertain the many different nations there were on board, found there were eight, all black (with the exception of one) belonging to the forecastle.[3] I could hardly believe it possible, there has been such harmony through the voyage.

29. I have just been looking on the chart—am astonished! to find the distance we have made the last three days. In a few hours shall probably be in sight of land. Those only who have been to sea can realize the joyful sensation one feels, when about to make their place of destination.

30. Went on deck this morning and sure enough the Isl[and] was in full view. The Kanackers [Kanakas] were

---

[1]This was Stephen A. Reynolds, though it is surprising since his unpleasantness about Mrs. Nye's singing class in the Charity School was no doubt still a vivid memory. Paty's Harbormaster Records lists the names of "S.A. Reynolds and Felipe Gomez, a school boy." No mention if made of a second boy.

[2]Some Mexican families in California sent their sons either to the Islands for education, or in some instances, to Chile, Mexico, or the American east coast. See Chapter II, *note* 74, *ante*.

[3]This is an error since some of the crew were Hawaiians, and Polynesians are not considered members of the black race.

singing and dancing at the sight of their native land.[4] I almost envied them. Ah! thought I, if the native feel such joy at the sight of home, what can be the feelings of the civilized! At 12 P.M. came to anchor, the wind not being favorable to come inside the harbor. We sailed from this Isl[and] April 19th, arrived Nov. 30th, having a pleasant voyage of seven months and eleven days. During the time, visited Columbia River, Oregon, from thence to Monterey, Santa Cruz, St. Francisco, St. Barbara, which was the last place, nineteen days passage. Had not been in the harbor long when Mr. Brewer came off and invited us to stop at his house, which I assure you seems to me almost like getting to my own dear home again. And now, that I am on land once more, I find my time wholly occupied. I shall not be surprised if my journal is treated with entire neglect.

---

[4]The crew consisted of Hawaiians. Anthropologically, Hawaiians are Polynesians.

Epilogue

Although Mrs. Nye's journal ends at this point, more of her interesting story may be gleaned from other papers in the Nye Collection, consisting of sixty items, which was presented to the Hawaii State Archives in December 1928, by a granddaughter, Lydia Bradford Parker of Plymouth, Massachusetts. Foremost in interest among these are several letters. The first written from Honolulu under the date of February 27, 1844:

My Dear Mother

Hearing a vessel was to sail for Mazatlan, I haste to embrace the opportunity of writing you but with sensations far different from any I ever experienced. Yes! it is with a parent's feelings I now address you. On the 30th of January I became the mother of a beautiful daughter, with black hair—black eyes—fair complexion, and in every way a good and quiet child—I may as well have said handsome but I leave that for you to decide—suffice it to say, she is an increasing comfort to us. By this time you are ready to say, why not tell me how *you* do? Considering the short time which has elapsed since my confinement (which was rather severe) I feel very well. I did not leave my room for three weeks—but this last week I have gained very fast—have rode several times—and even walked a short distance. It is a beautiful climate for the sick—having the windows and doors open the year round, one does not lose the air, consequently can get up much sooner *here* than in a land of snow and ice, which generally follows the month of Jan[uary]. Me thinks I hear you ask, where is your husband all the while. Do you think he left me at such a moment? O No! but for his kindness and attention, I could not seemingly have borne my sickness—But the hand of the Lord was upon me, he heard, & answered my prayers, and gave me strength, equal to my day—

While lying in bed with my infant besides me, my feelings would often overpower me, at the thought of my Mother! Could I but have had my *Mother* to come in and look upon me and clasp the little one—and congratulate me upon the birth of my first born—but rest assured dear Mother! I had every possible comfort and attention from my husband and friends. Mrs. B[rewer] and Mrs. More [Moore] were ever ready to wait on me while my nurse is very good. But I have something yet to say, which may disturb your feelings for the moment, but upon reflection, I hope it will meet your approbation. If nothing prevents, we commence housekeeping on the coming week. Boarding here is very expensive, and now that we have a family we think it better to keep house while we stop here; which I know not how long it will be, though it is hard to say it will exceed three years as business is now—but I shall *never cease* to talk, and think of *home* & its endearments. We have a neat little cottage about one mile or two from the town, which is much more healthy. During my sickness, Gorham has been making some alterations for my comfort. Yesterday I rode out to it, and to my surprise, found it all furnished, carpets down, everything ready, waiting only for me to be *well*, which I hope soon to be. My babe is very quiet. In the enclosed you will find a lock of her hair. Mrs. Martha Paty buried a dear child last week at the age of ten months.[1] The rest of the Plymouth people are well. Eli [Grimes] is on the Coast. Last Sunday Capt. Couch from Newburyport[2] arrived bringing no letters for me, which greatly distressed me, since then I have learned she was not advertised. It is now a year since he left *here*, by him I sent my Journal of my passage out. I have not heard from home since last March, but from other sources I have learned of several vessels that are on there way out, by them I hope to hear. By Capt. Rogers we sent a roll of satin & silk, two aprons to Mrs. Shaw to be delivered to you.[3] I have several sheets all written while on the Coast, which I have had no chance to send.

---

[1]Undoubtedly, the infant was the same child whose birth Mrs. Nye recorded on May 30, 1843. See Chapter II, *note* 110, *ante*.

[2]The American brig *Chenamus*, Captain Couch from Newburyport, arrived in Honolulu on February 23. It sailed for the Columbia River with a sizeable complement of passengers on April 2. *The Friend*, 2 (March 2, 1844), 32; (April 4, 1844), 44.

Remember my love to all my friends and do write often. Please give one of these little locks of hair to little Jane for Lydia A. looks just as she did when a week old. So I bid you goodbye for this time and hope this will find you in health is the wish of your Afft. Daughter

L. R. Nye

Accompanying this letter to Mrs. Drew in New England was another written by Captain Nye.

Dear Mother

I join with Lydia in sending you a few lines to let you know our situation, health, & whereabouts. We are residing at the house of Mr. C[harles] Brewers at present with our little family which now numbers three & the greater praise due to the giver of all good gifts is, Lydia has quite recovered from a very severe confinement & has presented me with a beautiful Daughter—we call it Lydia Atwood Nye—I think you would like to see it as it is called the *Belle* of Honolulu of all the Daughters this year—as it is Leap Year all are daughters—she is beautiful and quiet—her ma is now setting feeding her—hair and Eyes black as a crow.

Thanks to the Ruler of All things I was able to be with Lydia in all her Confinement. In fact I have never been from her since we first met at this place. I have a little cottage about a mile from the City where we think of going to House Keeping about the 2nd of next month as it is quite Expensive boarding at the price asked here today. $2 per day or $60 per month. We can live much cheaper and comfortable by ourselves what time we stay. My stay here will be about 2 months more. My ship is here. I weight [wait] for Mr. Thompson & Jones from Mazatlan,[4] then make a voyage to Cali-

[3]The *William and Elisha*, Captain Rogers, entered Honolulu October 21, 1842, and sailed on January 2, 1843, on a whaling expedition. Already six months at sea, the ship returned on October 22 and sailed for New York on December 10, 1843. Paty's Harbormaster Records; *The Friend*, 1 (Dec. 2, 1843), 75; 2 (Jan. 1, 1844), 8.

[4]They arrived on the bark *Concepción*, Captain Rossum, April 22, after a passage of twenty-five days. Not long after leaving Honolulu, on May 25 it returned, leaking so badly it had to be condemned. *The Friend*, 2 (May 1, 1844), 52; *The Polynesian*, new series, 1 (June 1, 1844), 2.

fornia & back to this place. The vessel that takes this letter the mail will close at 3 P.M.[5] It is now 2-30 P.M. Must conclude by sending love to all the family & best love to you.

I remain Your Affectionate Son,

Gorham H. Nye

A guest list in Mrs. Nye's handwriting enumerates the names of 130 callers who came to extend their good wishes "when we commenced housekeeping" in Nuuanu Valley. Included among these are the names of twenty-four sea captains, the consular representatives, missionaries, and most of the other foreign residents—or as William Paty would have summed it up, "all the respectable residents of Honolulu."[6]

Another item in the Nye Collection is a Baptismal Certificate:

> This certifies that Lydia Atwood Nye,[7] daughter of Capt. G. H. and Mrs. L. R. Nye, was baptized by me in the Seamen's Chapel, Honolulu, H.I. on the 5th day of May 1844. She was at that time three months and six days old.
>
> Samuel C. Damon,
> Pastor, Oahu Bethel Chapel

Mrs. Nye and Lydia, her baby daughter, did not accompany the captain on his next voyage to the Coast. Sailing on May 28 or 29, 1844, the *Fama* cleared Honolulu for California. The passengers included: "J. C. Jones, Esq.; Mr. Jos. Thompson; Captain E[liab] Grimes; Mr. Dedman [Joel P. Dedmond]; and Mrs. John Paty, with two children."[8] The vessel returned from Santa Barbara, after a voyage of twenty-one days, to the Islands, April 10, 1845, with a cargo of "hides, horses, lumber, etc."[9]

[5]Possibly the schooner *Ho'oikaika* which sailed for Mazatlán on February 28. *The Friend*, 2 (March 2, 1844), 32.

[6]See Appendix I for the list of Mrs. Nye's visitors.

[7]Later she took the name Gorham in place of Atwood, since Atwood is marked out and Gorham written above it in pencil.

[8]*The Friend*, 2 (June 1, 1844), 60. Paty's Harbormaster Records give the sailing date as May 29.

[9]*The Friend*, 3 (April 15, 1844), 61.

When Captain Nye sailed from Honolulu on his next voyage, May 6, 1845, Mrs. Nye and child were on board, along with two other passengers, Mr. Nadal and Mr. Ellsworth.[10] However, it would prove her last voyage with her husband.

The Larkin Papers reveals some interesting correspondence between John C. Jones, Jr., in Santa Barbara and Thomas Oliver Larkin in Monterey in respect to this last voyage of the *Fama*. Under date of June 2, 1845, Jones wrote:

> I was sorry to hear of the arrival of the *Fama*. I had hopes she would have succeeded in getting a freight at the Islands for the United States. There will be but little or nothing done this year in the way of hides and tallow, especially on this part of the Coast. From this to San Diego, there will be no cattle killed excepting such as are killed by hunger.[11]

Thus it becomes apparent that the drouth Mrs. Nye mentioned in her journal in 1843, as having deprived Monterey and Santa Barbara of rain for more than two years, was continuing.

It seems to have persisted unbroken until the fall of 1845, for Jones writes again, November 3, 1845:

> We have had almost a flood of rain in this part of the country and what is remarkable not strong winds; the grass is springing up beautifully and the country all around is covered with green.[12]

Evidently panicked by the prospect of the imminence of war between the United States and Mexico, Jones secured passage to the States for himself and family on the *Admittance*, which sailed from San Diego, January 26, 1846, with a cargo of "33,500 hides."[13] Mrs. James Stevens and her captain-husband, Mrs. Nye's friend in Santa Barbara, were also passengers homeward bound.[14]

Other letters to Larkin from Alpheus B. Thompson reveal the fate of the *Fama*. The first of these, from Santa Barbara, was dated March 6, 1846:

---

[10] *Ibid.*, 3 (May 16, 1844), 76; *The Polynesian*, new series, 1 (May 10, 1845), 209. The departure date in the latter is given as May 5.

[11] Hammond, ed., *Larkin Papers*, III:221.

[12] *Ibid.*, IV:85.

[13] Letter dated January 24, 1846. *Ibid.*, p. 181.

[14] The vessel sailed for Boston on January 26 from San Diego. *Ibid.*, p. 185; Ogden, "Trading Vessels on the California Coast," pp. 1050–1052.

> The Am Ship Fama was wrecked near this place on the 26th of last Month. The Cargo will probably all be saved or nearly all, a part in a damaged state.
>
> The Goods on Freight I believe have all been landed. The Wreck, and Cargo belonging to the Owners of the Fama will be sold for the benefit of whom it shall or may concern. Please inform me in your official capacity [American consul] with respect to the Goods on freight, whether they can be delivered to the Shippers or Consignees with the expense of landing, Cartage Storage 7c charged, or whether they must be abandoned or sold.[15]

From Thompson's second letter, March 20, 1846, also from Santa Barbara, further details are supplied:

> The Cargo of the Fama is all on Shore and much will be saved from the Wreck. I shall have the Crew to pay here which will annoy me some, but will be able to get through without a great deal of trouble.
>
> The Ship was underway to come inside the Kelp to receive fifty horses onboard when an order was given to remain outside until the Weather should appear better. The next day at 2 P.M. the Chain was slipped and the Ship went to sea in Company with the Sterling and at 12.30 A.M. she was on Shore at the Salt Ponds a Wreck, the Crew and all Saved, the Captain and Family not on board.[16]

Then from "Angs.," the old name for Los Angeles among foreigners on the Coast, written May 13, 1846: "Your draft in favor of Don Jose Noriega was by me accepted payable on my return to Santa Barbara, as I had scraped up all the Cash at that place that I could for payment of the Crew of my late Ship Fama."[17]

Thus Captain Nye and his family were detained on the Coast for a period of months while he took care of all the many details pertaining to the "late Ship *Fama*," her freight and cargo, even though actual war between Mexico and the United States had commenced little more than sixty days after the wreck had occurred. Indeed, it was not until October 13, 1846, on the return voyage of the *Brooklyn*, Captain Abel W. Richardson, after delivering Sam Brannan and his group of Mormon Saints to San Francisco, that we find "Captain Nye, lady, and daughter" listed as

---

[15]Hammond, ed., *Larkin Papers*, III:237.

[16]*Ibid.*, p. 262.

[17]*Ibid.*, p. 369.

passengers for Honolulu. They had taken passage at Santa Barbara on September 30.[18]

On their arrival, October 13, perhaps they may once more have occupied their Nuuanu cottage for a period of several months. In any event, *The Friend* for February 1, 1847, lists as a passenger for California sailing from Honolulu on the *Joven Guipuzcoana*, the name of "G. H. Nye, Mariner."[19]

Judging from a receipted bill in the Nye Collection for "15 weeks board and room for herself and daughter—$120," which is dated "24 May 1847" and is made out to Mrs. Nye and signed by Samuel C. Damon, it appears that the two lived in the Damon household after the captain's departure for the Coast. Many farewell notes from Honolulu friends, which are also included in the collection, indicate preparations for a return to New England; and a passenger list for the *Montreal*, Captain Justus Doane, which sailed for the United States via Hong Kong on May 25, 1847, included "Mrs. Nye and child."[20]

When the *Montreal* arrived in Hong Kong, after a forty-day passage, it took on board a cargo of teas and sailed August 7 for New York. Shortly after, Captain Doane took ill and the vessel put back into Hong Kong to await his recovery. Once again, on August 20, it headed for the Atlantic coast.[21] On reaching its destination, we lose sight of Mrs. Nye. Her later years are shrouded in darkness.

What Captain Nye found to do on the Coast remains uncertain, for further correspondence between John C. Jones and Thomas O. Larkin gives a clear picture of what had happened to the hide business. From West Newton, Massachusetts, October 8, 1848, Jones wrote:

> What do you think of the price of hides? They have been down as low as six cents but are now eight, and it will be a long time, if ever, they go above that price. More than enough cattle are now raised in this country to supply it with hides, and California salted hides are in bad repute; in Europe they will not sell at any price. The cargo of the Admittance is not yet sold—a part of the cargo of the Sterling were sold at 6 cents. That concern will not realize 50 cents on the dollar. Don't ship any hides to this country—send the gold.[22]

---

[18] *The Friend*, 4 (Oct. 15, 1846), 158.
[19] *Ibid.*, 5 (Feb. 1, 1847), 23.
[20] *Ibid.*, 5 (June 1, 1847), 87.
[21] *Ibid.*, 6 (Feb. 1, 1848), 16.
[22] Hammond, ed., *Larkin Papers*, VIII:6.

Although Jones states elsewhere in this letter, "I hear nothing from Mr. Thompson nor do I know what he is doing", it seems evident from a brief letter of Thompson's addressed to Talbot H. Green, one of Larkin's business associates, that he may have entered the lumber business on a larger scale, for under date of October 4, 1847, at San Francisco, he wrote: "You will please send me two mills-saw to Mr. William H. Davis to this place by the first opportunity."[23] If this assumption is correct, it may be that Captain Nye was associated with him, since it will be recalled that Mrs. Nye mentioned in her journal during her first visit to the Coast that the two were co-owners of a mill at Sonoma and that Thompson depended on the captain's good judgment to aid him in making decisions concerning it.

The gold rush provided Captain Nye a splendid opportunity for financial advancement. Speculative land fever swept the San Francisco Bay area. Formerly worthless land rapidly became priceless. Population growth demanded buildings. Building materials commanded a high premium. Like Larkin and some of the more experienced old California hands, Nye made considerable money in land and lumbering.

At the height of the stampede to San Francisco, the golden door to the mines, Nye took passage on the *Connecticut*, Captain David P. Penhallow, for Honolulu. Departing San Francisco on September 2, 1849, fifteen days later, he landed at Honolulu.[24] What brought him back to the Islands is unclear, but one surmise would be business.

In a letter written to Mrs. Nye in Plymouth by Julia M. Damon from Honolulu, dated November 27, 1849, one gleans some of the captain's motives and plans.

> My dear Mrs. Nye—
>
> Your kind letters of January 1st & March 6th have but just been received & I hasten to reply, as you say you do not often hear from these parts. Mr. D[amon] has written to you once or twice & I have also, but you may not have received the letters.

[23] *Ibid.*, VII:7.

[24] *The Friend*, 7 (Oct. 1, 1849), 56.

Your husband took tea with us a few evenings since, in good health & spirits—he says he hears often from you & told us how delighted he was with Lydia's daguerreotype which you sent him. He has now been in Honolulu nearly two months—has a pleasant house near by ours, & we frequently see him, indeed, he says he visits no where else, & I think he is quite "a stayer at home," for I seldom pass his door, but I see him "in his easy chair" with a book in his hand. I sent him your letters & the papers to read, & in return he sent me some of the finest oranges I ever saw here. It has been his intention to visit the States, & a few months since, he got as far as Mazatlan, on his way, but something happened to prevent. Still he does not give up the idea, but says he may be at home in six months. If reports are true any reasonable man would be satisfied with the fortune he has made. In his land speculations he has been particularly fortunate & I should judge from what he said fifty thousand [dollars] was a low estimate of his property (though of course I do not know); he intends in a few weeks to return to California to close up his business & then he says "go home for good." I sincerely hope he will, for this separation of families I do not believe in. Mr. Damon left us *four* months last summer (for a trip to Oregon & California) & I made up my mind then, that if he went again I would go with him.[25]

I must tell you something of your old friends & of the changes that have taken place since you left, tho' I suppose Mrs. Wm. Paty has told you everything before this.[26] There is hardly a lady in the place who was here when you left, but a number of new ones—Mr. Marshall's new wife & sister Mrs. Lee[27]—Mrs. Dr. Lathrop, Mrs.

---

[25]The diary of his trip was published in six installments in *The Friend,* 7 (Sept. 1, 1849–Dec. 20, 1849). He sailed April 17, 1848, and returned in August.

[26]See Chapter II, *note* 6, *ante*, for William Paty.

[27]James F. B. Marshall's first wife, Eunice H. Marshall, from Charlestown, Massachusetts, died July 28, 1846. Their infant son, Thomas Hooper Marshall, born August 29, 1844, preceded his mother in death, July 10, 1845. Marshall, as Peruvian consul, sailed on the *Brutus*, Captain Adams, for New York, November 8, 1847, taking both bodies with him for reburial in Massachusetts. While in the East, he married Martha A. T. Johnson at Charlestown, October 4, 1848. He returned with his bride on the *Leland*, from Boston, Captain Eldridge, after a 144-day voyage to Honolulu, March 12, 1849. *The Friend,* 3 (July 16, 1845), 109; 5 (Nov. 18, 1847), 64; 7 (Jan. 1, 1849), 7; 7 (April 2, 1849), 32.

William L. Lee, formerly of Sandy Hill, New York, married Catherine E. Newton, Albany, New York, on the *Leland*, March 11, 1849. Reverend Samuel C. Damon performed the marriage rite. *Ibid.*, 7 (April 2, 1849), 32.

Bates, Mrs. Harris[28]—& many others—Mrs. Dr. Wood's sister was married a few weeks since to Dr. Hoffman & Miss Tewkesbury to a Mr. Gilmore of Kauai[29]—It is reported that young Bishop is soon to be married to Bernice, one of the young chiefs![30] What think you of that! It is not more surprising to us that a thousand events which are daily occurring around us. You know Honolulu is always a great place for excitement, but it has been far more so than ever, since the *gold* discovery—our population is constantly changing, vessels are daily arriving from California with many passengers & Honolulu bids fair to become quite a City—only three or four years since your husband did most of the business of California! What a change!

Soon after you left—Mr. Dudoit's family (perhaps you know) removed to Kauai where they have resided ever since.[31] A few weeks since their little Julia Ann was drowned in Wailula river. She was bathing with little Alice Brown & her mother sat on the bank watching them, when suddenly the current took them down the stream, they were taken up by the natives almost instantly, but with all the means they could use they could not restore the sweet child to life.[32] Mrs. Penhallow has also lost a little daughter (eighteen months old) the past summer.[33] Mrs. Hooper lost her infant on her

[28]It may be that these ladies were the wives of George A. Lothrop, M.D., A. B. Bates, attorney at law, and C. C. Harris, destined to become Hawaii's chief justice. *The Friend*, new series, 2 (Nov. 1, 1853), 77; 30 (Aug. 1, 1881), 69; *The Polynesian*, new series, 5 (Jan. 27, 1849), 145. The latter could have been the Mrs. Harris who arrived from San Francisco with two children on the *Mary*, Captain Parker, August 30, 1849. *The Friend*, 7 (Sept. 1, 1849), 48.

[29]Maria Louise Morse married Dr. Edward Hoffman in Honolulu, November 1, 1849, Reverend Samuel C. Damon presiding. She came to Oahu on the *Montreal*, Captain Doane, May 3, 1847, the same vessel Mrs. Nye sailed home on. *Ibid.*, 5 (May 15, 1847), 79; 7 (Nov. 1, 1849), 72.

Ellen B. Tewkesbury (sometimes spelled Tewksbury) of Charleston, Massachusetts, arrived in Honolulu, March 21, 1846, on the *Boston*, Captain Knox, after a 129-day voyage. She married George Gilmore of Koloa, Kauai, November 15, 1849, Reverend Damon performing the nuptial. *Ibid.*, 4 (April 1, 1846), 55; 7 (Nov. 15, 1849), 77. It is possible she made a round trip voyage to Boston, for a "Miss Tewksbury" is listed as a passenger on the outbound *Angola*, Captain Varney, for Boston, October 3, 1846. *Ibid.*, 4 (Oct. 15, 1846), 158–159.

[30]Charles R. Bishop married Bernice Pauahi, June 4, 1850, Reverend Richard Armstrong presiding. *Ibid.*, 8 (July 1, 1850), 56.

[31]For Jules Dudoit, see Chapter II, *note* 30, *ante*.

[32]The tragedy occurred on July 22. Julia Ann was Dudoit's eldest daughter. *Ibid.*, 7 (Oct. 15, 1849), 64.

[33]Mary Ann, daughter of Captain David P. Penhollow and his wife, Mary F. Penhollow, died on August 21, 1849, at eighteen months. *Ibid.*, 7 (Sept. 1, 1849), 48.

passage to California; she has returned to H[awaii] to spend the winter.[34] Mrs. Thompson now lives in the house opposite to ours, her husband having bought it of Mr. Marshall.[35] Of Mrs. Grimes you probably know more than I do, as she has gone home.[36] Our neighbor Mrs. Ladd, remains almost as precisely as you left her.[37] Her husband is in Cal & doing *very well* as also Mr. Hooper & Mr. Brinsmade.[38] She sends love, as would others if they knew I was writing. I hope to see you some day, either home, or in America!

Sister Margarette sends *much* love—Mr. D[amon] also—Sammy sends love to Lydia. If you think of it, give my love to Mrs. Paty—but by *no means* show this *hasty* letter to *anyone*, I must write *hurriedly* or not *at all.* Give my love to your good mother & Lydia & write again soon, you will get some sort of an answer—With much "aloha"

Yours truly,
Julia M. Damon

As the combined result of uncertainty regarding California land titles following statehood, compounded by squatters who could not be legally evicted until the former had been settled in the courts, and the abatement of the gold fever, the great California land speculation bubble burst before Captain Nye got his affairs in order, as Mrs. Damon says he expected to do early in 1850. Without doubt, he took a tremendous financial loss. Land values in San Francisco dropped from seventeen million dollars in 1850–1851 to eleven million the year following. General confidence on the part

[34]Mrs. William Hooper made a number of round trips to San Francisco where her husband had business interest.

[35]Probably Mrs. Frederick W. Thompson whose husband was an auctioneer. The dwelling was purchased from J. F. B. Marshall. Richard Greer, "Honolulu in 1847," *The Hawaiian Journal of History*, IV (1970), 63, 69.

[36]Presumably the widow of Eliab Grimes.

[37]Mrs. Abigail Ladd, wife of William Ladd, a native of Concord, New Hampshire, resided on Nuuanu Road. She died, age seventy-three, January 19, 1863. *The Friend*, new series, 12 (Feb. 2, 1863), 16.

[38]William Hooper and Peter A. Brinsmade were in partnership with William Ladd. They had a "commission merchant" business in San Francisco, although Honolulu based. *Bogardus' Business Director for San Francisco* . . . (San Francisco, 1850), p. 3. See also Chapter II, *note* 10, *ante*.

of the public, due to the heavy losses incurred, was not restored until the early 1860s.

In his "Pioneer Index," Hubert H. Bancroft notes Captain Nye "is said to have made and lost a fortune in San Francisco, and to have gone east in 1853."[39] If that is true, then Nye left early in that year for Plymouth for on July 5, 1853, he wrote a plaintive and poignant letter to his friend William Heath Davis. That letter described his miserable existence in Plymouth and his contempt for his wife's family and relatives.

My dear William

I wish I could been with you on the fourth. There woul[d] been more to see there than here for here there was nothing but a few Boys firing crackers. All the men were to Boston to see the great fireworks; some of the white niggers out to hear them Preach & pray to the Black men. Nothing left here but a lot of gossiping old maids. If the town had caught fire I should had a fine time in seeing the petticoats flying in the blaze and smoke.

You have an old relation yet alive, one of your grandfather's sisters. She wants to hear from one of the family before she leaves this world. All your Aunts were named for your grandfather's sisters. She wants when I see you again to give you her best love and tell you to write her a line.

I am here and want to get out of this hole. It is so lonesome that at times hardly know whether I am dead or alive. I have got my wife home and more thanks to My God for so great relief and blessing. I call it a relief for it has been a heavy burden to me the last part of my life. It has allmost [*sic*] drove me out of this world two or three times. I think now that a new plan will be best take[n]—a fair start in the world alone where I can earn another dollar never to place it where it will be shut up from me in some Bank in Boston in some others name so that I am as bad as a beger [*sic*]. It[s] worse—a Beger [*sic*] with money I cannot move out of the place for want of means. There is no business here. Day work I cannot do at 75 cts for day [or] keep ship for $15 pr month. It would take me a long time to earn enough to git [*sic*] out to California. Help me out. There is no

[39] Bancroft, *California*, IV: 756.

one here. I am a stranger. No one knows me or I know no one. They are half ant men.

If you could accommodate me to git [*sic*] out I will repay you with the greatest pleasure as I begin the world a fresh start. It will begin with care, prudence, and Temperance. My frolicking [*sic*] days are over. My health now is first rate. I think that my not taking any spirits has been the reason and shall take no more.

There is no news here. I would send you the paper but there is nothing in it but advertisements, them you don't want it. The winter is coming on by and by that will give me some hard times—cramp rheumatism—everything cold weather is master of for this is a very cold place. There is none colder. I am in hopes through the blessing of God that providence will help be out of this by the last of October.

Four or Five hundred dollars is nothing to you. There has been times that it was nothing to me. I am too proud to ask for a gift, a loan only. I can keep your Ware house, see to any of your grain business. Alone by myself soon pay up.

William be shure [*sic*] and answer this as soon as you receive it as after the time of first of Nov I may be gone from here and don't want Money or Letters that are answers to any of mine to fall in the hands of any of the family here in Plymouth. The Letters they would tell me of but the Money never. My Best Regards to all your family.

Wishing you health & prosperity,

Yours,

Excuse haste Gorham H. N.[40]

This letter makes it clear that Captain Nye was dead broke. How he was making ends meet remains unknown. Nor is there any evidence that Davis came through with a loan to make it possible for Nye's longed-for return to California. When the opportunity came, however, he left his wife and daughter forever, for he did return, whether by the generosity of Davis or some other party. On his return to California—date unknown—he is reported living "in

[40]Gorham H. Nye to William Heath Davis, July 5, 1853, *William Heath Davis Collection*, Box 171, California State Library, Sacramento.

and about Santa Cruz County" as detailed in the newspaper account which follows. In 1865 his former Chinese steward, hearing of Nye's "straightened circumstances," made it possible for him to journey to the Islands for a last sojourn there.

A news story from the Calistoga *Tribune*, April 6, 1871, copied in Sacramento *Union*, July 8, and in *The Hawaiian Gazette* the following September 13th noted:

> On the Fourth of April, Capt. Gorham H. Nye paid Calistoga a visit for the first time in many years. Captain Nye may be called the Pioneer of pioneers, having arrived at Monterey in 1824 as master of a whaleship from Nantucket. From that time to 1831 he made three successive voyages to California from Plymouth, Mass., the last time coming in his own vessel and entering into the hide and tallow trade. He has never seen home since, having made Honolulu his depot, from whence he shipped his trade 'around Cape Horn'. For many years past, the Captain has resided in and about Santa Cruz County, among the old Californians—friends of his young days—most of whom, however, he has outlived. When running his vessel to the Islands, he had a Chinese steward, who remained on Hawaii when the Captain retired from the business, and in a few years became the wealthy proprietor of a sugar plantation. Some six years ago, hearing that his old Captain was in straightened circumstances, he requested Captain John Paty, who was at that time master of a Honolulu packet, to offer him a home on Hawaii, as long as he should wish, and advanced money for his passage. Captain Nye accepted the offer, and proceeded to the Islands, where he remained about two years, and then returned to his old California friends. Captain Nye is in his 90th year, and bears his age remarkably well.

Although the report exaggerates Nye's age and misstates a few facts, it points to another incomplete episode in the captain's life, namely, his farewell sojourn in the Islands. This much is known. He sailed to Honolulu on September 7, 1865, from San Francisco on the *Whistler* with his longtime friend Captain John Paty, commanding, who was accompanied by his wife, Mary Ann, a lady who holds the record for sailing with her husband on numerous voyages.[41] The ship reached Oahu, September 24, after a routine passage. If the Calistoga *Tribune's* account is accurate, Nye's passage was paid by his former Chinese steward. This generous gesture would reinforce the notion that the old mariner was in dire straits.

As to who was host to Nye during his three years and three months' residence in the Islands, one can deduce from existing evidence that it was a longtime Chinese resident, Aiko (Lum Jo in Chinese), also variously referred to as Ahco and Aicho.

The case for Aiko is found in a 1875 article which states: "In 1841 thatched buildings were put up in Iole, Kohala, by the Governor [Kuahihi of Hawaii], in pursuance with Aiko, a Chinaman, who had previously followed the sea in some capacity under Capt. Brewer. Aiko himself followed immediately and put up his [sugar] mill. . . ."[42] Since Captain Nye worked for Brewer, it may well be that Aiko served with him as a steward during some of his voyages before settling down on the big island, Hawaii, to engage in the early phases of sugar cane production and milling.

William Heath Davis, early business pioneer in what was then Yerba Buena, later San Francisco, offers a compelling confirmation of Aiko as Nye's steward. He records in his memoirs this pointed observation:

> Several years anterior to 1838 there was a Chinaman on board the brig *Bolivar Liberator*, Captain Nye, as a servant in the cabin, and he remained on the coast during the stay of the vessel. Probably this man of the Celestial empire was the first that visited California until the commencement of 1848.[43]

The actual year of the voyage Davis alludes to might be 1836, for in that year Nye became captain of the *Bolivar Liberator*, a 224-ton brig, jointly owned by P. I. Farnham and Company, Salem, Alpheus B. Thompson, California, and John C. Coffin, Jr., Honolulu. The ship sailed from Oahu on March 26 and reached Mon-

---

[41] *The Friend*, new series, 14 (Oct. 2, 1865), 80.

[42] Thomas G. Thrum, "Notes on the History of the Sugar Industry of the Hawaiian Islands," *Hawaiian Almanac and Annual for 1875* (Honolulu, 1875), 36.

[43] Davis, *Seventy-Five Years*, p. 261.

terey on April 21. The cargo had merchandise valued at $30,000. In the ensuing months, the brig worked the coast between San Francisco and San Pedro, departing for its home port on October 18 with a cargo of cattle, hides, horses, and furs. It came to safe anchor at Oahu on November 6.[44]

Nye returned the following year, again in command of the same brig for a comparable voyage commencing February 11 with return to Honolulu on November 22. A third voyage, December 19, 1837, to December 11, 1839, followed. Interestingly, on this particular passage some "Kanakas" (Hawaiians) are enlisted as part of the crew, as was the case with all of Nye's crews.[45]

If Davis is correct in his recollections that "Several years anterior to 1838 there was a Chinaman on board the brig *Bolivar Liberator*, Captain Nye," the voyages of 1836 and 1837 qualify, mayhap also the two-year voyage, 1837–1839. It may well be that Aiko was a steward on all these trips. Indeed, there is the prospect that he might have served with Nye even earlier when Nye was master of the brig *Loriot*, 1833–1835, his first command.[46] Further, there is the likelihood that Aiko continued to serve with Nye on the *Bolivar Liberator* 1840–1843 voyage as well, the latter trip being Nye's last captaincy of the brig, one which was followed in 1843 with the command of the ill-fated brig *Fama*, 1843–1846. Mrs. Nye in her journal of the 1843 *Fama* voyage refers in one place to "my boys" helping her take care of the cabin and in another to the steward serving a picnic on shore.[47] Certainly Captain Nye would have wished his wife well attended on their sea voyage together. Would he not seek to have a reliable steward whom he knew and trusted? And would that not be Aiko?

It appears doubtful that the Chinese steward served on Nye's

---

[44]Ogden, "Trading Vessels on the California Coast," p. 720. Faxon Dean Atherton was the clerk on the brig's voyages of 1836 and 1837–1839. Unfortunately, in his diary he makes no reference to a Chinese steward as a crew member. See Nunis, ed., *Diary of Faxon Dean Atherton, passim.*

[45]Ogden, "Trading Vessels on the California Coast," pp. 766, 810–811.

[46]*Ibid.*, pp. 640, 709.

[47]Entries for May 22 and June 13, 1843. The steward and his cooking are also mentioned in entries for August 14 and September 11. See Chapters III and IV, *ante*.

last command, the *Joven Guipuzcoana* in 1847, for that Peruvian-registered bark, departing Honolulu, March 5, on arrival at San Pedro, April 8, spent five months making two round trips between that southern port and San Francisco. On anchoring at the latter, September 2, the ship disappears from view. Thus did Nye's seafaring career end, quietly and obscurely.[48]

Although its unclear precisely when Aiko forsook life at sea for land, he probably made that decision on or before Nye's last voyage on the *Fama*, 1845–1846, when it was shipwrecked near Santa Barbara, February 26, 1846.[49] When Aiko opted for shore life, he became a very successful landowner, but not without trial and tribulation. Due to increases in rent and other charges, he had to sell his first plantation and relocate near Hilo "where he carried on a plantation with success for many years, and where he now resides [in 1875]."[50]

Much is known about Aiko's life. Born in China in 1799, he appeared in the Islands sometime between 1820–1836, possibly with Charles Brewer, if the 1875 account is relied upon. It appears he settled in Waimea about 1835–1836. He married a native woman, Maria Kaahapea; they had one child, a daughter, Amelia, born in Waimea in December 1836. By 1845 he had an acre of land in the *ahupuaaa* of Kaukuau, Hilo, and gradually prospered. A telling point is that by 1846 he also owned a store, a bowling alley, chartered ships, bought, sold, and leased property, which testily to his economic diversification, enterprise, and financial resources. In 1848, he applied for a Hawaiian passport that stated he was fifty years old and described him as five feet, six inches tall. The passport made it possible for him to join the gold rush to California. Heading for San Francisco, is it not likely he renewed contact with Nye, then residing in that city?

Whatever the contact the two may have had or not in the Bay

---

[48]*Ibid.*, pp. 1076, 1117, 1334. The Calistoga *Tribune's* April 6, 1871, story on Nye, in my view, has to be discounted. The paper remarked: "When running his vessel to the Islands, he had a Chinese steward, who remained on Hawaii when the Captain retired from the business, and in a few years became the wealthy proprietor of a sugar plantation." Since Aiko was prospering so well by 1846, as detailed later in the narrative, he probably quit the sea at least prior to the *Fama's* last voyage that ended in a shipwreck near Santa Barbara.

[49]Ogden, "Trading Vessels on the California Coast," p. 1177.

[50]Thrum, "Notes on the History of the Sugar Industry of the Hawaiian Islands," p. 36.

city, Aiko returned to Hilo some time later and resumed his profitable activities. In January 1862, like his wife and child, he became a Catholic. Perhaps the more interesting piece to the puzzle is that in 1869 he sold his then twenty acres of land at Wainaku and "possibly retired from sugar growing." It was in January of that same year that Nye returned to California! As for Aiko, he lived until 1895, dying in Hilo at the venerable age of ninety-five.[51]

Again this much is known. On January 26, 1869, Nye sailed from Honolulu on the *Comet*, Captain Abbott, bound for San Francisco.[52] He would never again visit the Islands.

Bancroft completes the story by stating that Captain Nye "From 1871, lived with Charles Krug in St. Helena, [California]. He died in '78 at the age of 73."[53] Nye was actually seventy-six at the time of his death on October 31, 1878.[54]

So passed one of the last of the hide and tallow ship captains. The final chapter in the history of the California-Hawaiian trade remains to be written. When it is, the name of Captain Gorham H. Nye will find frequent mention. And Lydia Rider Nye can lay claim to having kept the only known journal of a sea captain's wife during a trading venture along the Pacific Coast in the early 1840s.

---

[51]Peggy Kai, "Chinese Settlers in the Village of Hilo before 1852," *The Hawaiian Journal of History*, VIII (1974), 56–59.

[52]*The Friend*, new series, 19 (Feb. 4, 1869), 16.

[53]Bancroft, *California*, IV: 758.

[54]San Jose *Pioneer*, Nov. 16, 1878.

Appendixes

Appendix I

Lydia Rider Nye's Guest Book Kept in Honolulu

March 1844: List of those who called on us when we commenced housekeeping. [*Note*: In the list maintained by Mrs. Nye, she rarely gives first names or initials. Interestingly, she separates the men from the women callers. In presenting her list, I have taken the liberty of doing two things: (1) supplied full names and/or initials and correct spelling where needed; and (2) provided identifications either to notes in the text or reference data where it has been possible to locate information pertaining to the person mentioned. References to the actual notes are given by chapter and note number, II:26; Prologue, P:1; Epilogue, E:1. The list is presented as recorded by Mrs. Nye.]

Captain David P. Penhallow, Harbormaster (V:33)
General William Miller, British consul in Hawaii[1]
Mr. Frank (Francis) Johnson, merchant[2]
Mr. John Dominis (II:26)
Mr. O. P. Ricker (II:16)
Rev. Samuel C. Damon (I:23)
Captain J. Porter[3]
Mr. Donfesto
Rev. Mr. Richard Armstrong (II:59)
Mr. William Paty (II:6)

[1]General Miller took up his post in Honolulu as consul general on February 3, 1844, having visited Oahu as early as 1831. He also served in that capacity for all the Pacific islands, headquartered in Honolulu. His health dictated relocation to Peru. He departed the Islands on September 9, 1859, and died October 31, 1861. Kuykendall, *Hawaiian Kingdom, 1778–1854*, p. 234; Baker, *Honolulu in 1853*, p. 25.

[2]"Register of Foreigners Residing in Honolulu," *The Friend*, 5 (Jan. 15, 1847), 10 (hereinafter cited "1847 Register").

[3]Captain F. J. Porter was senior partner in the importing and commission firm of Porter & Ogden, both Englishmen. He committed suicide August 11, 1854. *The Friend*, new series, 3 (Sept. 1, 1854), 57.

Mr. James Gleason (II:14)
Mr. Charles Brewer (II:1)
J. Chambers, master of HMS *Modeste*[4]
J. M. Hobbs, purser on the *Modeste*
Mr. Hiram Grimes (II:18)
Mr. Jones
Captain Cornelius Hoyer (II:95)
Mr. Jules [Julius Alexander] Anton, merchant[5]
Mr. Gamaliel Drew (II: 69, 106)
Captain S. H. Edwards, master American whaleship *France*[6]
Mr. Cushing[7]
Captain Gouch (E:2)
Captain Eliab Grimes (II:18)
Captain John Wilson (II:62)
Captain James G. Scott[8]
Captain John Meek (IV:64)
Captain Charles Humphries (Humphreys)[9]
Mr. William Hooper, American consul (II:10)

---

[4]H.M.S. *Modeste* arrived at Honolulu on February 22, 1844, from Mazatlán. It sailed on June 11 for the Columbia and the Pacific Northwest Coast. James Chambers was master. *The Friend*, 2 (March 2, 1844), 32; (July 1, 1844), 68.

[5]His brother Louis was long-time Danish consul in Honolulu. Baker, *Honolulu in 1853*, p. 27.

[6]The *France*, 411 tons, from Sag Harbor, arrived at Honolulu on March 4, 1844. It had been at sea for eight months and had a catch of 1,200 bbls. sperm oil. Paty's Harbormaster Records.

[7]A William Cushing reached Honolulu on the brig *Chenamus*, Captain J. H. Couch, from Newburyport on February 23, 1844. *The Friend*, 2 (March 2, 1844), 32; (March 23, 1844), 35.

[8]Scott, a native of Scotland, came to California in 1828 as a supercargo, rising steadily to become a captain in his own right. Settling down in Santa Barbara in 1830, he continued to be active in maritime affairs. In March 1844, he was in Honolulu to buy the schooner *Juanita* in partnership with Captain John Wilson. In 1845 he purchased the Mission San Luis Obispo and was grantee to the Rancho Cañada de Chorro. He died in Santa Barbara in 1851. Bancroft, *California*, V:714; Ogden, "Trading Vessels on the California Coast," p. 1124.

[9]Correct spelling is Humphreys. Charles Humphreys had been in the employ of the Hudson's Bay Company since 1833, rising from seaman to master. In 1837 he was appointed captain of the *Columbia* serving on the Pacific Northwest Coast. He sailed the vessel back to England in 1842, departing in September again for the Columbia River. In November 1844, he was transferred to the *Beaver*. In the fall of 1845 his health broke, due to stress no doubt since his mind was affected, and was invalided out of service, returning to England on the *Cowlitz*, where he arrived in 1846 and was discharged from HBC service. Rich, ed., *McLoughlin Letters*, 1839–44, V:391–392. His visit to Mrs. Nye coincided with the arrival of the *Columbia* at Oahu on February 27, through its departure for return to the Columbia River was on April 2, 1844. Paty's Harbormaster Records.

Captain [Thomas] Bailee [Baillie] ship *Modeste*[10]
Captain Upham[11]
Captain Turner[12]
Captain Brown[13]
Captain Morgan[14]
Mr. Thapt
Mr. Dedman (Joel P. Dedmond)[15]
Captain Warner[16]
Mr. William Ladd, merchant (II:10)
Captain Rossum, master Guatemalan barque *Conception* [*Concepción*][17]
Rev. Mr. Timothy Dwight Hunt[18]
Mr. Henry Dimond (II:71)
Rev. Lowell Smith (II:2)
Captain John C. Dominis (II:26)
Captain Weston (P:15)
Captain Bennett[19]

---

[10]See *note*, 4, *ante*.

[11]The New Bedford 365-ton whaleship *Euphrates*, Captain Upham, reached Honolulu April 12. At sea twenty-two months, it had amassed 450 bbls. sperm and 550 bbls. whale oil. It weighed anchor on April 16. Paty's Harbormaster Records.

[12]Master of the *Janus*, 321 tons, which arrived April 9, 1844. *Ibid.*

[13]Master of either the whaleship *Henry*, 333 tons, out of Sag Harbor, nine months at sea with a catch of 400 bbls. whale oil and 100 bbls. sperm oil, that visited Honolulu April 7–25, or the 441-ton whaler, *Hannibal*, out of New London, six months at sea, April 12–18, 1844. *Ibid.*

[14]Master of the Stonington-based whaleship *Herald*, 241 tons, which reached Oahu April 12, twenty-eight months out, which 1,250 bbls. sperm oil on board. *Ibid.* (Departure date unknown.)

[15]Dedmond, an American carpenter, may have settled in California as early as 1838. Later he made such a claim after returning from an undetermined stay in Honolulu. He returned to California on the *Fama* with Captain Nye, sailing from Honolulu at the end of May 1844 and arriving at Monterey on June 23. He became a naturalized Mexican citizen and obtained the Rancho San Juan in the Sacramento Valley. Later he worked as a surveyor for Thomas O. Larkin, having sold his land to John A. Sutter. Thereafter, he drops from sight. Bancroft, *California*, II:773; Ogden, "Trading Vessels on the California Coast," p. 1117.

[16]Master of the whaleship *Samuel Robertson*, 421 tons, out almost thirty months with a cargo of 110 bbls. sperm oil on board, which arrived April 3, 1844. Paty's Harbormaster Records. (Departure date unknown.)

[17]The bark arrived on April 22. Shortly after it left Honolulu on May 25, 1844, it returned leaking so badly that it was condemned. *The Friend*, 2 (May 1, 1844), 52; *The Polynesian*, 1 (June 1, 1844), 2.

[18]The Rev. Hunt's and his wife's biographies are found in *Missionary Album*, pp. 118–119.

[19]Captain of the Sag Harbor whaleship *Henry Lee*, 409 tons, which called September 16–25, 1844, had on board 2,600 bbls. whale oil. Paty's Harbormaster Records.

Mr. E. C. Webster, merchant[20]
Captain Gardner[21]
Captain S. Dike (Dyke)[22]
Captain Brown, master American whaleship *Hannibal*[23]
Mr. William T. Faxon[24]
Mr. Hayden
Captain William A. Leidsdorff, master *Julia Ann*[25]
Mr. Evans
Mr. George Brown, U.S. commissioner[26]
Mr. Edwin O. Hall (II:75)
Mr. Samuel N. Castle (II:24)
Doctor Gerrit P. Judd (II:24)
Mr. Prichar[d]
Mr. Beal
Mr. A. S. Cook, teacher at Royal School[27]
Mr. James F. B. Marshall (E:27)
Mr. Joseph P. Thompson, Santa Barbara merchant[28]

---

[20]So listed in "1847 Register," p. 11.

[21]Gardner was master of either the whaler *Warren*, 382 tons, at sea fourteen months with 1,700 bbls. whale oil, which called October 14–November 4, 1844, or the New Bedford whaler *Milo*, 398 tons, out sixteen months with 100 bbls. sperm and 2,400 bbls. whale oil, which arrived at Honolulu on October 28, 1844. Paty's Harbormaster Records.

[22]Master of the New Bedford whaler *Canton*, 404 tons, out twenty-three months with 2,200 bbls. whale oil. It arrived Honolulu on November 1, 1844. *Ibid.*

[23]This New London whaler sailed on May 27 for the Northwest Coast having been at sea seven months. *The Polynesian*, 1 (June 1, 1844), 7.

[24]Faxon came to California in 1840 and took charge of Thomas O. Larkin's store in Monterey in 1841. In 1842 he went to Honolulu staying until 1844 when he returned to Monterey. He left the coast for good in 1846 on the *California*, homebound for Boston. Bancroft, *California*, III:735; Ogden, "Trading Vessels on the California Coast," p. 1156.

[25]Leidesdorff, a Danish West Indies mulatto, came to California as master of the *Julia Ann* in 1841, making numerous voyages to Hawaii thereafter. Making fledgling San Francisco his home port, he acquired property and became a naturalized Mexican citizen. He died in May 1849 at the age of thirty-eight. Bancroft, *California*, IV:711.

[26]Promptly after Congress enacted an appropriation for providing a U.S. commissioner for the Sandwich Islands, March 1, 1843, George Brown was appointed to the post. He reached Honolulu October 16, 1843, being presented to the king two weeks later. Kuykendall, *Hawaiian Kingdom, 1778–1854*, pp. 196, 234.

[27]"1847 Register," p. 10.

[28]Thompson, a native of Massachusetts, reputedly reached California in 1840, although he may have arrived several years earlier. He returned again in 1844 on the *Fama*, sailing from Honolulu on May 29, 1844, settling down first at Santa Clara, then San Francisco, later Napa. Bancroft, *California*, V:747; *The Polynesian*, 1 (June 1, 1844), 7.

Mr. Stephen Reynolds (II:73)
Mr. Luff, visitor[29]
Mr. Dunn
Mr. Lawrence
Mr. Malcolm
Mr. John Coffin Jones, Jr. (V:89)[30]
Mr. E. H. Boardman, watchmaker[31]
Doctor Robert W. Wood (II:27)
Mr. John Ricord, lawyer[32]
Mr. George B. Rowell (I:3)
Mr. G. T. Allan, merchant[33]
Doctor James W. Smith, missionary physician[34]
Rev. Mr. Titus Coan[35]
Captain Page, master U.S. Sloop *Levant*[36]
Captain Abraham B. Russell (II:82)
Mr. G. D. Gilman, storekeeper[37]
Captain Justus Doane (I:1)
Mr. Benson[38]
Mr. Gay[39]
Mr. Helicon
Captain Nichols, master British ship *William Ackers*[40]
Mr. Frederick W. Thompson, auctioneer[41]

---

[29] A. A. Luff was on the *Lausanne* bound for Oregon. The ship arrived at the end of April and sailed on May 23. *Ibid.; The Friend*, 2 (May 1, 1844), 52.

[30] Jones, native of Boston, was appointed U.S. agent (consul) in Hawaii on September 19, 1820, and continued until removed on April 19, 1838, at the same time serving as business agent for the Boston firm of Marshall & Wildes. Kuykendall, *Hawaiian Kingdom, 1778–1854*, pp. 98, 167n; Baker, *Honolulu in 1853*, p. 28.

[31] "1847 Register," p. 10.

[32] *Ibid.*, p. 11.

[33] *Ibid.*, p. 10.

[34] Dr. and Mrs. Smith's biographies are in the *Missionary Album*, pp. 177–178.

[35] *Ibid.*, pp. 70–71.

[36] *The Polynesian*, 1 (June 1, 1844), 7.

[37] "1847 Register," p. 111.

[38] E.S. Bensen was on board the *Lausanne* bound for Oregon. The vessel arrived on April 27 and sailed on May 23. *The Friend*, 2 (Aug. 1, 1844), 52.

[39] A. O. Gay was a passenger on the *Globe*, Captain Doane, from Boston via Tahiti, arriving on July 15, 1844. *The Friend*, 2 (Aug. 1, 1844), 76.

[40] The vessel arrived on June 26 after a passage of twenty-five days from Mazatlán and sailed in early September. *Ibid.*, 1 (June 29, 1844), 23; 2 (Sept. 4, 1844), 88.

[41] "1847 Register," p. 11.

Mr. Wilson Baker
Mrs. David P. Penhallow (P:33)
Miss Mary Ann Miller[42]
Mrs. Charles M. More [Moore] (II:5)
Mrs. Jules Dudoit, wife French consul (née Anna Corney [II:30])
Mrs. Mary A. Paty (II:6)
(Illegible name: Mrs. ?)
Miss F. Cormie
Mrs. O. P. Ricker (née Sarah Piper [II:16])
Mrs. Samuel C. Damon (née Julia Sherman Mills [I:23])
Mrs. John Dominis (II:26)
Mrs. Sullivan[43]
Mrs. Grimes[44]
Mrs. Martha Paty (II:6)
Mrs. William Ladd (I:10)
Mrs. Cornelius Hoyer (II:95)
Miss Elizabeth Dowsett[45]
Mrs. D. Dowsett (possibly Mrs. Mary Dowsett, widow [II:35])
Mrs. Joseph O. Carter (II:49)
Mrs. Richard Armstrong (II:59)
Mrs. Horton O. Knapp (II:4)
Mrs. Lowell Smith (II:2)
Mrs. Henry Dimond (II:71)
Mrs. Robert W. Wood (II:27)
Mrs. Edwin O. Hall (II:75)
Miss Sarah A. Goodale (II:105)
Mrs. Burnham
Mrs. Weston, wife of Captain Weston, master of the *Congaree* (P:15)
Mrs. James F. B. Marshall (V: 27)

---

[42]The niece of the newly appointed British consul to the Sandwich Islands, Miss Miller arrived with her uncle on H.M.S. *Hazard*, Captain Bell, from Mazatlán, February 3, 1844. The second daughter of Edward Miller, Count of Cambridge, she subsequently was married by the British consul to Andrew S. Hammond, eldest son of Vice Admiral Sir Graham E. Hammond and commander of H.M.S. *Salamander*, in Tahiti on November 13, 1844. *The Friend*, 2 (Feb. 14, 1844), 20; 3 (Jan. 1, 1844), 8.

[43]Mrs. Maria T. Sullivan of Boston was married to Frederick W. Thompson in Honolulu, September 24, 1844, by the Rev. Abbe Desiré Maigret. *Ibid.*, 2 (Sept. 4, 1844), 88.

[44]This would be Mrs. Hiram Grimes since Eliab Grimes never married.

[45]Miss Elizabeth Dowsett sailed for the United States on the Marcia in the fall of 1846. *Ibid.*, 4 Nov. 2, 1846), 166.

Miss Marshall, daughter
Mrs. Gary[46]
Mrs. Gerrit P. Judd (née Laura Fish [II:24])
Mrs. Andrew Johnstone (née Rebecca Worth [II:58})
Mrs. William Hooper (II:10; P:38)
Mrs. Milo Calkins (II:105)
Mrs. John Ladd (IV:37)
Mrs. Goodale[47]
Mrs. Timothy D. Hunt (née Mary Halsted Hedges)[48]
Mrs. Lowell Smith (née Abagail W. Tenny [II:2])
Mrs. Gardner
Miss Whitney[49]
Mrs. Charles Brewer(II:1)
Mrs. Sherman Peck, wife of merchant[50]
Mrs. Gamaliel Drew (II:106)
Mrs. Samuel N. Castle (née Angeline L. Tenny [II:105])
Mrs. Daniel Chamberlain (née Mary Patton [II:25])

---

[46]The wife of the Rev. George Gary bound for Oregon for the Methodist Episcopal mission. The Garys left New York, November 30, 1843, on the *Lawrence*. They reached Honolulu on April 24, 1844, and sailed on the bark *Brothers of Guernsey*, Captain Flere, for the Columbia River on May 2. Carey, ed., "Diary of Rev. George Gary," *Oregon Historical Quarterly*, 24 (March 1923), 68–70.

[47]The wife of Warren Goodale who served the Hawaiian government as collector general of customs. Mr. Goodale (born July 2, 1826; died February 22, 1897), after resigning from his post, remained for the rest of his life a resident. Warren Goodale, "Honolulu in 1853," *Papers of the Hawaiian Historical Society*, No. 10 (Honolulu, 1897), 1–10; Privy Council Records, vol. 7, p. 135; vol. 11, p. 133, HSA.

[48]See Missionary Album, pp. 118–119, for biographical sketch.

[49]Samuel Whitney and his wife Mercy (Partridge) reached Hawaii on the brig *Thaddeus*, April 4, 1820, dedicated as the first missionaries. They had two daughters, Maria Kapule (1820–1900) and Emilie Elizabeth (1827–1898). One of these young ladies was Mrs. Nye's visitor. Ibid., pp. 198–199.

[50]"1847 Register," p. 10.

Appendix II

William Paty's Journal Account of the British Seizure of Honolulu, 1842

William Paty's journal provides this graphic description of the events that unfold on February 8, 1842.

❦ ❦ ❦

Saturday 18th [February]. This morning all was bustle and excitement. It has proved the most eventful and extraordinary day that I ever witnessed. I have often (when reading of wars, particularly among the South America States) tried to imagine what might be the feelings of the quiet inhabitants of a village when notified that a few hours would turn their peaceful *home* into a scene of violence, slaughter and destruction. Today I have had opportunity to realize their feelings. It was generally supposed that the King would not comply with the demands of Lord Paulet, in event of which war must ensue as will be explained in the following notices issued from the U.S. Consulate at about 10

To All Americans resident at Honolulu

I am requested by Captain J. C. Long of the U.S. Ship *Boston* to give publicity to the following letter received last evening.

Her Brittanic Majesty's Ship
Wahoo, Feb. 17, 1843

Sir

I have the honor to notify you that her Brittanic Majesty's Ship *Carysfort* under my command will be prepared to make an immediate attack upon this town at 4 P.M. today [Saturday] in the event that the demands now forwarded by me to the King of these Islands not being complied with at this time.

I have the honor to be Sir—
Yor Mo. Obt. Humble Servant
(signed) Geo. Paulet
Captain

I am further requested by Capt. Long to tender to all American Citizens his ship as an asylum for their families and property in event of any hostile movement on the part of the British force now in this harbor.

(signed) Wm. Hooper
Acting U.S. Consl. Agt.

Office of U.S. Agency
Oahu Sandwich Islands
Feb. 18, 1843
To the Commanders of American Vessels in the Port of Honolulu
Gentlemen

I have to request that you will cause all boats belonging to your reprective ship to be manned and sent to Mr. Reynolds' wharf to render any assistance which may be required by citizens of the United States resident here, pending the difficulties between this Govt. and that of Great Britain and oblige

Your Most Obt. St.
(signed) W. Hooper
Acting U.S. Consul Agent

Office of the U.S. Consl.
Agency, Oahu, S.I.
February 18, 1843.

From 10 O.c. till 2 O.c. our street presented a most extraordinary spectacle, for a town usually as quiet as this. The streets were crowded with carts containing Money Chests, Book Safes, Trunks, Personal Clothing etc., all hastening towards the Wharfs to be placed on board the Ships (particularly the *Wm. Gray*) for Safety. All the English women and children in the place (except Dudoit, French Consul, family) were sent on board of an English Brig *Julia* lying outside. The American women and children and Dudoit's family prepared themselves to go on board the U.S. Ship *Boston* at 2 O.c. Such was the state of affairs until about 1 O.c. P.M. with a 'rumor' informed us that the threatened attack would not take place, which was soon confirmed by the following notice

To All Americans Resident at Honolulu Notice
Office of the U.S. Consl.
Agency, Oahu
Sandwich Islands, February 18, 1843

The undersigned has the pleasure to announce to the citizens of the United States, resident at the Sandch. Islands that he has received Official information from the Governor of this Island announcing to him that the difficulties between this Government and that of Great Britain are in the process of amicable adjustment.

(Signed) Wm. Hooper
Acting U.S. Consl. Agent

❦ ❦ ❦

Originals of these documents which William Paty quotes in his journal are in the Foreign Office and Executive Papers, 1790–1845, HSA. The documentary sources which fully detail Lord Paulet's actions in Oahu in late February and early March 1843 are printed in full in *British and Foreign State Papers, 1842–1843*, Vol. XXXI (London, 1858), pp. 1022–1035, and the background documents for the abortive action taken by Paulet in demanding the cession of the Hawaiian Islands are printed in *England. Foreign Office Confidential Prints* (London, 1843), Document C, pp. 1–27, and Document D, pp. 1–31, British Library, London.

Appendix III

An Account of the British Restoration of the Hawaiian Kingdom

An interesting side light on the restoration is to be found in an original letter preserved in the Hawaii State Archives from Paul Kanoa, acting governor of Oahu, to his friend, Timoteo Ha'alilio, absent in Europe as one of the three commissioners of the Hawaiian Kingdom, dated Honolulu, October 5, 1843. The typed translation reads:

> After the [British] flag had been up for four months during which time riots were frequent, the Admiral arrived from Valparaiso, to put a stop to the actions of Lord Geo. Paulet, having been informed of these things by a letter from John Meek which had been written from the Piia, that boat having been ordered to go to Valparaiso, and the Hooikaika to Magdalena where the new Consul was located. The Admiral arrived here on the 25th of July and immediately solicited an interview with the King. In their interview he acted as befitting a good officer, he was very kind and just. He condemned all the actions of Lord Geo. Paulet and did not uphold him in one single thing. The orders which had been given him had been destroyed and he had done things of his own will and had obeyed the orders of the Consul. The King and the Admiral showed himself to be just and considerate and conducted things in such a way as to do honor to Great Britain. Even now he is good and kind and in no way does he abuse the people nor the Chiefs. On the sixth day of his stay here that being the 31st day of July, the British flag was lowered and the Hawaiian flag hoisted at (Kula-o-ka-hua) [now Thomas Square] east of the City. A great gathering was held in this place, the officers and men from three British Warships were there, salutes were fired and evolutions performed by the marines. At this gathering the King issued a proclamation pardon-

ing all those who were in irons and all those who had been convicted under the laws of the land. . . .

Here is another thing, when the flag was hoisted on the 31st day of July, Kamehameha III proclaimed that, "There shall be no work during the first ten days in August. The Government shall be closed and everybody shall make these days, days of rejoicing because the country has been restored." We had much feasting in these ten days. Two were given in Nuuanu in honor of the Admiral and foreigners, one at your estate in Kanaana . . . and one at Waikiki.

❦ ❦ ❦

Commentary on Letter. According to Paty's Harbormaster Records, the *Piia* or *Victoria,* so named by the British, did not sail for Valparaíso to make contact with Admiral Thomas until March 17, a full twenty days after the cession had been made. Since the voyage, for a vessel of her size, required more than two months, Lord Paulet undoubtedly felt this would provide Alexander Simpson with sufficient time to reach London before Thomas could act.

John Meek, former harbormaster and pilot for Honolulu, was a native of Marblehead, Massachusetts, who first arrived in the Sandwich Islands in 1809 as first officer of a trading ship plying between the Northwest Coast and China. He settled in Oahu in 1812. Later he became a livestock breeder of some note. He was a firm friend of the kings and high chiefs from Kamehameha I on. He died January 29, 1875, age eighty-three. *The Friend*, new series, 24 (Feb. 1, 1875), [10]. He made the voyage to Valparaíso apparently as a crew member or pilot, perhaps having had it in mind from the outset to communicate directly with Admiral Thomas if opportunity arose, since he obviously did not trust Paulet to render an objective report of what had transpired.

Thomas, although without specific instructions from the Foreign Office or Admiralty, abrogated the cession in light of Lord Aberdeen's policy regarding British relations with Pacific island rulers. Kuykendall, *Hawaiian Kingdom, 1778–1854,* p. 186.

Since all Hawaiian flags had been confiscated and destroyed by the British under Paulet's orders, Admiral Thomas had a new flag made on his ship, the *Dublin*, and presented it to Kamehameha III. It was embossed with an olive branch and a crown superimposed on the central area. A second Hawaiian flag used during the restoration ceremonies was made and presented to the king by Honolulu merchants Peirce & Brewer.

Appendix IV

King Kamehameha III Gala Luau Celebrating Restoration of the Hawaiian Kingdom

The account of the gala luau given by King Kamehameha III for Admiral Thomas is reproduced from Gorham Gilman's manuscript, Gilman Collection, Hawaiian Historical Society, Honolulu, and quoted by permission.

❦ ❦ ❦

August 2d, [1843]. Wednesday. Today his Majesty gives a public feast to *all* who will attend. There are no invitations given but to the public characters. Parties commenced moving out at about 10 o'clock at which hour His Majesty and Suite went out. Mounting at 12 in company with some of the officers of the "Constellation"—we started up the valley. It was a beautiful day, the breeze just strong enough for comfort without raising the dust, the Sun just bright enough. The Valley is a very beautiful one highly cultivated mostly by the natives, and the broad green leaf of the "kalo" can be seen on both sides of the way. The Summer cottages of the residents are in this valley. Some of them very pretty and helping to make up the picture. The natural scenery also is very grand and it forms a side (the valley) that one does not soon tire from enjoying. Large numbers of the natives were passing along, some on foot, some on horses, or anything else that could carry them, all flocking to the place of festivity for they were also to share in the good thing, the bounty of their King. After riding about three miles or half an hour we came in sight of the place. It is a pleasant spot in the valley on a gentle assent [*sic*] and among a fine grove of trees. (Said to be the pleasantest place in the whole valley.) In a few moments we were among the crowd on a master field or some such place. Men, women, children, horses, jackasses, mules, carts, carriages—the place was thronged and not a little noise from the natives in charge of the horses. Giving our horses to a native, we entered the house where we soon discovered that *ceremony* had been left downtown for, some had hats on, some off and every one seemed to please himself and enjoy themselves as they best could. The ladies were most all present, and added much to the enjoyment of the day and the gaiety of the scene. The children were also in the room playing about and seeming to enter with whole hearts in the pleasure. . . . His Majesty was moving about among his guests, talking with all and appeared to enjoy himself as did some of the nobility. Some of them make a very graceful appearance on the floor and would grace any drawing room. . . .

The Band from HBMS Dublin were in attendance and contributed to the pleasure of all. They played some fine music. The Ladies and some of the officers got up a little dance and seemed to have a pleasant time . . . about 2 P.M. our attention was directed to a long string of natives passing with food . . . here a lot of Poi—a large Hog taking two natives to carry him—fowls—fish—Kalo—Turkies, in fact every thing that could be got was there, all neatly done up in the native stile [*sic*]. The procession was some time in passing and there must have been 150 to 200 natives I should think.

Soon after dinner was announced. The Band led the way through the trees to the place where the table was laid. And here a sight met the eye. . . . A long avenue of trees was lined with the Flags of the nations friendly to this Government while at the head was suspended the Hawaiian Flag, forming a canopy under which His Majesty seated himself . . . and the Admiral on his right and Com. Jones on his left, with the Consuls in their vicinity. . . . The table was "Mother earth" and the cloth her own, consisting of a broad leaf called the "Ki" leaf which is both smooth and broad and by lying them regularly they formed a very good substitute for a cloth. . . .

It was a very laughable affair to get seated particularly for those who had their pants strapped pretty tight down. Such bursting of buttons, breaking of straps to say nothing of the inconvenience, but all got down to some way or another for most had pretty good appetites judging from the way that the things disappeared . . . as I have said before everything that could be had in the market was there, the food well cooked, and it had justice done to it. . . . His Majesty had provided by each plate a good Bowl of Poi and neither were there wanting knives, forks, spoons and all the other necessaries of the table—and if a person went away hungry it was not the fault of His Majesty.

There was no stronger drink than Lemonade, which was much better than all the wines he could have had for some would probably used them too freely. . . . Everything passed off well and the dinner will long be remembered . . . parallel to the table set for us there were two tables laid for the natives that were amply supplied with fish, poi, Kalo, etc., and the natives did not let them go a begging you had better believe. . . .

After the company had returned to the house, the ladies and gentlemen sang the "Restoration Anthem" to His Majesty the King, and to old Admiral Thomas. [The text for the anthem is printed in *The Friend,* 2 (March 1844), 28–29.] The Old Gentleman was so much affected that his voice failed him, which he was obliged to use his handkerchief. Soon after the anthem was sung the company began to leave. . . .

About an hour after we left the King came down with music, flags, etc., a long procession. The cheering as His Majesty rode through the streets was long and loud. . . . It is a day that will dwell long in memory. (Editorial structure supplied.)

Gilman states in his account that Lord Paulet did not appear at either the actual Restoration Ceremonies on the plain or the service of Thanksgiving in Kawaiaha's Church which followed. His excuse, illness. He sent a subordinate officer as substitute.

Appendix V

Sir George Simpson's Description of the California Hide and Tallow Trade

Sir George Simpson gives the following account of the hide business in his *Narrative of a Journey Round the World,* I:291–292, which he credits to Richard Henry Dana.

> When the hide is taken from the bullock, holes are cut round it near the edges, by which it is staked out to dry. In this manner it dries without shrinking. After they are thus dried in the sun, they are received by the vessels, and brought down to the depot. The vessels land them, and leave them in large piles near the houses. Then begins the hidecurer's duty.
>
> The first thing is to put them in soak. This is done by carrying them down at low tide, and making them fast, in small piles, by ropes, and letting the tide come up and cover them. Every day we put in soak twenty-five for each man, which, with us, made a hundred and fifty. There they lie forty-eight hours, when they are taken out, and rolled up, in wheelbarrows, and thrown into vats. These vats contain brine, made very strong, being sea-water, with great quantities of salt thrown in. This pickles the hides, and in this they lie forty-eight hours; the use of the seawater, into which they are first put, being merely to soften and clean them. From these vats they are taken, and lie on a platform twenty-four hours, and then are spread upon the ground, and carefully stretched and staked out, so that they may dry smooth.
>
> After they were staked, and while yet wet and soft, we used to go upon them with our knives, and carefully cut off all bad parts: the pieces of meat and fat, which would otherwise corrupt and affect the whole if stowed away in a vessel for months; the large flippers, the ears, and all other parts that prevent close stowage. This was the most difficult part of our duty, as it required much skill to take everything necessary off, and not to cut or injure the hides. It was

> also a long process, as six of us had to clean a hundred and fifty, most of which required a great deal to be done to them, as the Spaniards are very careless in skinning their cattle. Then, too, as we cleaned them while they were staked out, we were obliged to kneel down upon them, which always gives beginners the back-ache . . .
>
> This cleaning must be got through with before noon, for by that time they get too dry. After the sun has been on them for a few hours, they are carefully gone over with scrappers, to get off all the grease which the sun brings out. This being done, the stakes are pulled up, and the hides carefully doubled, with the hair side out, and are left to dry. About the middle of the afternoon they are turned upon the other side, and at sundown piled up and covered over. The next day, they are spread out and opened again, and at night, if fully dry, are thrown upon a long horizontal pole, five at a time, and beat with flails. This takes all the dust from them. Thus, being salted, scraped, cleaned, dried, and beaten, they are stowed away in the house.

Richard Henry Dana, Jr.'s account is found in his *Two Years Before the Mast,* edited by John H. Kemble (2 vols; Los Angeles, 1964), I:153–156.

Bibliography
&
Index

Bibliography

Manuscript Sources

BANCROFT LIBRARY, University of California, Berkeley

Adele Ogden, "Trading Vessels Along the California Coast, 1786–1848," typed manuscript.

CALIFORNIA STATE LIBRARY, Sacramento

Letter: Gorham H. Nye to William Heath Davis, Plymouth, Massachusetts, July 5, 1853. William Heath Davis Collection, Box 171.

HENRY E. HUNTINGTON LIBRARY, San Marino, California

Diary of Francis Mellus.

HAWAIIAN HISTORICAL SOCIETY, Honolulu

Gorham Gilman Collection.

HAWAIIAN STATE ARCHIVES, Honolulu

Harbormaster Records: Arrival and Departures, Honolulu Harbor, October 21, 1842–December 31, 1849.

William Paty's Journal, January 1, 1842–January 28, 1845.

Letter: Paul Kanoa to Timoteo Ha'alilio, Honolulu, October 5, 1843 Lydia Rider Nye Collection.

Privy Council Records.

Stephen Reynolds Journal, 1823–1842, typed manuscript.

NEW ENGLAND HISTORIC GENEALOGICAL SOCIETY, Boston

Vital Records, Plymouth, Massachusetts, copied by Mrs. Ella F. Huntoon, 1897.

PERSONAL CORRESPONDENCE

Letter: Ms. Agnes C. Conrad, Hawaii State Archivist, to Doyce B. Nunis, Jr., March 19, 1969.

PUBLIC RECORD OFFICE, Kew, Richmond, Surrey, England

Foreign Office Papers:

Richard Charlton to George Canning, June 30, 1828, F.O. 58/5, fo. 11.

Richard Charlton to Lord Palmerston, October 27, 1841, F.O. 58/12, fo. 1086.

Valparaíso English Residents to Lord Aberdeen, December 9, 1840, F.O. 16/46, fos. 141–141b, 135–140.

San Diego Historical Society

Henry Delano Fitch Notebook.

Santa Barbara Mission Archive–Library

Marriage Records.

Presidio Baptismal Records.

Presidia Burial Register, 1782–1848.

Primary Printed Sources

Books

Alexander, James M. *Mission Life in Hawaii: Memoir of Rev. William P. Alexander.* Oakland, California, 1888.

Bingham, Hiram. *A Residence of Twenty-One Years in the Sandwich Islands.* Hartford and New York, 1849. Second printing, Canadaigua, New York, 1855.

Bogardus' Business Directory for San Francisco. San Francisco, 1850.

Brewer, Charles A. *Reminiscences.* Jamaica Plains, New York [c. 1844].

Brown, D. Mackenzie, ed. *China Trade Days in California: Selected Letters From the Thompson Papers.* Berkeley and Los Angeles, 1947.

Brown, John H. *Reminiscences and Incidents of Early Days of San Francisco.* San Francisco, [1886].

Davis, William Heath. *Seventy-Five Years in California.* Edited by Harold D. Small. San Francisco, 1967.

Gleason, Duncan and Dorothy Gleason, eds. *Beloved Sister: The Letters of James Henry Gleason, 1841 to 1845.* Glendale, California, 1978.

Hammond, George P., ed. *The Larkin Papers.* Berkeley and Los Angeles, 1951–1964. 10 vols.

Howay, F[rederic] W., ed. *The Voyage of the New Hazard.* Salem, Massachusetts, 1938.

Jackson, Donald and Mary Lee Spence, eds. *The Expeditions of John Charles Fremont, Volume I: From 1838–1844.* Urbana, Illinois, 1970.

Jessett, Thomas E., ed. *Reports and Letters of Herbert Beaver, 1836–1838.* Portland, Oregon, 1949.

Judd, Laura F. *Honolulu: Sketches of Life in the Hawaiian Islands from 1828 to 1861.* Edited by Dale L. Morgan. Chicago, 1966.

Lloyd's Register of British and Foreign Shipping from July 1, 1843, to June 30, 1844. London, 1844.

Nunis, Jr., Doyce B., ed. *The California Diary of Faxon Dean Atherton 1836–1839*. San Francisco, 1964.

Petit-Thouars, Abel A. du. *Voyage due monde sur la frigate la* Venus, *pendant les annees, 1836–1839*. Paris, 1840–1845. 4 vols.

Report of the Proceedings and Evidence in the Arbitration Between the King and Government of the Hawaiian Islands and Messrs. Ladd & Co., Before Messrs. Stephen H. Williams and James F. B. Marshall. Honolulu, 1846.

Rich, E. E., ed. *McLoughlin's Fort Vancouver Letters, Second Series, 1839–44*. London, 1943.

_____, ed. *Simpson's 1828 Journey to the Columbia*. London, 1947.

_____ and A. M. Johnson, eds. *A Journal of a Voyage From the Rocky Mountain Portage in Peace River to the Sources of Finlays Branch and North West Ward in Summer 1824*. London, 1955.

Ruschenberger, W[illiam] S. D. *A Voyage Around the World*. Philadelphia, 1838.

Sandels, G. W. Waseurtza. *A Sojourn in California by the King's Orphan*. San Francisco, 1945.

Simpson, Sir George. *Narrative of a Voyage Round the World*. London, 1847. 2 vols.

Simpson's Boston Directory 1840. Boston, 1840.

Simpson's Boston Directory 1843. Boston, 1843.

Thurston, Lorrin A., ed. *The Fundamental Law of Hawaii*. Honolulu, 1904.

Wilkes, Charles. *Narrative of the United States Exploring Expedition*. Philadelphia, 1845. 6 vols.

Wolcott, Marjorie T., ed. *Pioneer Notes From the Diaries of Judge Benjamin Hayes, 1849–1875*. Los Angeles, 1929.

Articles

Brewer. Henry B. "Log of the *Lausanne*—V." Edited by John M. Cause. *Oregon Historical Quarterly*, XXX (March 1929).

Camp, Charles L., ed. "The Chronicles of George C. Yount, California Pioneer of 1836." *California Historical Society Quarterly*, II (April 1923).

Carey, Charles H., ed. "Diary of Reverend George Cray—IV." *Oregon Historical Quarterly*, XXIV (December 1923).

Cartright, Bruce. "Honolulu, 1809–1810." *Paradise of the Pacific*, 38 (December 1925).

Gilman, Gorham D. "1848—Honolulu As It Is." Edited by Jean S. Sharpless and Richard Greer. *The Journal of Hawaiian History,* IV (1970).

Gleason, Duncan, ed. "James Henry Gleason: Pioneer Journal and Letters, 1841–1846." *Quarterly Historical Society of Southern California,* XXXI (March–June 1949).

Goodale, Warren, "Honolulu in 1853." *Papers of the Hawaiian Historical Society,* No. 10 (Honolulu, 1897).

Green, Mrs. Edward C., ed. "Journal of Captain John Paty, 1807–1868." *California Historical Society Quarterly,* XIV (December 1935).

Greer, Richard. "Honolulu in 1847." *The Journal of Hawaiian History,* IV (1970).

Marshall, James F. B. "An Unpublished Chapter in Hawaiian History." *Harper's,* XLVII (September 1883).

"Methodist Annual Reports Relating to the Willamette Mission, 1834–1848." *Oregon Historical Quarterly,* XXVI (June 1925).

The Missionary Herald, XXXVIII (June 1842).

Piper, Nellie B., ed. "The Diary of Henry Bridgeman Brewer: Being a Log of the Lausanne and the Time-book of the Dalles Mission." *Oregon Historical Quarterly,* XXIX (June 1928); (December 1928).

Rockwood, E. Ruth, ed. "Diary of Reverend George H. Atkinson, D.D." *Oregon Historical Quarterly,* XL (June 1939).

Secondary Printed Sources

Books

Alexander, Mary C. and Charlotte P. Dodge. *Punahau, 1841–1941.* Berkeley and Los Angeles, 1941.

Anderson, Rufus. *History of the Sandwich Island Missions.* London, 1872.

Baker, Ray J. *Honolulu in 1853.* N.p., n.d.

Bancroft, Hubert H. *History of California.* San Francisco, 1884–1890. 7 vols.

_____. *History of Oregon.* San Francisco, 1886–1888. 2 vols.

_____. *California Pastoral.* San Francisco 1888.

Baur, K. Jack. *Surfboats and Horse Marines: U.S. Naval Operations in the Mexican War, 1846–48.* Annapolis, Maryland, 1969.

Bradley, Harold W. *The American Frontier in Hawaii: The Pioneers, 1789–1843.* Stanford, California, 1942.

Callahan, Edward W., comp. *List of Officers of the Navy of the United States and Marine Corps from 1775 to 1900.* New York, 1901.

Corning, Howard M. *Dictionary of Oregon History.* Portland, 1956.

Cowan, Robert C. *Ranchos of California.* Fresno, 1956.

Damon, Ethel M. *Early Hawaiian Churches.* Honolulu, 1924.

_____. *The Stone Church at Kawaiahao.* Honolulu, 1925.

Dobbs, Caroline C. *Men of Champoeg.* Portland, Oregon, 1932.

Drury, Clifford M., ed. *First White Women Over the Rocky Mountains.* Glendale, California, 1963–1966. 3 vols.

Evans, Elwood. *History of the Pacific Northwest: Oregon and Washington.* Portland, Oregon, 1889.

Eveleth, Ephraim. *History of the Sandwich Islands, with an account of the American mission established there in 1820.* Philadelphia, 1831.

Fairburn, William A. *Merchant Sail.* Center Lowell, Massachusetts, 1945–1955. 6 vols.

Gast, Ross H. *Contentious Consul: A Biography of John Coffin Jones.* Los Angeles, 1976.

Geiger, O. F. M., Maynard. *Franciscan Missionaries in Hispanic California, 1769–1848: A Biographical Dictionary.* San Marino, California, 1969.

_____. *History of Mission Santa Barbara, 1782–1965.* Santa Barbara, 1965.

Genini, Ronald and Richard Hitchman. *Romualdo Pacheco: A Californian in Two Eras.* San Francisco, 1988.

Gudde, Ewin G. *California Place Names.* Rev. ed., Berkeley and Los Angeles, 1969.

Hamersly, Thomas H. S. *General Register of the United States Navy and Marine Corps.* Washington, D.C., 1882.

Harvey, Paul, ed. *The Oxford Companion to English Literature.* Oxford, England, 1967.

Hawaiian Mission Children's Society. *Portraits of American Missionaries to Hawaii.* Honolulu, 1901.

Hines, Gustavus. *Oregon: Its History, Condition, and Prospects.* Buffalo, 1851.

_____. *Wild Life in Oregon.* New York, 1881.

Hines, Harvey K. *An Illustrated History of Oregon.* Chicago, 1873.

Hitchcock, Charles H. *Hawaii and Its Victorians.* Honolulu, 1911.

Hittell, Theodore H. *History of California.* San Francisco, 1898. 4 vols.

Hough, Henry B. *Whaling Wives.* Boston, 1953.

Hussey, John A. *The History of Fort Vancouver and Its Physical Structure.* Portland, 1957.

Jarves, James J. *History of the Hawaiian or Sandwich Islands.* 2nd ed., Boston, 1843.

Johnson, Allen and Dumas Malone, eds. *Dictionary of American Biographies.* New York, 1928–1936. 20 vols.

Joseting, Edward. *Hawaii, An Uncommon History.* New York, 1972.

Judd, Bernice. *Voyages to Hawaii before 1860.* Honolulu, 1974.

Kirker, Harold. *California's Architectural Frontier.* San Marino, California, 1960.

Kuykendall, *The Hawaiian Kingdom, 1778–1854.* Honolulu, 1938.

_____. *The Hawaiian Kingdom, 1854–1874.* Honolulu, 1953.

MacArthur, Lewis A. *Oregon Geographic Names.* Portland, 1953.

Martínez, Pablo L. *Guia Familiar de Baja California, 1700–1900.* Mexico, D.F., 1965.

McGraw-Hill Encyclopedia of Science and Technology. 3rd rev. ed., New York, 1971.

Missionary Album: Portraits and Biographical Sketches of American Protestant Missionaries to the Hawaiian Islands. Honolulu, 1969.

Montgomery, Richard G. *The White-Headed Eagle: John McLoughlin, Builder of an Empire.* New York, 1935.

Navy Department, Naval History Division, comps. *Dictionary of American Naval Fighting Ships.* Washington, D.C., 1959–1981. 8 vols.

Nunis, Doyce B., Jr. *The Trials of Isaac Graham.* Los Angeles, 1967.

Nye and Best. *A Genealogy of the Nye Family.* N.p., 1907.

Pethick, Derek. *First Approaches to the Northwest Coast.* Vancouver, 1976.

Scott, Harvey W. *History of the Oregon Country.* New York, 1924.

Simpson, Alexander. *The Sandwich Islands, Progress of Events since their Discovery.* London, 1851.

Smith, Bradford. *Yankees in Paradise.* Philadelphia and New York, 1956.

Soulé, Frank, *et al. Annals of San Francisco,*. New York and San Francisco, 1855.

Taber, Robert M. and Harold W. Dubach. *1001 Questions Answered About the Ocean and Oceanography.* New York, 1972.

[Thompson and West]. *History of Santa Barbara County.* Oakland, 1883.

Thurston, Lucy. *Life and Times of Lucy C. Thurston.* Ann Arbor, Michigan, 1883.

Trochiana, H[enry] A. Van Coenen. *Story of the Mission Santa Cruz.* San Francisco, 1933.

Tyler, David B. *The Wilkes Expedition.* Philadelphia, 1968.

Underhill, Reuben L. *From Cowhides to Golden Fleece.* Stanford, California, 1946.

Venn, J.A., comp. *Alumni Cantabrigienses, Part II: From 1752 to 1900.* Cambridge, England, 1940–1954. 16 vols.

Weber, Francis J. *Francisco Garcia Diego, California's Transition Bishop.* Los Angeles, 1971.

ARTICLES

Alexander, W. A. "The Oahu Charity School." *Sixteenth Annual Report of the Hawaiian Historical Society.* Honolulu, 1908.

Baldwin, J. R. "England and the French Seizure of the Society Islands." *Journal of Modern History,* X (June 1938).

Ballou, Howard M. and George R. Carter. "The History of the Hawaiian Mission Press, with a Bibliography of the Earlier Publications." *Papers of the Hawaiian Historical Society,* No. 14. Honolulu, 1908.

"Beginnings and Development of Trade on the Pacific Coast of North America." [Mercantile Trust Company of California] *Monthly Review,* XII, Pts. 8–9 (March–April 1923).

Brooke, Jr., George M. "The Vest Pocket War of Commodore Jones." *Pacific Historical Review,* XXXI (August 1962).

[Brooke, R. S.]. "Alcalde Grants in the City of San Francisco." *The Pioneer,* I (April 1854).

Burgess, Sherwood D. "Lumbering in Hispanic California." *California Historical Society Quarterly,* XLI (September 1962).

Day, Mrs. F. H. "Sketches of Early Settlers of California: Captain John Paty." *The Hesperian,* III (September 1859).

_____. "Sketches of Early California Settlers: George C. Yount." *The Hesperian,* II (March 1859).

Early, Mabel D. "Biographical Narrative of Bennett Family." *The Pony Express,* XVII (September 1950); (November 1950).

Holden, E. D. "California's First Pianos." *California Historical Society Quarterly,* XIII (March 1934).

Hoyt, Helen P. "Hawaii's First English Newspaper and Its Editor." *Sixty-Third Annual Report Hawaiian Historical Society.* Honolulu, 1954.

Johnson, Donald D. "Powers in the Pacific: Tahiti and Hawaii, 1825–1850." *Sixty-Sixth Annual Report of the Hawaii Historical Society.* Honolulu, 1957.

Jones, Idwal. "Dona Josefa." *Westways,* 43 (May 1951).

Jore, Leonce A. "Captain Jules Dudoit, the First French Consul in the Hawaiian Islands, 1837–1867, and his Brig Schooner, the *Clementine.*" Translated by Dorothy B. Aspinwall. *Sixty-Fourth Annual Report of the Hawaiian Historical Society.* Honolulu, 1955.

Judd, Bernice. "Koloa: A Sketch of Its Development." *Forty-Fourth Annual Report of the Hawaiian Historical Society.* Honolulu, 1935.

Kai, Peggy. "Chinese Settlers in the Village of Hilo Before 1852." *The Hawaiian Journal of History,* VIII (1974).

Kovacevic, Ante. "On the Descent of John Owen Dominis, Prince Consort of Queen Liliuokalani." *The Hawaiian Journal of History,* X (1976).

Lamb, W. Kaye. "The Mystery of Mrs. Berkeley's Diary." *British Columbia Historical Review,* 6 (January 1942).

McArthur, Lewis A. "Oregon Geographic Names." *Oregon Historical Quarterly,* XXVII (March 1926); XXVIII (March 1927).

Meany, Edmond S. "Washington Geographic Names." *Washington Historical Quarterly,* VIII (October 1917); IX (January 1918).

Taylor, Clarice B., in collaboration with George Mirairda. "Tales About Hawaii: Honolulu Street Names—4." *Honolulu Star-Bulletin,* January 30, 1956.

Thrum, George G. "Notes on the History of the Sugar Industry of the Hawaiian Islands." *Hawaiian Almanac and Annual for 1875.* Honolulu, 1875.

Wipple, A.B.C. "The Hard-Luck Frigate [U.S.S. *Constellation*]." *American Heritage: The Magazine of History,* 7 (February 1956).

"Yerba Buena Biographies." *California Historical Society Quarterly,* XIV (June 1935).

Newspapers

California Star, November 18, 1848.

Calistoga *Tribune,* April 6, 1871.

The Friend [Honolulu]: Volumes 1–5, 1843–1847; New Series, Volumes 6–24, 1857–1875.

Hawaiian Spectator [Honolulu], 2 (April 1839).

Honolulu *Advertiser*, July 28, 1926; October 14, 1928.

Los Angeles *Star*, March 1, 1869.

Oakland *Tribune*, March 4, 1928.

The Polynesian [Honolulu]: Volume 1, 1840; New Series, Volume 1–5, 1844–1849.

Sacramento *Bee*, September 17, 1961.

Sacramento *Union*, November 19, 1857; September 10, 1859; July 8, 1871; February 1, 1873; May 25, 1874; August 5, 1943.

San Diego *Union*, May 6, 1954; June 15, 1873; March 14, 1926; July 20, 1930.

San Francisco *Alta California*, February 15, October 24, November 8, 15, 1849; October 7, 1865; July 10, 1871.

San Francisco *Bulletin*, April 23, 1896.

San Jose *Pioneer*, November 16, 1878; February 15, 1893.

Sandwich Island Gazette [Honolulu], May 26, November 11, 17, 1838.

Valparaíso *Mercurio*, July 12, 13, August 2, 7, 10, 11, 26, 30, 1842.

Theses and Dissertations

Miller, Ronald L. "Henry Delano Fitch." Ph. D. Dissertation, University of Southern California, 1972.

Index

The Journal of a Sea Captain's Wife, 1841–1845,
has been published in an edition of
seven hundred and fifty copies.
The book has been designed and produced
under the direction of Robert A. Clark,
and printed by Thomson-Shore, Inc., of
Dexter, Michigan.